226 Best-Selling
LUXURY
HOME PLANS

Photo by Dave Dawson

DESIGN 9838, page 126

HOME PLANNERS, LLC
Wholly owned by Hanley-Wood, LLC
Tucson, Arizona

Published by Home Planners, LLC
Wholly owned by Hanley-Wood, LLC
3275 West Ina Road, Suite 110
Tucson, Arizona 85741

Distribution Center:
29333 Lorie Lane
Wixom, Michigan 48393

Patricia Joseph, President
Jan Prideaux, Editor In Chief
Morenci Wodraska, Editor
Teralyn Morriss, Graphic Designer

Photo Credits
Front Cover: ©Dave Dawson
Back Cover: ©Jon Riley

10 9 8 7 6 5 4 3 2 1

Printed in the United States of America.

Library of Congress Catalog Card Number: 00-134203

ISBN softcover: 1-881955-76-1

On the front cover: Architectural elegance at its finest, Design 9838 is a perfect example of the symmetry of stone and stucco. For more information about this design, see page 126.

On the back cover: Page 17 provides a closer look at Design 9661.

DESIGN 3638, page 157

TABLE OF CONTENTS

EDITOR'S NOTE

As you study the plans on the following pages, we invite you to examine the best of what nature's light has to offer. Creative planning utilizes this wonderful gift for optimum dramatic effect. You'll find plans to enrich the colors and textures of the home's interior as well as providing magnificent views of the landscape beyond. Consider the warm welcome received from a two-story foyer drenched in sunlight. Enjoy sun rooms and panoramic windows that provide a front-row seat to the everchanging seasons. Natural light streaming through properly placed windows or glass doors can bring the rich colors of a room to their full potential. And light filtered through a stained-glass window or transom can add a touch of fantasy or color to any room. As you will discover in the chapters that follow, the light-enhancing combinations and possibilities of good design are virtually boundless. To help you plan the cost of your dream home, our Quote One™ estimating service is available for many of our plans. The Quote One™ logo has been placed on the plan pages for easy reference. For additional information regarding this invaluable service, please see page 230. The sky's the limit— and the best part—the view can be found within the comfort of your own home!

About the Designers

The Blue Ribbon Designer Series™ is a collection of books featuring the home plans of a diverse group of outstanding home designers and architects known as the Blue Ribbon Network of Designers. This group of companies is dedicated to creating and marketing the finest possible plans for home construction on a regional and national basis. Each of the companies exhibits superior work and integrity in all phases of the stock-plan business including modern, trendsetting floor planning, a professionally executed blueprint package and a strong sense of service and commitment to the consumer.

Design Basics, Inc.

For nearly a decade, Design Basics, a nationally recognized home design service located in Omaha, has been developing plans for custom home builders. Since 1987, the firm has consistently appeared in *Builder* magazine, the official magazine of the National Association of Home Builders, as the top-selling designer. The company's plans also regularly appear in numerous other shelter magazines such as *Better Homes and Gardens, House Beautiful* and *Home Planner.*

Design Traditions

Design Traditions was established by Stephen S. Fuller with the tenets of innovation, quality, originality and uncompromising architectural techniques in traditional and European homes. Especially popular throughout the Southeast, Design Traditions' plans are known for their extensive detail and thoughtful design. They are widely published in such shelter magazines as *Southern Living* magazine and *Better Homes and Gardens.*

Alan Mascord Design Associates, Inc.

Founded in 1983 as a local supplier to the building community, Mascord Design Associates of Portland, Oregon began to successfully publish plans nationally in 1985. With plans now drawn exclusively on computer, Mascord Design Associates quickly received a reputation for homes that are easy to build yet meet the rigorous demands of the buyers' market, winning local and national awards. The company's trademark is creating floor plans that work well and exhibit excellent traffic patterns. Their motto is: "Drawn to build, designed to sell."

Larry E. Belk Designs

Through the years, Larry E. Belk has worked with individuals and builders alike to provide a quality product. After listening to over 4,000 dreams and watching them become reality all across America, Larry's design philosophy today combines traditional exteriors with upscale interiors designed for contemporary lifestyles. Flowing, open spaces and interesting angles define his interiors. Great emphasis is placed on providing views that showcase the natural environment. Dynamic exteriors reflect Larry's extensive home construction experience, painstaking research and talent as a fine artist.

Larry W. Garnett & Associates, Inc.

Starting as a designer of homes for Houston-area residents, Garnett & Associates has been marketing designs nationally for the past ten years. A well-respected design firm, the company's plans are regularly featured in *House Beautiful, Country Living, Home* and *Professional Builder.* Numerous accolades, including several from the Texas Institute of Building Design and the American Institute of Building Design, have been awarded to the company for excellence in architecture.

Home Planners

Headquartered in Tucson, Arizona, with additional offices in Detroit, Home Planners is one of the longest-running and most successful home design firms in the United States. With over 2,500 designs in its portfolio, the company provides a wide range of styles, sizes and types of homes for the residential builder. All of Home Planners' designs are created with the care and professional expertise that fifty years of experience in the home-planning business affords. Their homes are designed to be built, lived in and enjoyed for years to come.

Donald A. Gardner, Architects, Inc.

The South Carolina firm of Donald A. Gardner was established in response to a growing demand for residential designs that reflect constantly changing lifestyles. The company's specialty is providing homes with refined, custom-style details and unique features such as passive-solar designs and open floor plans. Computer-aided design and drafting technology resulting in trouble-free construction documents places the firm at the leading edge of the home plan industry.

The Sater Design Collection

The Sater Design Collection has a long established tradition of providing South Florida's most diverse and extraordinary custom designed homes. Their goal is to fulfill each client's particular need for an exciting approach to design by merging creative vision with elements that satisfy a desire for a distinctive lifestyle. This philosophy is proven, as exemplified by over 50 national design awards, numerous magazine features and, most important, satisfied clients. The result is an elegant statement of lasting beauty and value.

Home Design Services, Inc.

For the past fifteen years, Home Design Services of Longwood, Florida, has been formulating plans for the sun-country lifestyle. At the forefront of design innovation and imagination, the company has developed award winning designs that are consistently praised for their highly detailed, free-flowing floor plans, imaginative and exciting interior architecture and elevations which have gained international appeal.

Making The Most Of Natural Light

S un—our source of heat and light. Though reasons are not entirely understood, the sun rejuvenates our human spirit and creates an environment where human, animal and plant life flourishes. Therefore, it makes a great deal of sense to harness this resource and incorporate it into our home's design whenever possible.

The following pages contain homes filled with natural light that are suited for all regions, whether they have cool, temperate or warm climates. Depending on your needs, your home may be situated on your building site to take maximum advantage of the brilliant benefits of sunlight. Exteriors are enhanced by light-filled entrances and window treatments, while panoramic windows and walls, glass doors, sun rooms and greenhouses add depth and dimension, enriching the color and texture of the interiors.

Grand entrances, bathed in light, furnish a bright introduction whether formal or informal. In chapter one, examples of these include the formal traditional style of Design 3310 found on page 7, and Design 8086 on page 22. A warm welcome—farmhouse style—can be seen on page 15 (Design 3615) and page 34 (Design 9767). It is obvious that unique window treatments enhance the appearance of a home's exterior. But they also provide an interior focal point that frames the view overlooking a favorite landscape, creating a beautiful outdoor canvas. Picture the beautiful scene presented from the front window of Design 9538 on page 39, or the expansive stretch of beach that could be enjoyed from the rear window of Design 9987 (page 50).

Skylights, clerestories and transoms, found in chapter three, make the most of natural lighting, opening up ceilings as well as walls. The rear elevation of Design 9621 on page 75 provides a marvelous example of clerestory lighting, while Design 9124 (page 95) demonstrates the effective use of skylights both upstairs and down. Creative use of panoramic windows, glass walls and doors has a huge impact on the personality of your home. Expansive amounts of glass allow you to look through your walls rather than at them, and brighten even the darkest corners. Notice the rear floor plan of Design 9898 found on page 97. Unobstructed views of the deck and rear grounds beyond stretch across the width of the home on both floors. The one-story planning of Design 9203 found on page 124 provides another fine example.

The sun room was designed to take maximum advantage of light. Depending on its primary use, consideration should be given to how the sun room will be situated on the building site. If the space is to be used for its solar benefits, it is best that the sun room faces south. However, if it is to be used as a studio, northern exposure will provide the softest lighting for creating your works of art. No matter what its purpose, outstanding examples are found on page 176 (Design 9910) and page 182 (Design 8139). Not to be overlooked are options for individuals who wish to employ their green thumbs. Design 2883 located on page 193 provides an interesting option for a greenhouse or dining room while Design 2880 (page 198) provides a greenhouse ideally located adjacent to the kitchen, perfect for growing fresh herbs.

Whether overlooking a courtyard (see Design 3632, page 206), enjoying the coolness of a refreshing pool (see Design 8692, page 214) or attending a veranda where children play (Design 6611, page 212), views to sun spaces provide a tranquil place to enjoy the natural beauty of the outdoors. All you need to supply is the relaxation.

In a great variety of choices, the plans displayed in the following chapters offer a wealth of fine home-building opportunities. Find your favorite and let the sun shine in!

Design by
Home Planners

Design 3573

First Floor: 1,650 square feet
Second Floor: 1,508 square feet
Total: 3,158 square feet
Bonus Room: 275 square feet
Bedroom Option: 176 square feet

L **D**

● A design for the times, this beautiful transitional home may be built with a fourth bedroom and/or a first-floor bonus room. The entrance court introduces a covered porch. Inside, the tiled foyer offers a dramatic space comprised of a dining room on the left and, separated by a staircase, a living room on the right. Both rooms enjoy their own terrace. Casual living takes off in the family room with its terrace. An expansive kitchen backs up the plan and includes a walk-in pantry and an island countertop. Upstairs, overlooking the dining room, a hallway branches off into three bedrooms, including a delightful master suite. Here, highlights range from two balconies to a bath with a whirlpool tub.

QUOTE ONE™
Cost to build? See page 230 to order complete cost estimate to build this house in your area!

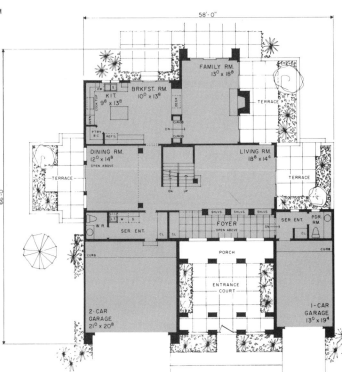

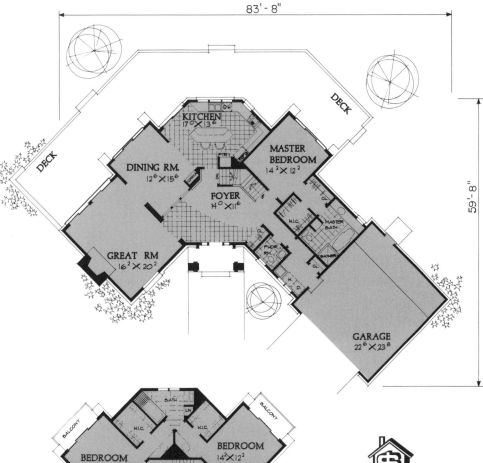

83' - 8"

59' - 8"

Design 3310

First Floor: 1,668 square feet
Second Floor: 905 square feet
Total: 2,573 square feet

L **D**

● If you're looking for a different angle on a new home, try this enchanting transitional house. The open foyer creates a rich atmosphere. To the left you'll find a great room with raised-brick hearth and sliding glass doors that lead out onto a wraparound deck. The kitchen enhances the first floor with a snack bar and deck access. The master bedroom, with balcony and bath with whirlpool, is located on the first floor for privacy. Upstairs, two family bedrooms, both with balconies and walk-in closets, share a full bath. Don't overlook the lounge and elliptical window that give the second floor added charisma.

QUOTE ONE™

Cost to build? See page 230 to order complete cost estimate to build this house in your area!

Design by
Home Planners

7

Design 8908

First Floor: 3,985 square feet
Second Floor: 2,278 square feet
Total: 6,263 square feet

● First and second-story bay windows with copper roofs and detailed brick arches at the front entry and veranda recall classic estate homes of the 1920's. The magnificent foyer features an impressive staircase and balcony. The gallery offers a view into the formal living room, which has a fireplace flanked by built-in bookcases and access to the terrace via French doors. Double doors open to a private master suite with an octagonal sitting area and corner fireplace. The formal dining room shares a two-way fireplace with the pub area. Three pairs of French doors provide a view from the kitchen and breakfast area into the sundrenched solarium/family room. Second-floor living space includes four bedrooms, a raised library/reading area and a huge game room.

Design by
Larry W.
Garnett &
Associates, Inc.

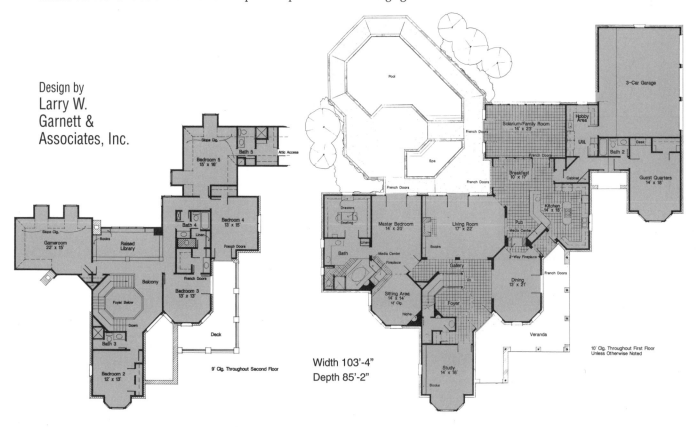

Width 103'-4"
Depth 85'-2"

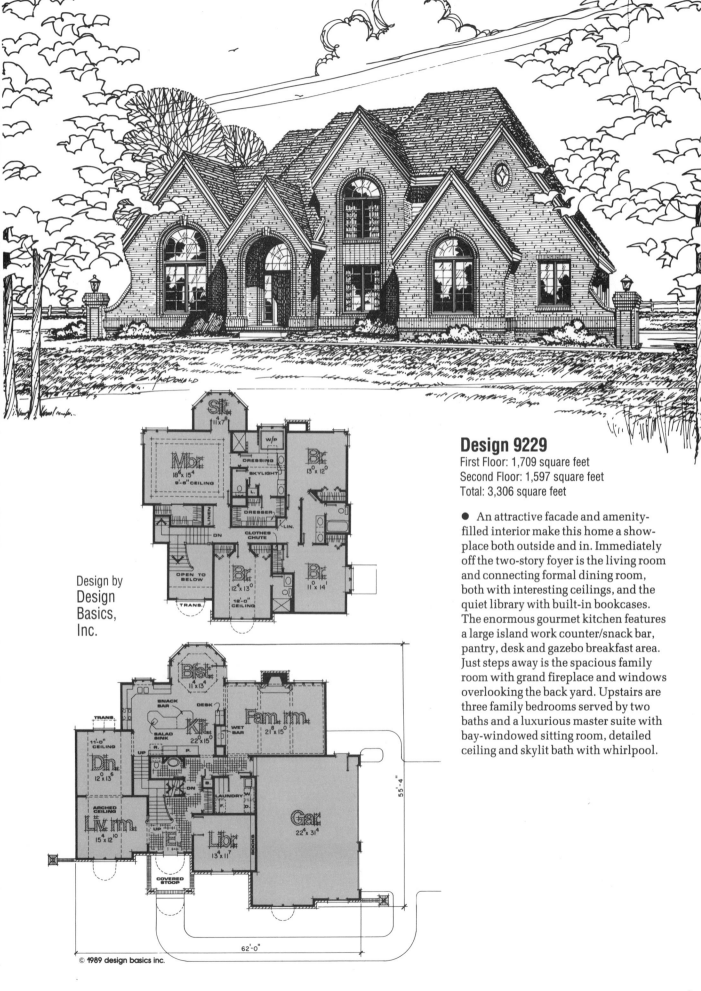

Design by Design Basics, Inc.

Design 9229

First Floor: 1,709 square feet
Second Floor: 1,597 square feet
Total: 3,306 square feet

● An attractive facade and amenity-filled interior make this home a show-place both outside and in. Immediately off the two-story foyer is the living room and connecting formal dining room, both with interesting ceilings, and the quiet library with built-in bookcases. The enormous gourmet kitchen features a large island work counter/snack bar, pantry, desk and gazebo breakfast area. Just steps away is the spacious family room with grand fireplace and windows overlooking the back yard. Upstairs are three family bedrooms served by two baths and a luxurious master suite with bay-windowed sitting room, detailed ceiling and skylit bath with whirlpool.

Design 3409

First Floor: 1,481 square feet
Second Floor: 1,287 square feet
Total: 2,768 square feet

L

● Glass block walls and a foyer with barrel vaulted ceiling create an interesting exterior. Covered porches to the front and rear provide for excellent indoor/outdoor living relationships. Inside, a large planter and through-fireplace enhance the living room and family room. The dining room has a stepped ceiling. A desk, eating area and snack bar are special features in the kitchen. The master suite features a large walk-in closet, bath with double bowl vanity and separate tub and shower, and a private deck. Three additional bedrooms share a full bath.

QUOTE ONE™

Cost to build? See page 230
to order complete cost estimate
to build this house in your area!

Design by
Home Planners

Width 64'
Depth 56'-2"

Quote One™

Cost to build? See page 230
to order complete cost estimate
to build this house in your area!

Design by
Home Planners

Design 3403

First Floor: 2,422 square feet
Second Floor: 714 square feet
Total: 3,136 square feet

L

● There is no end to the distinctive features in this Southwestern contemporary. Formal living areas are concentrated in the center of the plan, perfect for entertaining. To the right of the plan, the kitchen and family room function well together as a working and living area. Also note the separate laundry room. The optional guest bedroom or den and the master bedroom are located to the left of the plan. Upstairs, the remaining two bedrooms are reached by a balcony overlooking the living room and share a bath with twin vanities.

Width 77'-8"
Depth 62'

This home, as shown in the photograph, may differ from the actual blueprints. For more detailed information, please check the floor plans carefully.

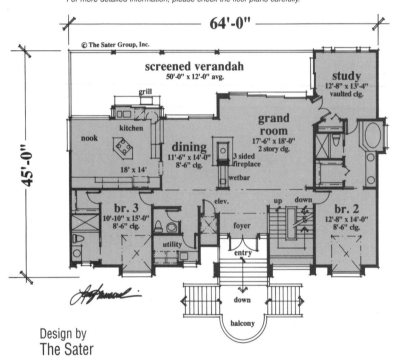

64'-0"

© The Sater Group, Inc.

45'-0"

screened verandah
50'-0" x 12'-0" avg.

grill

kitchen

nook

18' x 14'

dining
11'-6" x 14'-0"
8'-6" clg.

3 sided
fireplace

wetbar

**grand
room**
17'-6" x 18'-0"
2 story clg.

study
12'-8" x 13'-4"
vaulted clg.

br. 3
10'-10" x 15'-0"
8'-6" clg.

elev.

up   down

br. 2
12'-8" x 14'-0"
8'-6" clg.

utility

foyer

entry

down

balcony

Design by
**The Sater
Design Collection**

Design 6620

First Floor: 2,066 square feet
Second Floor: 810 sq. ft.
Total: 2,876 square feet
Lower Floor: 1,260 square feet

L

● If entertaining's your passion, then this is the design for you. With a large open floor plan and an array of amenities, every gathering will be a success. The foyer embraces livings areas accented by a glass fireplace and a wet bar. The grand room and living room each access a screened veranda for outdoor enjoyments. The gourmet kitchen delights with its openness to the rest of the house. A nook here also adds a nice touch. Two bedrooms and a study radiate from the first floor living areas. Upstairs—or use the elevator—is a masterful master suite. It contains a huge walk-in closet, a whirlpool tub and a private sun deck.

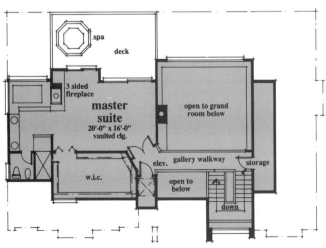

spa

deck

3 sided
fireplace

**master
suite**
20'-0" x 16'-0"
vaulted clg.

open to grand
room below

w.i.c.

elev.   gallery walkway   storage

open to
below

down

© The Sater Group, Inc.

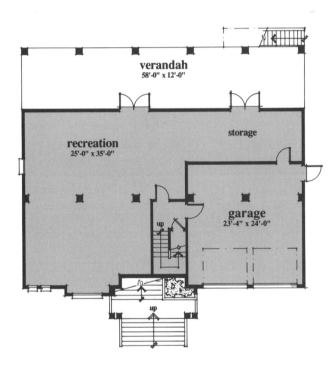

verandah
58'-0" x 12'-0"

recreation
25'-0" x 35'-0"

storage

garage
23'-4" x 24'-0"

up

up

Width 58'
Depth 54'

QUOTE ONE®

Cost to build? See page 230
to order complete cost estimate
to build this house in your area!

Design by
The Sater
Design Collection

Design 6622

Square Footage: 2,190
Basement: 1,966 square feet

● A dramatic set of stairs leads to the entry of this
home. The foyer leads to an expansive living room with
a fireplace and built-in bookshelves. A lanai opens off
this area and will assure outdoor enjoyments. For formal
meals, a front-facing dining room offers a bumped-out
bay. The kitchen serves this area easily as well as the
breakfast room. A study and three bedrooms make up
the rest of the floor plan. Two secondary bedrooms
share a full hall bath. A utility area is also nearby. In the
master suite, two walk-in closets and a full bath are
appreciated features. In the bedroom, a set of French
doors offers passage to the lanai.

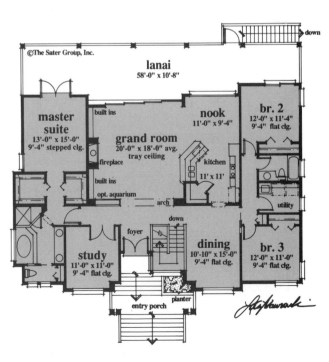

©The Sater Group, Inc.

lanai
58'-0" x 10'-8"

master
suite
13'-0" x 15'-0"
9'-4" stepped clg.

built ins

nook
11'-0" x 9'-4"

br. 2
12'-0" x 11'-4"
9'-4" flat clg.

grand room
20'-0" x 18'-0" avg.
tray ceiling

fireplace

kitchen
11' x 11'

built ins

opt. aquarium

arch

utility

study
11'-0" x 11'-0"
9'-4" flat clg.

foyer

down

dining
10'-10" x 15'-0"
9'-4" flat clg.

br. 3
12'-0" x 11'-0"
9'-4" flat clg.

entry porch

planter

down

BEDROOM
10⁴ x 14⁰
+ DORMER

DESK   BOOKS   DESK
HALL
RAILING
LINEN
DN
BATH

BEDROOM
11⁸ x 14⁰
+ DORMER

OPEN TO
FOYER BELOW

LEDGE   LEDGE

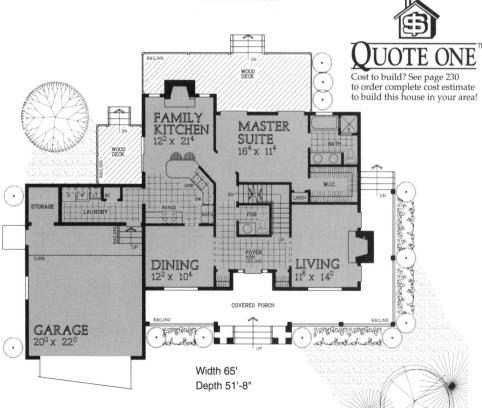

RAILING
WOOD DECK
DN

**FAMILY
KITCHEN**
12² x 21⁴

**MASTER
SUITE**
16⁴ x 11⁴

BATH
S

WOOD DECK
DN
RAILING

STORAGE
D W LT BC
LAUNDRY
RANGE
SINK
DW
REF
DN
PDR
W.I.C.
LINEN
DN

RAILING
UP

CURB

DINING
12² x 10⁴

FOYER
HIGH CEILING
UP
UP

LIVING
11⁸ x 14⁰

GARAGE
20⁰ x 22⁰

COVERED PORCH
RAILING
RAILING
UP

Width 65'
Depth 51'-8"

QUOTE ONE™

Cost to build? See page 230 to order complete cost estimate to build this house in your area!

Design 3467

First Floor: 1,276 square feet
Second Floor: 658 square feet
Total: 1,934 square feet

L

● Bold and beautiful, this Neoclassic farmhouse will delight family and friends alike. Lap wood siding combined with a standing seam metal roof provides a wealth of visual appeal. Inside, living takes off with a great kitchen and family room combination. Or take in brunch on the wood deck located just off this area. For more formal occasions, a split dining room and living room—with a fireplace—will serve well. A covered wraparound porch is accessible from both rooms and makes outdoor living a pleasure. Located at the rear of the first floor, the master bedroom extends the finest accommodations including a private bath and a walk-in closet. Upstairs, two bedrooms with dormers may be finished at a later date.

Design by
Home Planners

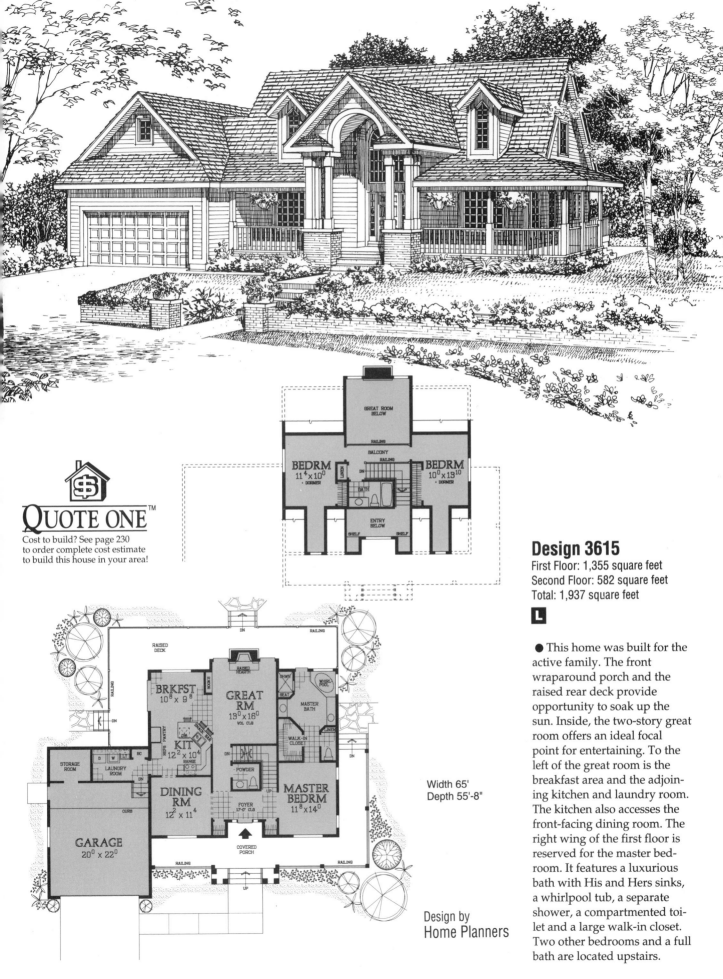

Quote One™

Cost to build? See page 230 to order complete cost estimate to build this house in your area!

Design 3615

First Floor: 1,355 square feet
Second Floor: 582 square feet
Total: 1,937 square feet

L

● This home was built for the active family. The front wraparound porch and the raised rear deck provide opportunity to soak up the sun. Inside, the two-story great room offers an ideal focal point for entertaining. To the left of the great room is the breakfast area and the adjoining kitchen and laundry room. The kitchen also accesses the front-facing dining room. The right wing of the first floor is reserved for the master bedroom. It features a luxurious bath with His and Hers sinks, a whirlpool tub, a separate shower, a compartmented toilet and a large walk-in closet. Two other bedrooms and a full bath are located upstairs.

Width 65'
Depth 55'-8"

Design by
Home Planners

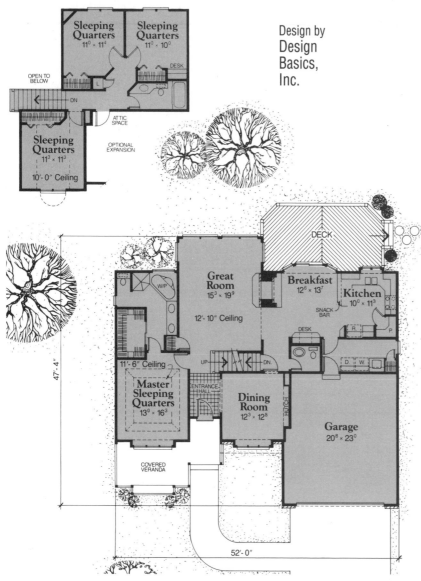

Design by
Design
Basics,
Inc.

OPEN TO BELOW

Sleeping Quarters
11⁰ × 11⁴

Sleeping Quarters
11⁰ × 10⁰

DESK

DN

ATTIC SPACE

Sleeping Quarters
11³ × 11³
10'-0" Ceiling

OPTIONAL EXPANSION

DECK

Great Room
15³ × 19⁹
12'-10" Ceiling

Breakfast
12⁶ × 13⁷

Kitchen
10⁰ × 11³

SNACK BAR

W/P

11'-6" Ceiling

DESK

UP

DN.

Master Sleeping Quarters
13⁰ × 16³

ENTRANCE HALL

Dining Room
12³ × 12⁸

HUTCH

Garage
20⁸ × 23⁰

COVERED VERANDA

47'-4"

52'-0"

Design 9288

First Floor: 1,421 square feet
Second Floor: 578 square feet
Total: 1,999 square feet

● Victorian details and a covered veranda lend peaceful flavor to the elevation of this popular home. A volume entry hall views the formal dining room and luxurious great room. Imagine the comfort of relaxing in the great room which features a 12'-10" ceiling and abundant windows! The kitchen/breakfast area includes a through fireplace, snack bar, walk-in pantry and wrapping counters. The secondary sleeping quarters have special amenities unique to each. A secluded main-floor master sleeping quarters features a vaulted ceiling, luxurious dressing/bath area and corner whirlpool tub. At 1,999 square feet, this home truly captures the simpler lifestyle of yesteryear!

Photos by Jon Riley

This home, as shown in the photograph, may differ from the actual blueprints. For more detailed information, please check the floor plans carefully.

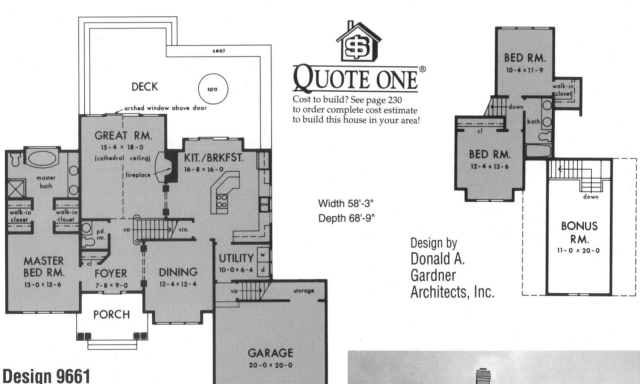

DECK

seat

spa

arched window above door

GREAT RM.
15-4 × 18-0
(cathedral ceiling)

fireplace

KIT./BRKFST.
16-8 × 16-0

master bath

walk-in closet

walk-in closet

up

sto.

pd. rm.

MASTER BED RM.
13-0 × 13-6

cl

FOYER
7-8 × 9-0

DINING
12-4 × 12-4

UTILITY
10-0 × 6-4

w

d

up

storage

PORCH

GARAGE
20-0 × 20-0

Quote One®

Cost to build? See page 230 to order complete cost estimate to build this house in your area!

Width 58'-3"
Depth 68'-9"

Design by
Donald A. Gardner Architects, Inc.

BED RM.
10-4 × 11-9

walk-in closet

down

bath

cl

BED RM.
12-4 × 13-6

down

BONUS RM.
11-0 × 20-0

Design 9661

First Floor: 1,416 square feet
Second Floor: 445 square feet
Total: 1,861 square feet
Bonus Room: 284 square feet

● An arched entrance and windows provide a touch of class to the exterior of this plan. The foyer leads to all areas of the house minimizing corridor space. The dining room displays round columns at the entrance while the great room boasts a cathedral ceiling, fireplace and arched window over exterior doors to the deck. In the master suite is a walk-in closet and lavish bath. On the second level are two bedrooms and a full bath. Bonus space over the garage can be developed later. The plan is available with a crawl-space foundation.

Design 8118

First Floor: 1,905 square feet
Second Floor: 855 square feet
Total: 2,760 square feet

Design by
Larry E. Belk
Designs

WIDTH 62'-6"
DEPTH 52'-10"

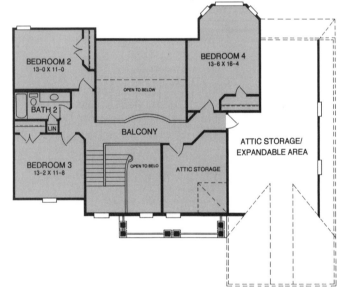

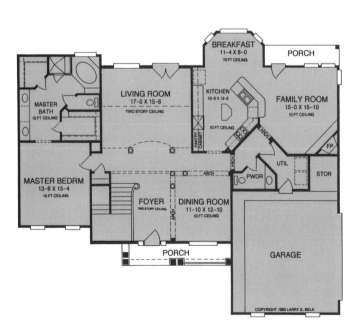

● An inviting front porch gives this elevation a homey feeling. Classic columns flank the entrance to the two-story living room. The island kitchen, bay-windowed breakfast room and large family room are open to one another, providing a spacious family retreat. The family room features a corner fireplace and access to the rear porch. The downstairs master bedroom includes a bath tailor-made for the working couple with His and Hers vanities and closets, a separate shower and a corner whirlpool tub. Upstairs, three roomy bedrooms and a bath, as well as a uniquely shaped balcony, complete the plan. An additional 336 feet is available for future expansion. Please specify crawlspace or slab foundation when ordering.

Design 8161

First Floor: 2,028 square feet
Second Floor: 558 square feet
Total: 2,586 square feet

● From the curb, this inviting entrance beckons family and friends to enter. The two-story foyer features a ledge perfect for displaying a special picture or tapestry. Arched openings form the entrance to the formal dining room and great room. An angled, see-through fireplace serves the great room, breakfast room and kitchen areas. The kitchen features an abundance of cabinet and counter space, a walk-in pantry and a built-in desk. A sitting area and a luxurious master bath enhance the private master suite. An adjacent secondary bedroom serves well as a guest room, a nursery or a study. Upstairs, two family bedrooms, a full bath and an expandable area complete the layout. Please specify slab or crawlspace foundation when ordering.

Design by
Larry E. Belk
Designs

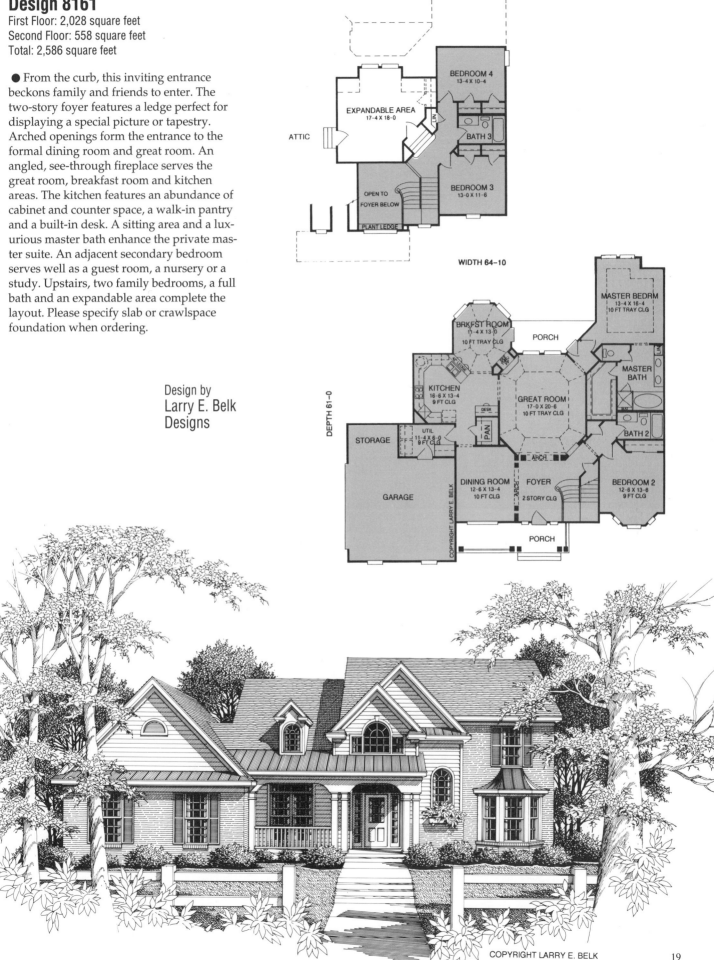

COPYRIGHT LARRY E. BELK

19

Design 3319
Square Footage: 2,274

L **D**

● This attractive bungalow design
separates the master suite from family bedrooms and puts casual living
to the back in a family room. The
formal living and dining areas are
centrally located and have access to
a rear terrace, as does the master
suite. The kitchen sits between
formal and informal living areas.
The two family bedrooms are found
to the front of the plan. A home
office or study opens off the front
foyer and the master suite.

Quote One™

Cost to build? See page 230
to order complete cost estimate
to build this house in your area!

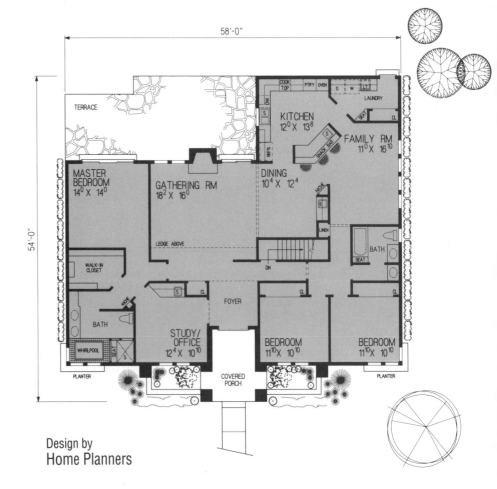

Design by
Home Planners

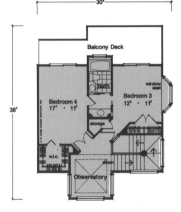

Design by
Home Design
Services, Inc.

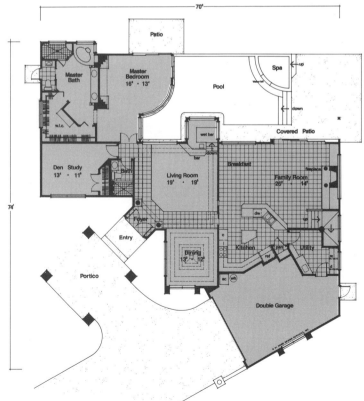

Design 8652

First Floor: 2,212 square feet
Second Floor: 675 square feet
Total: 2,887 square feet

● As you drive up to the porte cochere entry of this home, the visual movement of the elevation is breathtaking. The multi-roofed spaces bring excitement the moment you walk through the double-doored entry. The foyer leads into the wide glass-walled living room. To the right, the formal dining room features a tiered pedestal ceiling. To the left is the guest and master suite wing of the home. The master suite with its sweeping curved glass wall has access to the patio area. The master bath, with its huge walk-in closet, comes complete with a columned vanity area, soaking tub and shower for two. Two large bedrooms on the second floor share a sun deck and an activity area.

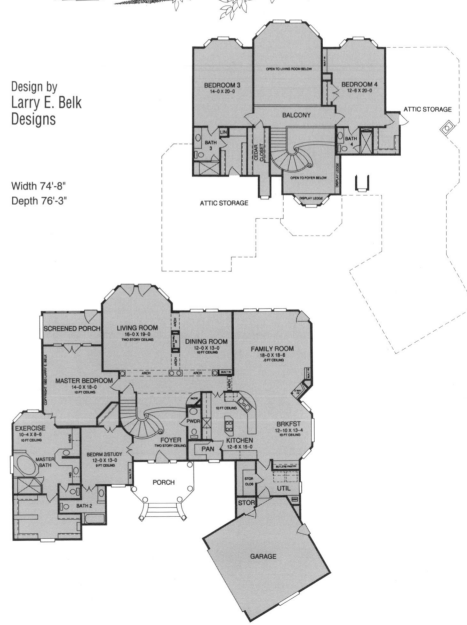

Design by
Larry E. Belk
Designs

Width 74'-8"
Depth 76'-3"

Design 8086

First Floor: 2,733 square feet
Second Floor: 1,003 square feet
Total: 3,736 square feet

L

● This Mediterranean-style villa is distinguished by a stunning, octagonal front porch. The second-story dormer above the porch accents the entry to this lovely home. The home is designed to capture views to the rear grounds and is perfect for a golf course or lake. Through arched openings flanked by columns, the adjoining living room and dining room open off the two-story foyer. A see-through fireplace separates the two rooms. The gourmet kitchen, family room and breakfast room are adjacent to one another. The master suite is at the rear of the home and provides access to a private screened porch. A curved staircase leads to two bedrooms on the second floor.

Design 3639

First Floor: 2,137 square feet
Second Floor: 671 square feet
Total: 2,808 square feet

L

● This stucco home provides a
wealth of livability for the entire
family. Inside, formal living areas
grab your attention with a dining
room and an elegant living room
that opens to a covered entertainment area outside. The family
room—with a fireplace—delights
with open views to the kitchen and
breakfast nook. The nearby "recipe
corner" includes a built-in desk.
The laundry room is fully functional with a laundry tub and a broom
closet. The two-car garage opens
off this area. On the left side of the
plan, the master bedroom suite
delights with a full, private bath
and a lanai perfect for a spa. A
large den could easily double as a
bedroom. Two bedrooms and a full
bath are located upstairs.

Design by
Home Planners

QUOTE ONE™
Cost to build? See page 230
to order complete cost estimate
to build this house in your area!

23

Design 8693

Square Footage: 1,433

● A volume entry and open planning give this house a feeling of spaciousness that goes far beyond its modest square footage. The foyer opens onto a large living and dining area that combines for flexible entertaining needs. The kitchen is planned to fulfill a "frugal gourmet's" dream and merges with the breakfast area for informal dining. Located to the rear for privacy, the master suite opens onto the patio and features a pampering bath with a huge walk-in closet. Two secondary bedrooms share a full hall bath.

Design by
Home Design
Services, Inc.

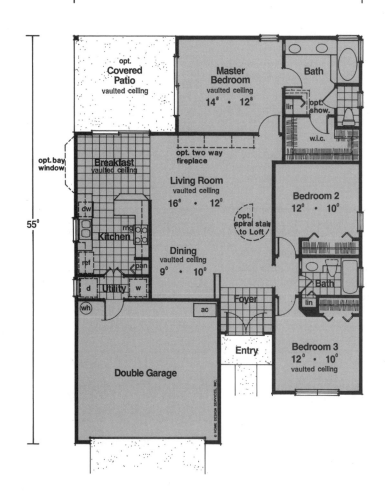

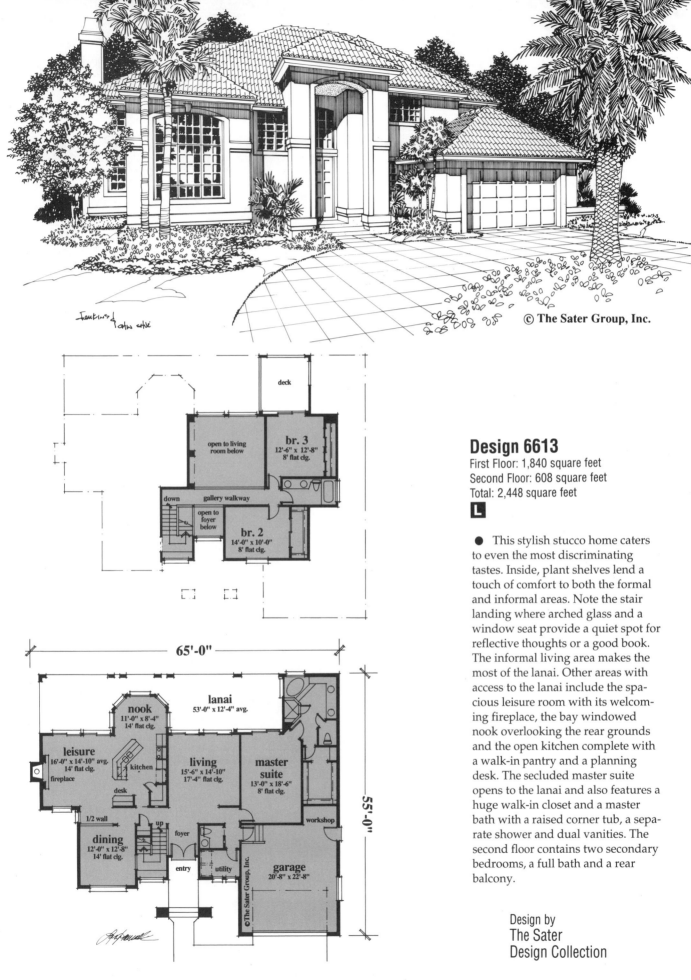

© The Sater Group, Inc.

deck

open to living room below

br. 3
12'-6" x 12'-8"
8' flat clg.

down | gallery walkway

open to foyer below

br. 2
14'-0" x 10'-0"
8' flat clg.

Design 6613

First Floor: 1,840 square feet
Second Floor: 608 square feet
Total: 2,448 square feet

L

● This stylish stucco home caters to even the most discriminating tastes. Inside, plant shelves lend a touch of comfort to both the formal and informal areas. Note the stair landing where arched glass and a window seat provide a quiet spot for reflective thoughts or a good book. The informal living area makes the most of the lanai. Other areas with access to the lanai include the spacious leisure room with its welcoming fireplace, the bay windowed nook overlooking the rear grounds and the open kitchen complete with a walk-in pantry and a planning desk. The secluded master suite opens to the lanai and also features a huge walk-in closet and a master bath with a raised corner tub, a separate shower and dual vanities. The second floor contains two secondary bedrooms, a full bath and a rear balcony.

65'-0"

nook
11'-0" x 8'-4"
14' flat clg.

lanai
53'-0" x 12'-4" avg.

leisure
16'-0" x 14'-10" avg.
14' flat clg.

fireplace

kitchen

desk

living
15'-6" x 14'-10"
17'-4" flat clg.

master suite
13'-0" x 18'-6"
8' flat clg.

1/2 wall

up

foyer

workshop

dining
12'-0" x 12'-8"
14' flat clg.

entry

utility

garage
20'-8" x 22'-8"

©The Sater Group, Inc.

55'-0"

Design by
**The Sater
Design Collection**

25

Design 8687

Square Footage: 2,278

● The grand entrance of this one-story home offers a fine introduction to an open, spacious interior. A welcoming formal living/dining room sized for large get-togethers extends from the foyer. To the left, a decorative niche distinguishes the master wing. The bayed master bedroom wall creates a sitting area with panoramic views. Amenities found in the master bath include a luxurious soaking tub, His and Hers walk-in closets and a compartmented toilet. The family wing boasts a large kitchen with a walk-in pantry, a nook and a uniquely angled family room crowned by a fireplace wall. Two family bedrooms of ample size with a split bathroom design complete this home.

Design by
Home Design
Services, Inc.

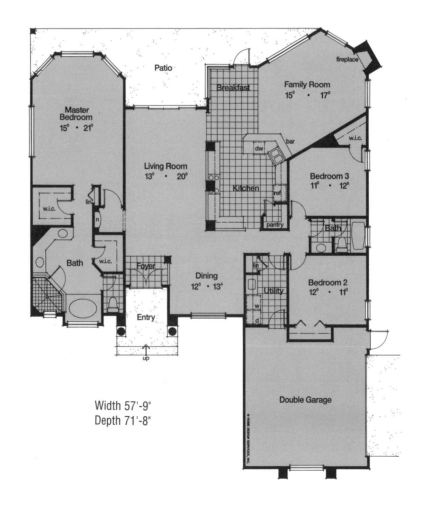

Width 57'-9"
Depth 71'-8"

Design 8688
Square Footage: 2,636

Width 71'-8"
Depth 71'-4"

● A towering entry welcomes you into the foyer of this soaring contemporary design. Interior glass walls supply openness to the den/study and mirror the arches to the formal dining room. The sunken living room has a bay-windowed wall that provides expansive views of the rear yard. Located to the rear, the master suite accesses the powder room/patio bath. Sliding glass doors from the suite open onto the patio. The master bath features His and Hers walk-in closets, a sunken vanity/bath area and a doorless shower. Casual living takes place in the family wing which holds the gourmet kitchen, the nook and a family room with a fireplace. Two secondary bedrooms share a private bath

Design by
Home Design Services, Inc.

w.i.c.

Bath

Bedroom 4
volume ceiling
14⁸ • 11⁰

fireplace

Family Room
volume ceiling
15⁸ • 20⁰

Nook

Covered Patio

Sitting

Bedroom 3
volume ceiling
11⁰ • 13⁰

dw

Kitchen

Living Room
volume ceiling
12⁰ • 18⁴

Pdr.

Master Bedroom
volume ceiling
12⁸ • 26⁰

Bedroom 2
volume ceiling
12⁰ • 12⁰

pantry

Bath

ref

n

lin

Utility

d

n

w

ac

wh

n

Dining
volume ceiling
11⁸ • 13¹⁰

Foyer

w.i.c.

w.i.c.

Double Garage

Entry

Bath

27

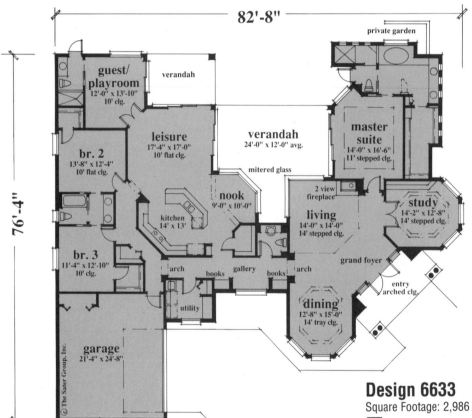

Design by
**The Sater
Design Collection**

Design 6633

Square Footage: 2,986

L

● Tropical living takes off in this super one-story home. Double doors lead to a lovely formal living area consisting of a living room, dining room and study. Through an archway, a gallery adds an air of distinction. The kitchen is open to a sunny nook and a bright leisure area for delightful dining and relaxing. A play room opens off this area and is sure to please the kids of the house. A full bath here leads outside. Two bedrooms nearby each sport a walk-in closet and utilize a full bath in between. The master bedroom suite enjoys a private bath with a whirlpool tub, dual lavs, a large walk-in closet and a compartmented toilet and shower.

Design 8032

First Floor: 2,520 square feet
Second Floor: 1,305 square feet
Total: 3,825 square feet

L

● Distinctive touches to this elegant European-style home make the first impression an unforgettable one. This home provides the perfect blend of charm and practicality. A unique two-story foyer is graced by a lovely staircase and a Romeo balcony overlook from the upstairs. To the right is the formal dining room, to the left, a study. Directly ahead, pass through two columns flanking the entry to the great room, taking note of the wall of windows and the French doors that lead to the rear grounds. Two-story, double-bay windows to the rear of the home form the keeping room and the breakfast room on one side and a marvelous master suite featuring a sitting room and a pampering bath on the other. A huge walk-in pantry and adjacent butler's pantry connect the dining room to the kitchen. Upstairs, three bedrooms and two full baths complete the plan. This home is also available in a 4,200 square-foot version.

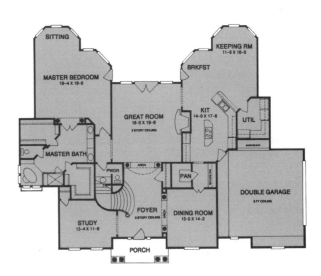

Design by
**Larry E. Belk
Designs**

Width 73'-8"
Depth 58'-6"

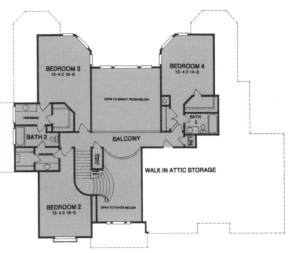

Design 8628

First Floor: 3,770 square feet
Second Floor: 634 square feet
Total: 4,404 square feet

● This fresh and innovative design creates unbeatable ambience. Octagon-shaped rooms, columns and flowing spaces will delight all. The breakfast nook and family room both open onto a patio—a perfect arrangement for informal entertaining. A private garden surrounds the master bath and its spa tub and enormous walk-in closet. The master bedroom delights with a fireplace and access to the outdoors. Additional family bedrooms come in a variety of different shapes and sizes; Bedroom 4 reigns over the second floor and features its own full bath.

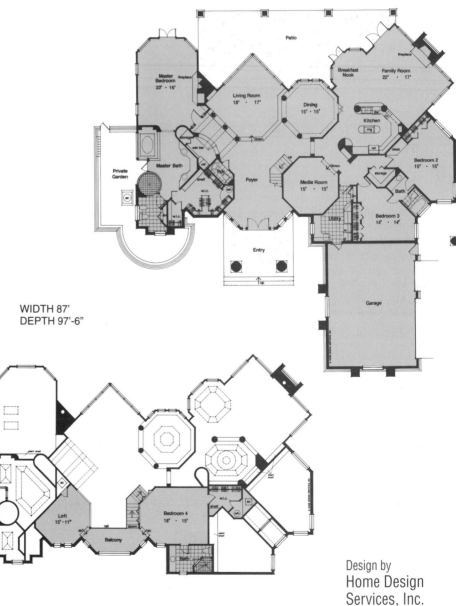

WIDTH 87'
DEPTH 97'-6"

Design by
Home Design
Services, Inc.

Design 6642

Square Footage: 3,743

L

● An exciting elevation makes the exterior of this home as special as the interior details. A custom grill archway and keystone columns add to the style. The gable roof detail at the entry is carried through to the rear of the house. Columns and archways grace the formal areas of the home. A bow window at the living room overlooks the lanai. A large nook, complete with a buffet server, highlights the family area. The master bedroom has a stepped ceiling and overlooks the lanai. The bath features His and Hers closets, a garden tub and an area for exercise equipment.

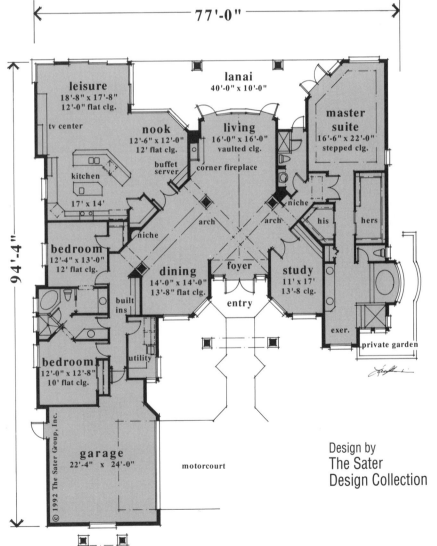

Design by
**The Sater
Design Collection**

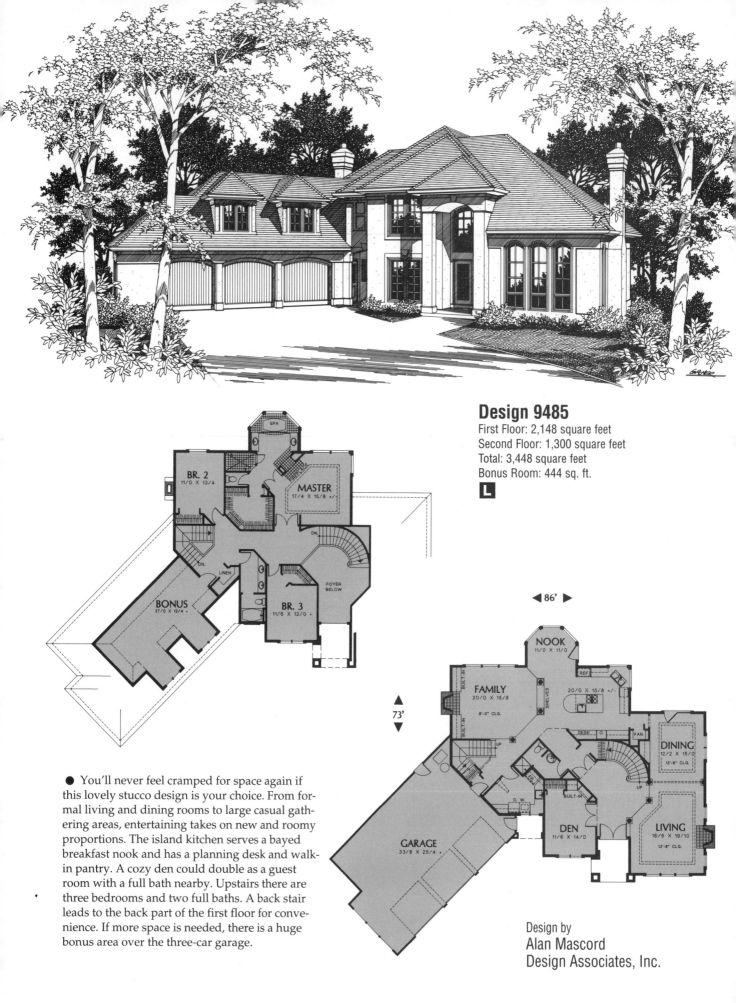

Design 9485

First Floor: 2,148 square feet
Second Floor: 1,300 square feet
Total: 3,448 square feet
Bonus Room: 444 sq. ft.

L

● You'll never feel cramped for space again if this lovely stucco design is your choice. From formal living and dining rooms to large casual gathering areas, entertaining takes on new and roomy proportions. The island kitchen serves a bayed breakfast nook and has a planning desk and walk-in pantry. A cozy den could double as a guest room with a full bath nearby. Upstairs there are three bedrooms and two full baths. A back stair leads to the back part of the first floor for convenience. If more space is needed, there is a huge bonus area over the three-car garage.

Design by
Alan Mascord
Design Associates, Inc.

◀ 71' ▶

GAMES RM.
26/8 X 19/0

OPTIONAL
WET BAR

BR. 2
12/8 X 12/8

BR. 3
13/0 X 13/0

STOR

LINEN

BR. 4
11/0 X 11/6

COVERED DECK

DECK

DINING
10/8 X 14/0

LIVING
16/8 X 15/0

BUILT-INS

NOOK
10/0 X 10/4

FAMILY
14/8 X 16/0

BOOKSHELF

MASTER
17/8 X 15/0

▲
56'
▼

GALLERY

SPA

BUILT-IN

GARAGE
32/4 X 23/2 +/-

DEN
12/4 X 14/4 +/-

Design by
**Alan Mascord
Design Associates, Inc.**

Design 9417

Square Footage: 2,196
Lower Level: 1,542 square feet

● This refined home is
designed for lots that fall off
toward the rear and works especially well with a view out the
back. The kitchen and eating nook
wrap around the vaulted family
room with its arched transom windows flanking the fireplace.
Directly off the nook is a covered
deck. Don't miss the huge game
room on the lower level.

Design 9767

First Floor: 1,841 square feet
Second Floor: 594 square feet
Total: 2,435 square feet
Bonus Room: 391 square feet

● Spaciousness and lots of amenities earmark this design as a family favorite. The front, wraparound porch leads to the foyer where a bedroom/study and dining room open. The central great room presents a warming fireplace, a cathedral ceiling and access to the rear porch. In the kitchen, oodles of counter and cabinet space are sure to satisfy. An adjacent bayed breakfast nook and a utility room with a pantry round out this side of the plan. In the master bedroom suite, a private bath with a bumped-out tub and a walk-in closet act as enhancements. Upstairs, two bedrooms flank a full bath. A bonus room over the garage allows for future expansion.

Design by
Donald A.
Gardner,
Architects, Inc.

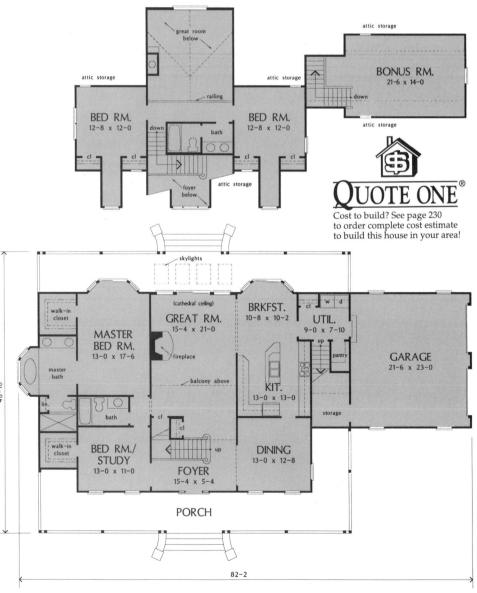

Quote One®

Cost to build? See page 230
to order complete cost estimate
to build this house in your area!

Enhanced Window Treatments

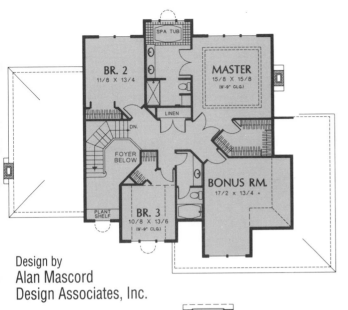

Design by
Alan Mascord
Design Associates, Inc.

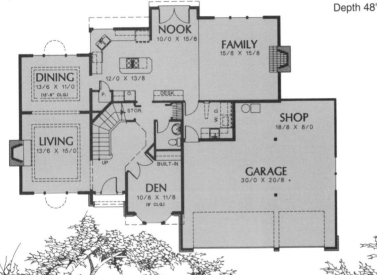

Width 63'
Depth 48'

Design 9542

First Floor: 1,465 square feet
Second Floor: 1,103 square feet
Total: 2,568 square feet
Bonus Room: 303 square feet

● Here's traditional style at its best! The bay-windowed den with built-in bookshelves is conveniently located to the front of the plan, making it ideal for use as an office or home-based business. To the left, the formal area contains a living and dining room, both with a tray ceiling. Cooks will find the kitchen a delight, with its sunlit corner sink, cooktop island, large pantry and built-in planning desk. A bumped-out eating nook opens to the rear yard through double doors. Completing the first floor is a spacious family room with a fireplace. The second floor contains the sleeping zone. A master suite with a relaxing spa tub, a separate shower and a huge walk-in closet is sure to please. Bedrooms 2 and 3 share a full bath. The three-car garage provides ample space for a workshop.

Design 3479

First Floor: 914 square feet
Second Floor: 1,050 square feet
Total: 1,964 square feet

L **D**

● This four-bedroom family home has a distinctive interior design. The gathering room features two bay windows, a sloped ceiling, a fireplace and a built-in entertainment center. A low wall separates the gathering room from the formal dining area. A rear terrace can be accessed from sliding glass doors here. Informal meals may take place in the bay-windowed breakfast nook. The kitchen includes a snack bar, a built-in planning desk and a walk-in pantry. The sleeping area is located quietly on the second floor. The master bedroom is highlighted by a sloped ceiling and includes two closets and a deluxe master bath with dual vanities and a whirlpool tub.

QUOTE ONE™

Cost to build? See page 230 to order complete cost estimate to build this house in your area!

Design by
Home Planners

Design 3439

First Floor: 1,424 square feet
Second Floor: 995 square feet
Total: 2,419 square feet

L

● Featuring a facade of wood and window glass, this home presents a striking first impression. It's floor plan is equally as splendid. Formal living and dining areas flank the entry foyer—both are sunken a step down. Also sunken from the foyer is the family room with attached breakfast nook. A fireplace in this area sits adjacent to a built-in audiovisual center. A nearby study with adjacent full bath doubles as a guest room. Upstairs are three bedrooms including a master suite with whirlpool spa and walk-in closet. Plant shelves adorn the entire floor plan.

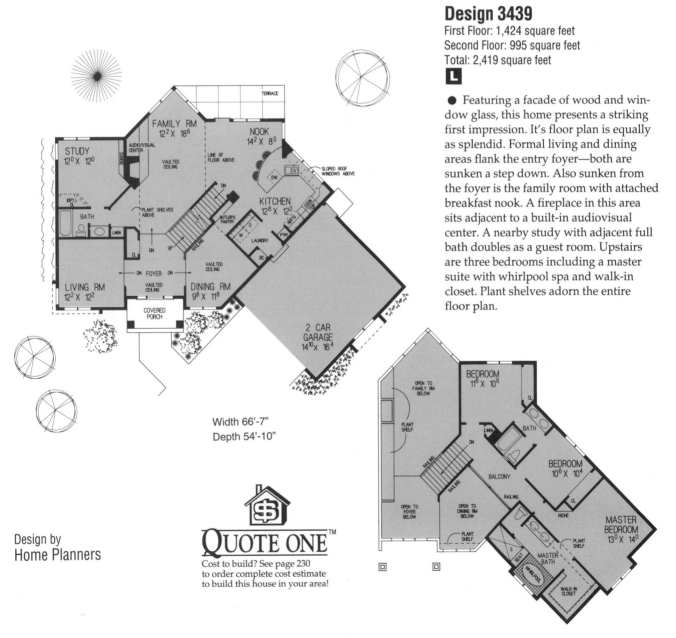

Width 66'-7"
Depth 54'-10"

Design by
Home Planners

QUOTE ONE™
Cost to build? See page 230 to order complete cost estimate to build this house in your area!

Design 9509

Main Level: 1,022 square feet
Upper Level: 813 square feet
Total: 1,835 square feet

L

● This house not only accommodates a narrow lot, but it also fits a sloping site. Notice how the two-car garage is tucked away under the first level of the house. The angled corner entry gives way to a two-story living room with a tiled hearth. The dining room shares an interesting angled space with this area and enjoys easy service from the efficient kitchen. A large pantry and an angled corner sink add character to this area. The family room offers double doors to a refreshing balcony. A powder room and a laundry room complete the main level. Upstairs, three bedrooms include a vaulted master suite with a private bath. Bedrooms 2 and 3 each take advantage of direct access to a full bath.

Design by
**Alan Mascord
Design Associates, Inc.**

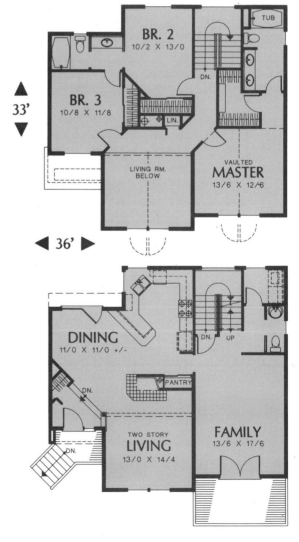

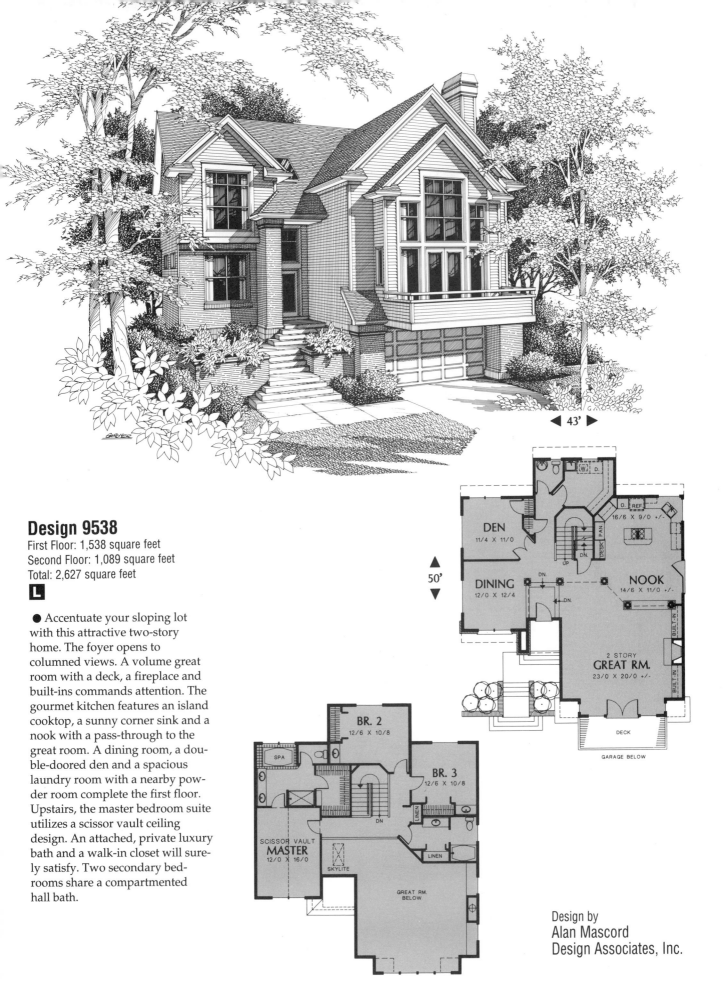

◄ 43' ►

Design 9538

First Floor: 1,538 square feet
Second Floor: 1,089 square feet
Total: 2,627 square feet

L

● Accentuate your sloping lot with this attractive two-story home. The foyer opens to columned views. A volume great room with a deck, a fireplace and built-ins commands attention. The gourmet kitchen features an island cooktop, a sunny corner sink and a nook with a pass-through to the great room. A dining room, a double-doored den and a spacious laundry room with a nearby powder room complete the first floor. Upstairs, the master bedroom suite utilizes a scissor vault ceiling design. An attached, private luxury bath and a walk-in closet will surely satisfy. Two secondary bedrooms share a compartmented hall bath.

50'

W. D.

O. REF.

DEN
11/4 X 11/0

16/6 X 9/0 +/-

DESK PAN.

UP
DN.

DINING
12/0 X 12/4

NOOK
14/6 X 11/0 +/-

DN.

DN.

BUILT-IN

BUILT-IN

2 STORY
GREAT RM.
23/0 X 20/0 +/-

BUILT-IN

DECK

GARAGE BELOW

BR. 2
12/6 X 10/8

SPA

BR. 3
12/6 X 10/8

LINEN

DN.

LINEN

SCISSOR VAULT
MASTER
12/0 X 16/0

SKYLITE

LINEN

GREAT RM.
BELOW

Design by
Alan Mascord
Design Associates, Inc.

39

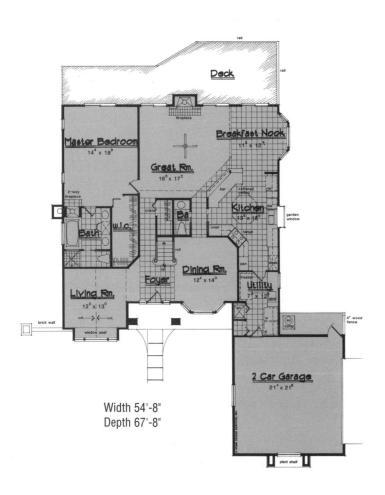

Width 54'-8"
Depth 67'-8"

Design by
Home Design
Services, Inc.

Design 8689

First Floor: 1,810 square feet
Second Floor: 922 square feet
Total: 2,732 square feet

● A Palladian window crowns this impressive entry and brings you into the foyer which separates the formal living and dining rooms. Efficient planning keeps the casual living area to the rear where the breakfast nook, the great room and the huge kitchen share views of the deck and backyard beyond. A fireplace flanked by sliding glass doors is the focal point of the great room, as is the bay window in the breakfast nook. The master suite features a large bedroom and a deluxe bath featuring a huge walk-in closet and a soaking tub with a see-through fireplace. Upstairs, Bedroom 2 has a private bath and a walk-in closet, while two other bedrooms share a full bath.

Design 6649

First Floor: 3,035 square feet
Second Floor: 945 square feet
Total: 3,980 square feet

L

● Rich custom details in this traditional home, such as archways and columns, provide luxury for the most discriminating homeowners. To the left of the foyer is the private master suite. The lavish bath contains a large walk-in closet, a double-basin vanity and a compartmented toilet. An adjacent study combines well with the suite. The dining room is perfect for formal occasions and the nearby kitchen with its island prep center and eating nook are ideal for casual meals. Completing this area is a leisure room with a built-in wet bar. The second floor accommodates a loft, two bedrooms with private baths, a large deck and a sun deck.

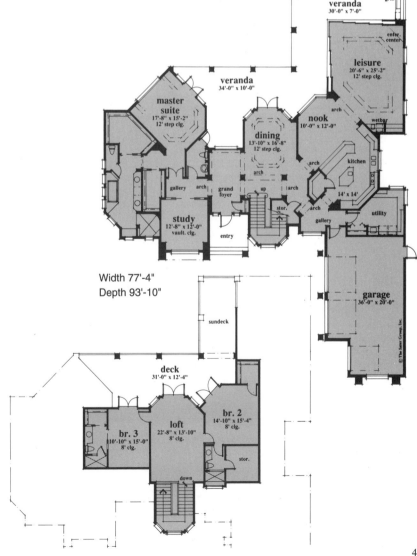

Width 77'-4"
Depth 93'-10"

Design by
**The Sater
Design Collection**

41

BEDRM
11⁸ X 11²

OPEN BELOW

RAILING

DN

LINEN

BEDRM
11⁸ X 10⁰

TUB

BATH

SHOWER

WHIRLPOOL

DN

RAILING

BALCONY
RAILING

MASTER
BEDROOM
16⁴ X 15⁰

MASTER
BATH

OPEN BELOW

Quote One™

Cost to build? See page 230
to order complete cost estimate
to build this house in your area!

Design by
Home Planners

Design 3452

First Floor: 1,689 square feet
Second Floor: 992 square feet
Total: 2,681 square feet

 L

● Clean lines and tasteful window treatment
create a pleasing facade. The formal living
room (with vaulted ceiling) and dining room
are open to each other. To the right of the foyer
is a parlor that may serve as a guest bedroom,
with a full bath nearby. The island kitchen easily serves the octagonal breakfast room and the
family room with a vaulted ceiling and a fireplace. A rear patio can be accessed from the
family room or breakfast room. Two stairways
lead to the second floor. Balconies overlook the
living and family rooms. The master bedroom
features a luxurious bath and a walk-in closet,
while two family bedrooms share a full bath.

FAMILY ROOM
20¹⁰ X 13⁴

BRKFST
10⁰ X 10⁰

SNACK BAR

DINING
ROOM
11² X 13⁰

UP

DN

SINK

PANTRY

KITCHEN
11⁸ X 15²

D. W. L.T.

REFG

OVEN

LAUNDRY

RAILING

CL.

CL.

PWDR. RM.

SHOWER

LIVING
ROOM
15⁰ X 15²
OPEN ABOVE

UP

PARLOR
10⁸ X 9²

GARAGE
19⁰ X 21²

FOYER

PORCH

49'-0"

55'-8"

This home, as shown in the photograph, may differ from the actual blueprints. For more detailed information, please check the floor plans carefully.

Design 2826 First Floor: 1,112 square feet
Second Floor: 881 square feet; Total: 1,993 square feet

D

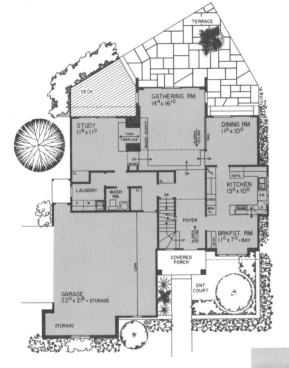

Width 49'
Depth 54'-4"

Design by
Home Planners

● This is an outstanding example of the type of informal, traditional-style architecture that has captured the modern imagination. The interior plan houses all of the features that people want most - a spacious gathering room, formal and informal dining areas, efficient, U-shaped kitchen, master bedroom, two children's bedrooms, second floor lounge, entrance court and rear terrace and deck. Study all areas of this plan carefully.

QUOTE ONE®
Cost to build? See page 230
to order complete cost estimate
to build this house in your area!

Design 3315

First Floor: 2,918 square feet
Second Floor: 330 square feet
Total: 3,248 square feet

L

● Besides the covered front veranda, look for another full-width veranda to the rear of this charming home. The master bedroom, breakfast room, and gathering room all have French doors to this outdoor space. A handy wet bar/ tavern enhances entertainment options. The upper lounge could be a welcome haven.

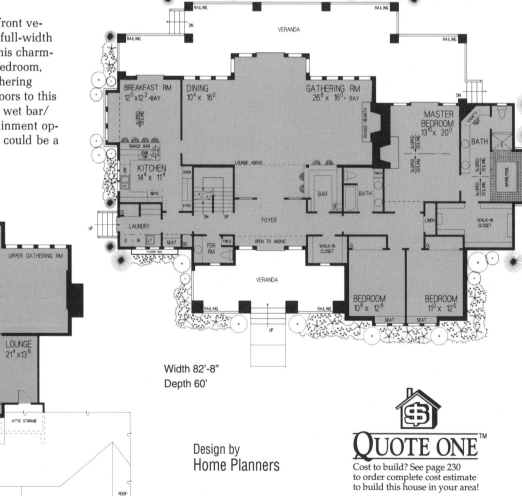

Width 82'-8"
Depth 60'

Design by
Home Planners

QUOTE ONE™

Cost to build? See page 230
to order complete cost estimate
to build this house in your area!

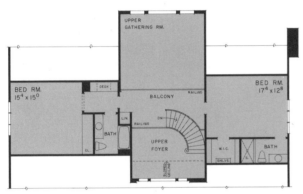

Design 3557

First Floor: 2,897 square feet
Second Floor: 835 square feet
Total: 3,732 square feet

L **D**

● The owners of this home will be giving themselves a real treat. A large master bedroom is accompanied by a pampering master bath and dressing area with walk-in closet. The master suite also provides access to the media room with bay window and fireplace. A sunken gathering room suits formal or informal occasions. The kitchen contains a snack bar and is convenient to the breakfast and dining rooms. Two large bedrooms upstairs are accompanied by two full baths.

Design by
Home Planners

Width 60'
Depth 58'-4"

QUOTE ONE™

Cost to build? See page 230
to order complete cost estimate
to build this house in your area!

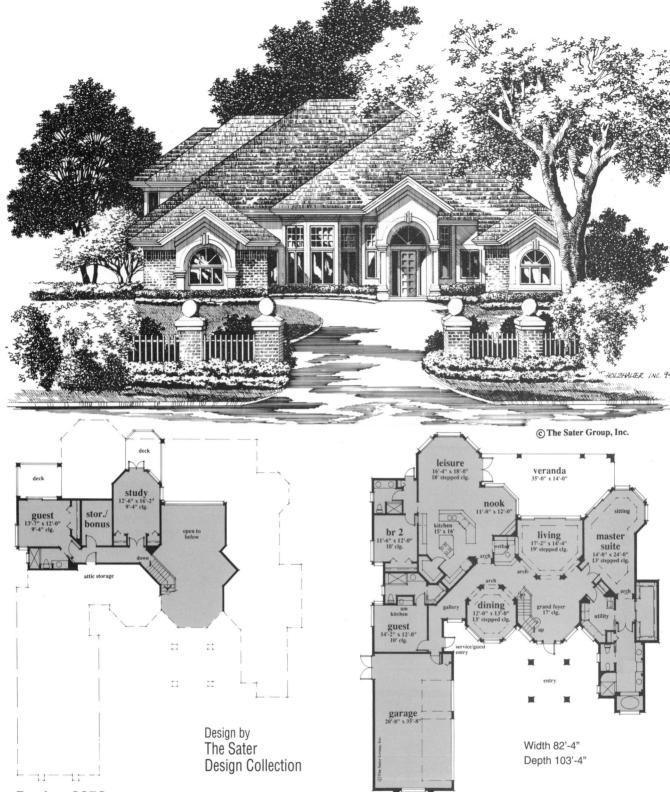

Design by
The Sater
Design Collection

© The Sater Group, Inc.

Width 82'-4"
Depth 103'-4"

Design 6650

First Floor: 3,092 square feet
Second Floor: 656 square feet
Total: 3,748 square feet

● Luxury is paramount in this four-bedroom traditional home. A columned entry leads to the grand foyer. The exclusive master suite is split from the two secondary bedrooms, residing to the right of the plan, and has a private entrance to the lanai. An arched entry provides access to large His and Hers closets and an extravagant master bath featuring a whirlpool tub and a separate shower. The central portion of the first floor contains the living area. The living room and adjacent dining room provide space for formal entertaining. For the best in casual living, the spacious kitchen, multi-windowed nook and leisure room are combined. The second floor contains a comfortable guest suite with a full bath and a study. Both enjoy private decks.

veranda
40'-0" x 9'-0"

leisure
19'-4" x 17'-4"
10' high clg.

optional entertainment center

fireplace

pantry

desk

living
20'-2" x 15'-8"
2 story clg.

nook
9'-0" x 11'-0"

kitchen
12' x 12'

master suite
15'-0" x 18'-2"
11' step clg.

up

utility

study
13'-4" x 12'-0"
12'-6" high clg.

foyer

dining
13'-6" x 14'-0"
vault. clg.

entry

garage
22'-4" x 42'-8"

deck

loft
19'-8" x 14'-4"

wetbar

down

open to living below

br. 3
16'-10" x 11'-4"
9'-4" clg.

br. 2
11'-4" x 14'-10"
9'-4" clg.

Width 76'
Depth 90'

Design by
**The Sater
Design Collection**

Design 6646

First Floor: 2,551 square feet
Second Floor: 1,037 square feet
Total: 3,588 square feet

L

● This beautiful home has many attributes. These include a bowed dining room and a living room with a fireplace and outdoor access. For family gatherings, the kitchen remains open to the living areas. A study off the foyer will be much appreciated. A full bath leads to the outdoors—perfect for poolside. The master suite enjoys its own personal luxury bath with a whirlpool tub, dual lavatories, a compartmented toilet and bidet and a separate shower. Dual walk-in closets provides ample storage space. Upstairs, two bedrooms share a full bath. A loft with a wet bar accommodates playtime. A wraparound deck is an added feature.

◄ 63' ►

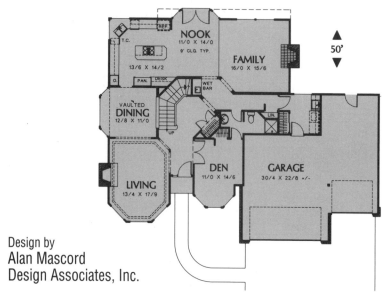

50'

Design by
Alan Mascord
Design Associates, Inc.

NOOK
11/0 X 14/0
9' CLG. TYP.

FAMILY
16/0 X 15/6

13/6 X 14/2

Vaulted
DINING
12/8 X 11/0

WET
BAR

UP

LIN.

DEN
11/0 X 14/6

GARAGE
30/4 X 22/8 +/-

LIVING
13/4 X 17/9

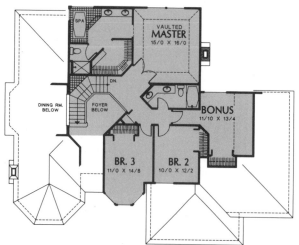

SPA

VAULTED
MASTER
15/0 X 16/0

DN.

DINING RM.
BELOW

FOYER
BELOW

BONUS
11/10 X 13/4

BR. 3
11/0 X 14/8

BR. 2
10/0 X 12/2

Design 9478

First Floor: 1,586 square feet
Second Floor: 960 square feet
Total: 2,546 square feet
Bonus Room: 194 square feet

L

● This exquisite plan features two tower structures that enhance its dramatic facade. Inside, it contains a beautifully functioning room arrangement that caters to family lifestyles. The living areas radiate around the central hallway which also contains the stairway to the second floor. The areas are large, open and convenient for both casual and formal occasions. Three bedrooms upstairs include two family bedrooms and a grand master suite with a bath fit for a king. An oversized walk-in closet and vaulted ceiling are found here. Bonus space over the garage can be developed at a later time to suit changing needs.

Design 9415

First Floor: 1,002 square feet
Second Floor: 784 square feet
Total: 1,786 square feet

● A two-story turret dominates the facade of this special home for narrow lots, adding significant appeal both inside and out. But don't let that distract your examination of the efficient floor plan. Besides extra space over the garage, a cozy nook with a bay window and a family room with a fireplace, the efficient kitchen provides expansive corner window treatments. The three bedrooms upstairs include a master suite with bay windows overlooking the front yard, a spa tub, a compartmented shower and toilet and a double vanity. Two additional bedrooms share a full bath.

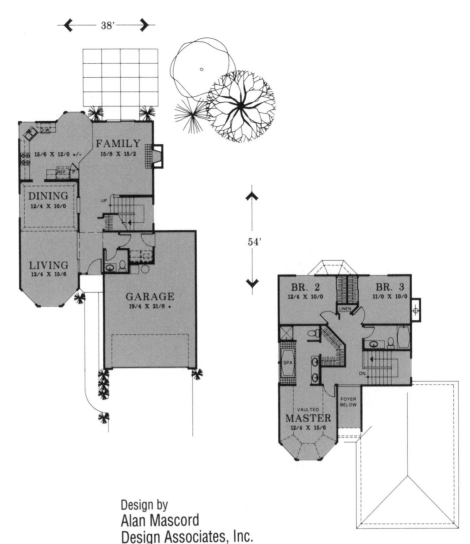

38'

54'

FAMILY
15/8 X 15/2

15/6 X 12/0 +/-

DINING
12/4 X 10/0

UP

LIVING
12/4 X 15/6

GARAGE
19/4 X 21/8 +

BR. 2
12/4 X 10/0

BR. 3
11/0 X 10/0

LINEN

DN.

SPA

FOYER
BELOW

VAULTED
MASTER
12/4 X 15/6

Design by
Alan Mascord
Design Associates, Inc.

Design 9987

First Floor: 1,341 square feet
Second Floor: 598 square feet
Total: 1,939 square feet

● Can't you smell the salty air, feel the ocean breezes and hear the crashing waves of the sea? What a beautiful home to enjoy these sensations from! Imagine sitting in the great room, perhaps with a crackling fire to warm the evening, or savoring leisurely mornings sipping your favorite beverage on the enclosed porch. After an afternoon of sailing, meal preparation is a breeze with a galley kitchen designed for efficiency. The first floor contains two bedrooms and a unique bath to serve family and guests. The second floor offers a private getaway with a master suite that supplies panoramic views from its adjoining sitting area. A master bath with His and Hers walk-in closets and a private deck complete the upstairs.

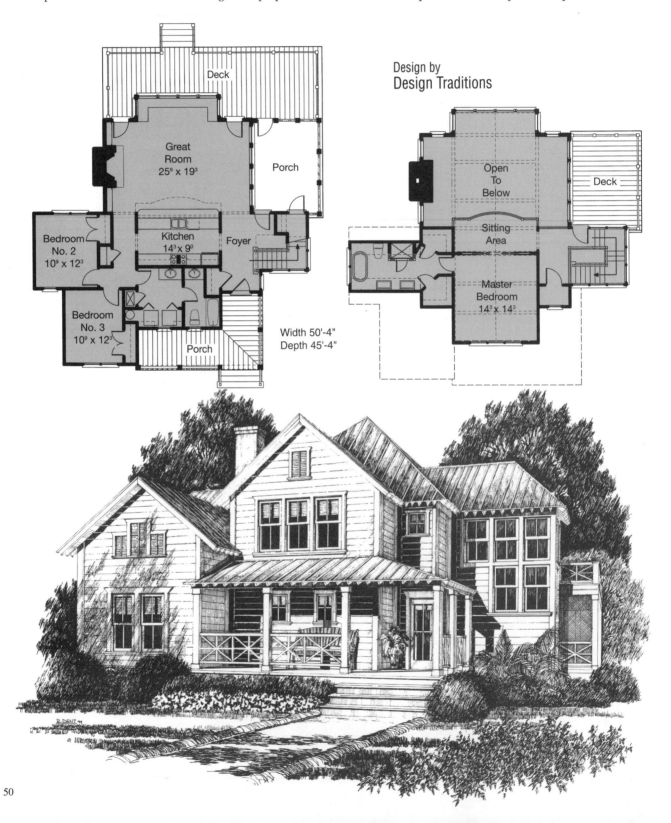

Design by
Design Traditions

Width 50'-4"
Depth 45'-4"

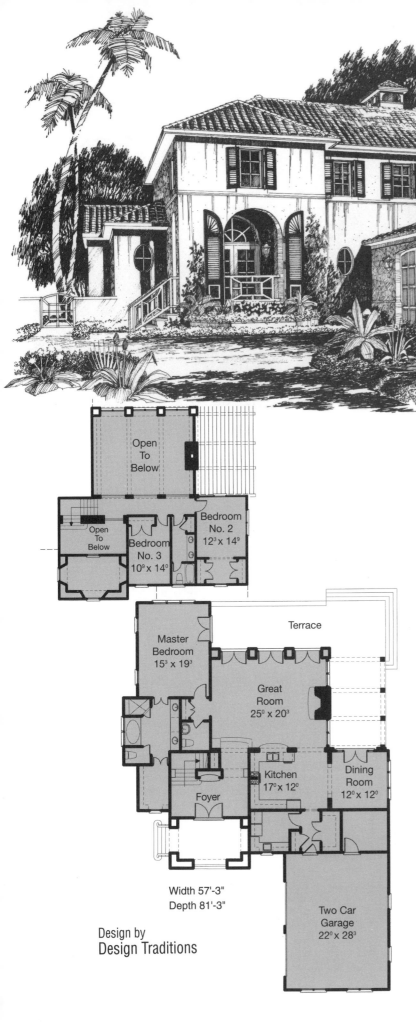

Open
To
Below

Open
To
Below

Bedroom
No. 3
10⁹ x 14⁰

Bedroom
No. 2
12³ x 14⁹

Master
Bedroom
15³ x 19³

Terrace

Great
Room
25⁰ x 20³

Kitchen
17⁰ x 12⁰

Dining
Room
12⁰ x 12⁰

Foyer

Width 57'-3"
Depth 81'-3"

Two Car
Garage
22⁰ x 28³

Design by
Design Traditions

Design 9989

First Floor: 2,058 square feet
Second Floor: 712 square feet
Total: 2,770 square feet

● If you have always dreamed of owning a villa, we invite you to experience the magic. Designed with a fine balance of formal and informal lifestyles in mind, this home fulfills both requirements. The charming exterior focuses on a rear terrace that surrounds the great room and is accessed from the dining room and master bedroom as well. French doors opening from the great room produce a superb marriage of indoor/outdoor relationships. A U-shaped kitchen is planned for convenience and serves the dining room and great room with equal ease. Views from the master bedroom combine with a relaxing master bath to creating a winning master suite. The second floor is comprised of two family bedrooms that share a full bath.

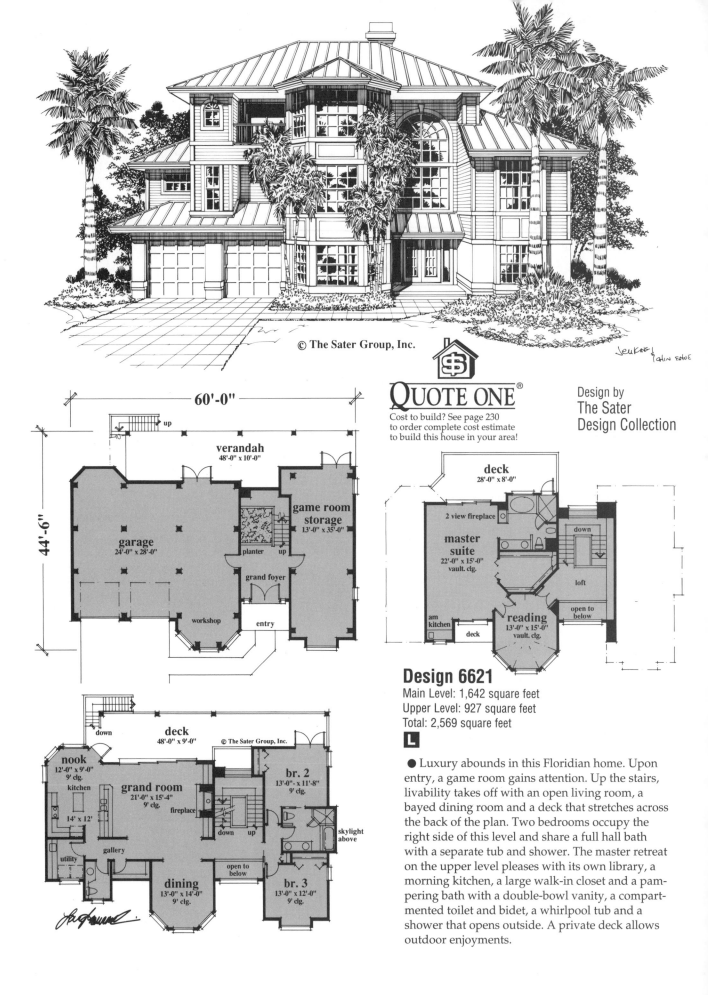

© The Sater Group, Inc.

60'-0"

44'-6"

up

verandah
48'-0" x 10'-0"

garage
24'-0" x 28'-0"

game room storage
13'-0" x 35'-0"

planter

up

grand foyer

workshop

entry

Quote One®

Cost to build? See page 230
to order complete cost estimate
to build this house in your area!

Design by
The Sater Design Collection

deck
28'-0" x 8'-0"

2 view fireplace

down

master suite
22'-0" x 15'-0"
vault. clg.

loft

am kitchen

deck

reading
13'-0" x 15'-0"
vault. clg.

open to below

Design 6621

Main Level: 1,642 square feet
Upper Level: 927 square feet
Total: 2,569 square feet

L

down

deck
48'-0" x 9'-0"

© The Sater Group, Inc.

nook
12'-0" x 9'-0"
9' clg.

kitchen

14' x 12'

grand room
21'-0" x 15'-4"
9' clg.

fireplace

br. 2
13'-0" x 11'-8"
9' clg.

down

up

skylight above

utility

gallery

open to below

dining
13'-0" x 14'-0"
9' clg.

br. 3
13'-0" x 12'-0"
9' clg.

● Luxury abounds in this Floridian home. Upon
entry, a game room gains attention. Up the stairs,
livability takes off with an open living room, a
bayed dining room and a deck that stretches across
the back of the plan. Two bedrooms occupy the
right side of this level and share a full hall bath
with a separate tub and shower. The master retreat
on the upper level pleases with its own library, a
morning kitchen, a large walk-in closet and a pampering bath with a double-bowl vanity, a compartmented toilet and bidet, a whirlpool tub and a
shower that opens outside. A private deck allows
outdoor enjoyments.

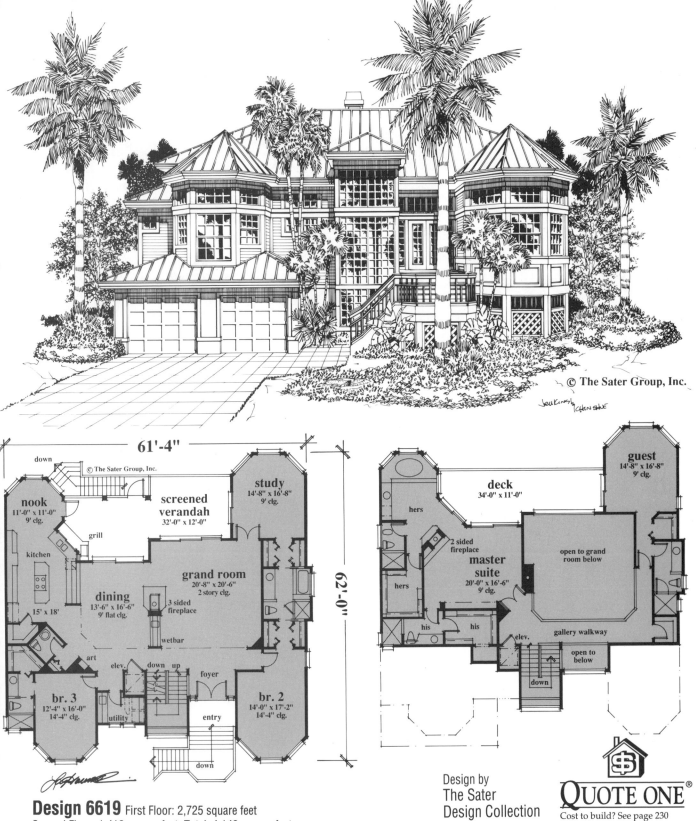

© The Sater Group, Inc.

Design 6619 First Floor: 2,725 square feet
Second Floor: 1,418 square feet; Total: 4,143 square feet

L

Design by
The Sater
Design Collection

Quote One®
Cost to build? See page 230
to order complete cost estimate
to build this house in your area!

● Florida living takes off in this wonderful design. A grand room gains attention as a superb entertaining area. A see-through fireplace here connects this room to the dining room. Sets of sliding glass doors offer passage to an expansive rear veranda. In the study, quiet time is assured—or slip out the doors and onto the veranda for a breather. A full bath connects the study and Bedroom 2. Bedroom 3 sits on the opposite side of the house and

enjoys its own bath. The kitchen is fully functional with a large work island and a connecting breakfast nook. Upstairs, the master bedroom suite is something to behold. His and Hers baths, a see-through fireplace and access to an upper deck all characterize this room. A guest bedroom suite is located on the other side of the upper floor and will make visits a real pleasure.

Design 9499

First Floor: 1,762 square feet
Second Floor: 1,233 square feet
Total: 2,995 square feet

L

● This stucco contemporary plan is resplendent and quite distinct with wide eaves and inventive window design. The floor plan adds some unique touches as well. The entry foyer leads to a formal living room and dining room on the left and a den or music room on the right. The family room is to the back of the plan and contains a warming corner fireplace. The kitchen is quite different--it boasts a two-story ceiling and is overlooked by the balcony upstairs. Bedrooms include two family bedrooms with shared bath and a master suite. The master includes a private balcony and pampering bath. Cove ceilings can be found in the master suite and also in the dining room and living room.

Design by
**Alan Mascord
Design Associates, Inc.**

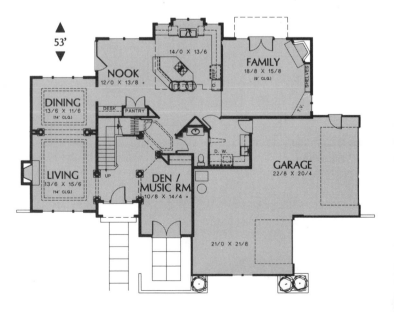

Design 6647

First Floor: 2,638 square feet
Second Floor: 1,032 square feet
Total: 3,670 square feet

● Unique window treatments, glass walls and French doors provide panoramic views from every room in this sophisticated two-story home. Natural light fills a two-story foyer that opens onto a study to the right and a formal parlor and dining room to the left. The leisure room located to the rear of the plan provides access to the veranda via three sets of French doors, creating a perfect setting for casual gatherings. The kitchen features an island cooktop and serves the sunny breakfast nook, as well as informal and formal areas with equal ease. The first-floor master suite is a private getaway that invites relaxation. His and Hers walk-in closets separate a luxurious master bath. The second floor contains three additional bedrooms—all with walk-in closets—and two full baths.

Design by
**The Sater
Design Collection**

Width 80'-4"
Depth 65'-4"

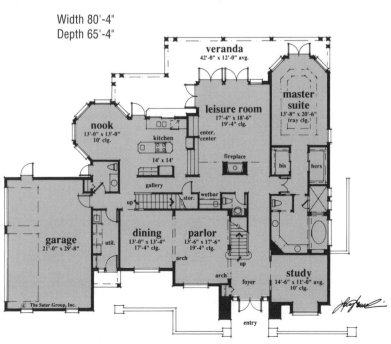

Design 3323

First Floor: 1,923 square feet
Second Floor: 838 square feet
Total: 2,761 square feet

L

● This two-story southwestern home was
designed to make living patterns as pleasant
as they can be. Take a step down from the
foyer and go where your mood takes you: a
gathering room with fireplace and an alcove
for reading or quiet conversations, a media
room for enjoying the latest technology, or to
the dining room with sliding glass doors to
the terrace. The kitchen has an island range
and eating space. Also on the first floor is a
large master suite including a sitting area
with terrace access, walk-in closet and
whirlpool. An elegant spiral staircase leads to
two family bedrooms sharing a full bath and
a guest bedroom with private bath.

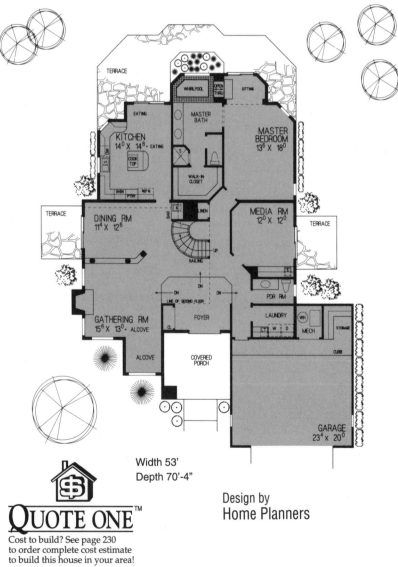

Width 53'
Depth 70'-4"

Design by
Home Planners

QUOTE ONE™

Cost to build? See page 230
to order complete cost estimate
to build this house in your area!

56

Design 9554

Main Level: 1,989 square feet
Upper Level: 1,349 square feet
Lower Level: 105 square feet
Total: 3,443 square feet

Cost to build? See page 230
to order complete cost estimate
to build this house in your area!

● Dramatic balconies and spectacular window treatment enhance this stunning luxury home. Inside, a through-fire-place warms the formal living room and a restful den. Both living spaces open onto a balcony that invites quiet reflection on starry nights. The banquet-sized dining room is easily served from the adjacent kitchen. Here, space is shared with an eating nook that provides access to the rear grounds and a family room with a corner fireplace perfect for casual gather-ings. The upper level contains two family bedrooms and a luxurious master suite that enjoys its own private balcony. The lower level accommodates a shop and a bonus room for future development.

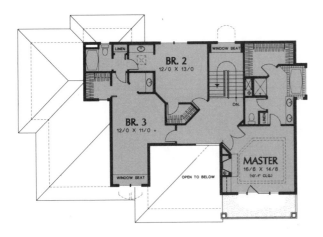

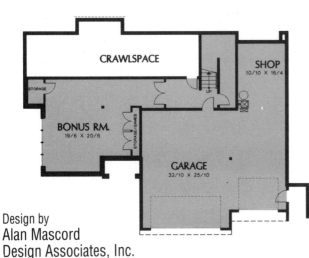

Design by
Alan Mascord
Design Associates, Inc.

Width 63'
Depth 48'

Design 8672

Square Footage: 2,397

● Low-slung, hipped rooflines and an abundance of glass enhance the unique exterior of this fine one-story home. Inside, the use of soffits and tray ceilings heighten the distinctive style of the floor plan. To the left, double doors lead to the private master suite which is bathed in natural light—compliments of an abundant use of glass—and enjoys a garden setting from the corner tub. Convenient planning of the gourmet kitchen places everything at minimum distances and serves the outdoor kitchen, breakfast nook and family room with equal ease. Completing the plan are two family bedrooms that share a full bath.

Design by
Home Design
Services, Inc.

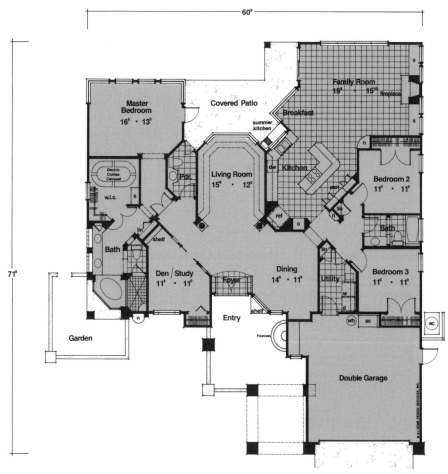

Photos by Allen Maertz

This home, as shown in the photograph, may differ from the actual blueprints. For more detailed information, please check the floor plans carefully.

Design by
Home Planners

WIDTH 154'
DEPTH 94'-8"

QUOTE ONE™

Cost to build? See page 230
to order complete cost estimate
to build this house in your area!

Design 3471

First Floor: 3,166 square feet
Second Floor: 950 square feet
Total: 4,116 square feet
Guest Living Area: 680 square feet

L

● Western farmhouse-style living is captured in this handsome design. The central entrance leads into a cozy parlor—half walls provide a view of the grand dining room. Entertaining's a cinch with the dining room's built-in china alcove, service counter and fireplace. The country kitchen, with a large island cooktop, overlooks the gathering room with its full wall of glass. The master bedroom will satisfy even the most discerning tastes. It boasts a raised hearth, porch access and a bath with a walk-in closet, separate vanities and a whirlpool. You may want to use one of the additional first-floor bedrooms as a study, the other as a guest room. To round out the first floor, you'll also find a clutter room with a pantry, freezer space and access to storage space. Two family bedrooms and attic storage make up the second floor. Note, too, the separate garage and guest house which make this such a winning design.

59

Design 8690

Square Footage: 3,556

● A beautiful curved portico provides a majestic entrance to this one-story home. Curved ceilings in the formal living and dining rooms continue the extraordinary style. To the left of the foyer is a den/bedroom with a private bath, ideal for use as a guest suite. The exquisite master suite features a see-through fireplace and an exercise area with a wet bar. A sumptuous soaking tub and island shower in the master bath invite relaxation. The family wing is geared for casual living with a powder room/patio bath, a huge island kitchen with a walk-in pantry, a glass-walled breakfast nook and a grand family room with a fireplace and media wall. Two family bedrooms share a private bath.

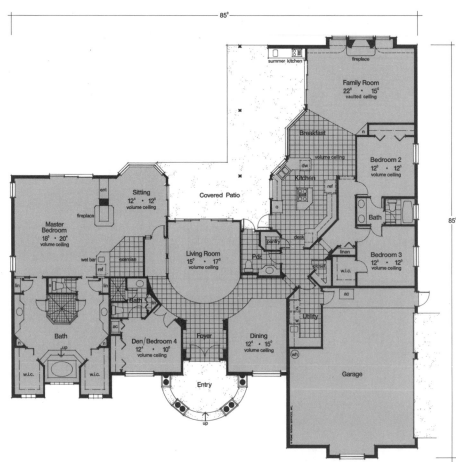

Design by
Home Design
Services, Inc.

Design 8663
Square Footage: 2,597

Design by
Home Design
Services, Inc.

● The angles in this home create unlimited views and spaces that appear larger. Majestic columns of brick add warmth to a striking elevation. Inside, the foyer commands special perspective on living areas, including the living room, the dining room and the den. The island kitchen services the breakfast nook and the family room. A large pantry provides ample space for food storage. In the master bedroom suite, mitered glass and a private bath set the tone for simple luxury. Two secondary bedrooms share privacy and quiet at the front of the house. The den may also convert to a fourth bedroom, if desired.

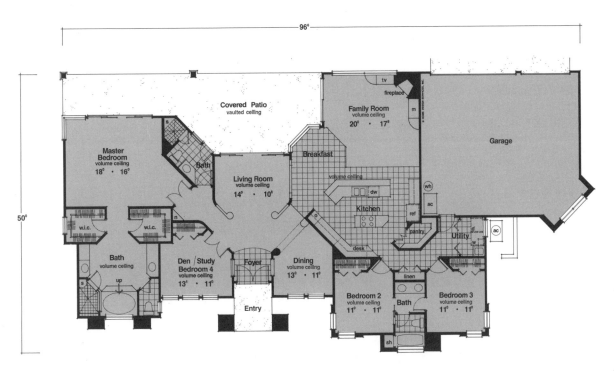

Design 8686
Square Footage: 2,104

● The playful use of Palladian and other window shapes, and massive columns, set the stage for this elegant one-story home. Inside, columns and floating soffits create an open, airy design. Formal living areas flank the foyer, while the rear of the plan is occupied by the more casual family room with its welcoming corner fireplace. The kitchen is efficiently placed to serve the informal breakfast nook and the formal dining room with ease. Split-bedroom planning separates the master suite from family bedrooms for privacy. The master bedroom opens onto the rear patio and features an opulent master bath complete with a corner tub. Secondary bedrooms share a unique pool bath. Bedroom 2 is ideally situated for use as a den or home office.

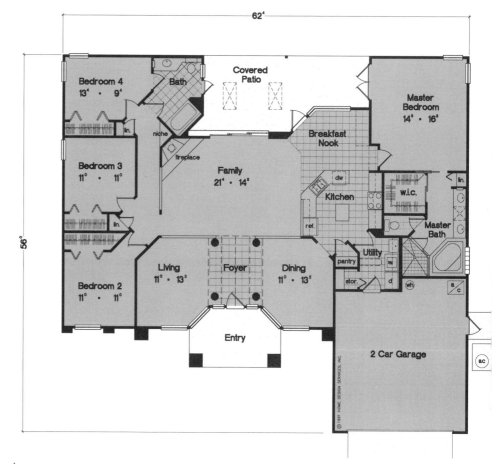

Design by
**Home Design
Services, Inc.**

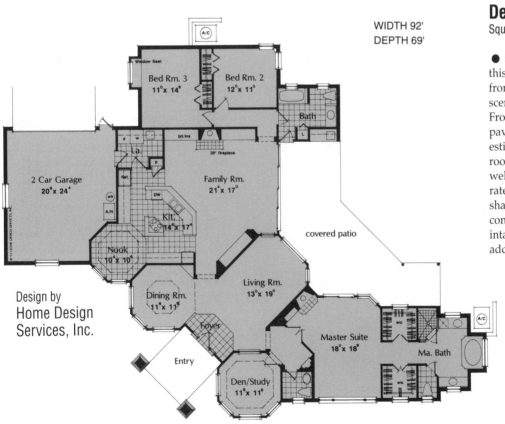

WIDTH 92'
DEPTH 69'

A/C

Window Seat

Bed Rm. 3
11⁰ x 14⁸

Bed Rm. 2
12⁰ x 11⁰

Bath

blt/ins

36" fireplace

La.

d w

p

2 Car Garage
20⁸ x 24⁴

Ret.

Family Rm.
21⁴ x 17⁰

A/H

DW

wh

Kit.
14⁸ x 17⁰

Nook
10⁸ x 10⁸

Dining Rm.
11⁸ x 11⁸

Living Rm.
13⁰ x 19⁰

covered patio

Foyer

wic

Design by
**Home Design
Services, Inc.**

Entry

Master Suite
18⁰ x 18⁸

Ma. Bath

A/C

Den/Study
11⁸ x 11⁸

wic

Design 8603
Square Footage: 2,656

● A graceful design sets
this charming home apart
from the ordinary and tran-
scends the commonplace.
From the octagon foyer
paved in granite to the interesting breakfast nook, dining
room and den/study, this
well-executed plan incorporates rooms of varying
shapes but keeps its original
concept of spaciousness
intact. A large covered patio
adds to the living area.

COPYRIGHT LARRY E. BELK

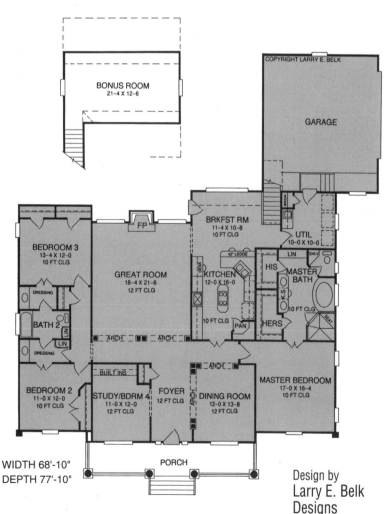

BONUS ROOM
21-4 X 12-6

COPYRIGHT LARRY E. BELK

GARAGE

BEDROOM 3
13-4 X 12-0
10 FT CLG

DRESSING

BATH 2

DRESSING

GREAT ROOM
18-4 X 21-6
12 FT CLG

FP

BRKFST RM
11-4 X 10-6
10 FT CLG

UTIL
10-0 X 10-0

LIN

42" LEDGE

HIS

MASTER
BATH

KITCHEN
12-0 X 16-0

K.S.

10 FT CLG

10 FT CLG

PAN

HERS

SEAT

ARCH

ARCH

BUILT INS

BEDROOM 2
11-0 X 12-0
10 FT CLG

STUDY/BDRM 4
11-0 X 12-0
12 FT CLG

FOYER
12 FT CLG

ARCH

ARCH

DINING ROOM
12-0 X 13-8
12 FT CLG

MASTER BEDROOM
17-0 X 16-4
10 FT CLG

WIDTH 68'-10"
DEPTH 77'-10"

PORCH

Design by
Larry E. Belk
Designs

Design 8143

Square Footage: 2,648
Bonus Room: 266 square feet

● This vintage elevation has all the
extras desired by today's homeowners.
Inside, 12' ceilings give the study, the
dining room, and the great room a large,
spacious feeling. Graceful arches are
flanked by stately columns. The kitchen
features a cooktop work island, a pantry
and a 42" eating bar. An optional bonus
room over the garage is a great place for
a play room or an in-home office. The
master suite includes His and Hers closets and an amenity-filled master bath.
Bedrooms 2 and 3 feature roomy closets
and each has access to a private dressing
area off of Bath 2. Please specify
crawlspace or slab foundation when
ordering.

64

This home, as shown in the photograph, may differ from the actual blueprints. For more detailed information, please check the floor plans carefully.

Photos by Bob Greenspan

Design 3558

First Floor: 2,328 square feet
Second Floor: 603 square feet
Total: 2,931 square feet

L **D**

● This home will keep even the most active family from feeling cramped. A broad foyer opens to a living room that measures 24 feet across and features sliding glass doors to a rear terrace and a covered porch. Adjacent to the kitchen is a conversation area with additional access to the covered porch, a snack bar, fireplace and a window bay. A butler's pantry leads to the formal dining room. Placed conveniently on the first floor, the master suite features a roomy bath with a huge walk-in closet and dual vanities. Two large bedrooms are found on the second floor.

Design by
Home Planners

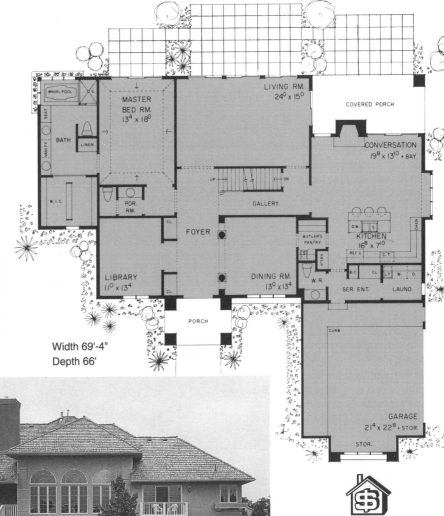

Width 69'-4"
Depth 66'

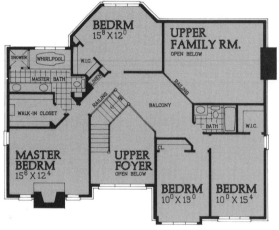

Design 3446

First Floor: 1,532 square feet
Second Floor: 1,200 square feet
Total: 2,732 square feet

 L **D**

● A unique facade harbors a spacious, two-story foyer with an angled stairway. To the left is the formal living room with a fireplace and half walls separating the formal dining room. To the right is a quiet den. The kitchen and breakfast room combination takes advantage of a sunny bay. The family room features a second fireplace and a vaulted ceiling with three skylights. Yet another fireplace is found in the master bedroom suite, which includes a pampering master bath with walk-in closet, dual vanities and a separate tub and shower. Bedroom 2 is set into a bay and features a walk-in closet. Two additional family bedrooms and a full bath round out the second floor.

Design by
Home Planners

Width 60'-4"
Depth 48'-8"

QUOTE ONE™

Cost to build? See page 230 to order complete cost estimate to build this house in your area!

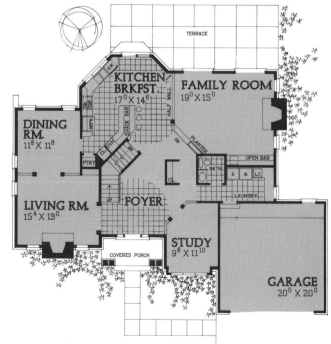

Design 7273

First Floor: 1,719 square feet
Second Floor: 1,688 square feet
Total: 3,407 square feet

● Two-story bays, luminous windows and brick details embellish this stately traditional home. Inside, the soaring foyer is angled to provide impressive views of a spectacular curving staircase and columns that grace and define the octagonal dining room. Although hard to choose, the home's most outstanding feature may be the sunroom which is highlighted by a dome ceiling and bowed windows. This room provides access to the multi-windowed great room and an expansive veranda for outdoor enjoyment. A cozy hearth room, breakfast room and kitchen complete the informal living area. The sumptuous master suite features a fireplace, a library and an opulent master bath with a gazebo ceiling and skylight above the whirlpool tub. Three secondary bedrooms and a bath complete the second floor.

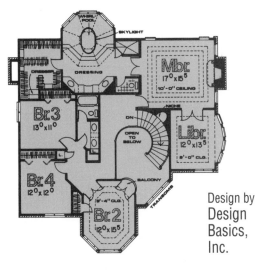

Design by
Design
Basics,
Inc.

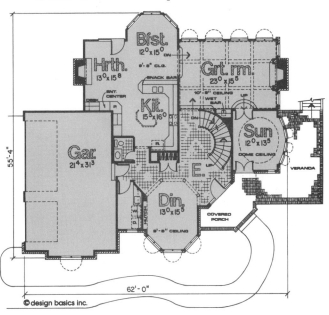

Design 8960

First Floor: 2,589 square feet
Second Floor: 1,037 square feet
Total: 3,626 square feet

● Finely detailed entry pilasters
and a second-story Palladian
window combine to create a
distinctive facade for this stately
home. The unique angled foyer
offers an uninterrupted view of
the sunken living room and dining room beyond. Skylights,
French doors, and a window
seat offer natural light to the
breakfast room and garden
room, while a two-story ceiling
adds a dramatic touch to the
kitchen. A window-walled
walkway with skylights leads
to the utility room and three-car
garage. The first-floor master
retreat offers a sitting room with
built-in media center, an elegant
bath with corner whirlpool tub,
and a glass-enclosed exercise
solarium. The second-floor
skylit game room overlooks the
kitchen below.

Design by
Larry W.
Garnett &
Associates, Inc.

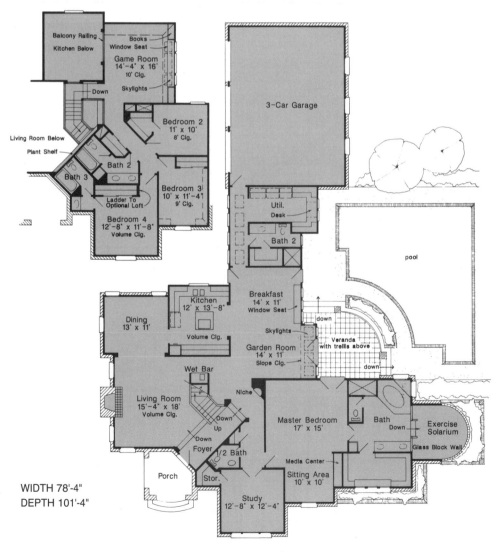

WIDTH 78'-4"
DEPTH 101'-4"

WIDTH 47'
DEPTH 54'-4"

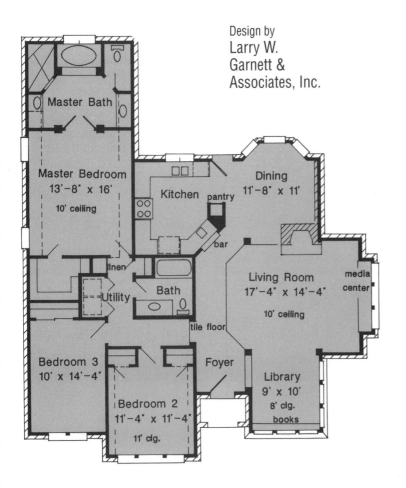

Design by
Larry W.
Garnett &
Associates, Inc.

Master Bath

Master Bedroom
13'-8" x 16'
10' ceiling

Kitchen

pantry

Dining
11'-8" x 11'

bar

linen

Utility

Bath

Living Room
17'-4" x 14'-4"

10' ceiling

media
center

tile floor

Bedroom 3
10' x 14'-4"

Foyer

Bedroom 2
11'-4" x 11'-4"

11' clg.

Library
9' x 10'
8' clg.

books

Design 9180
Square Footage: 1,824

● This traditional brick home pleases the eye with its sloping rooflines and multi-pane windows. The feeling carries to the interior where a library opens off the foyer and leads to a volume living room. Here, a window seat and a fireplace enhance the elegance of the room. A bayed dining room joins the living room with a column—note the wet bar that services the area around both the living and dining rooms. The kitchen will delight with its abundance of counter space and open plan. A back door leads to a quaint outdoor space. Three bedrooms grace the left side of the home and include a master suite with a lavish, private bath. It offers separate vanities, a compartmented toilet and a central, window-lit tub.

This home, as shown in the photograph, may differ from the actual blueprints. For more detailed information, please check the floor plans carefully.

Photo by Andrew D. Lautman

Design 2973

First Floor: 1,269 square feet
Second Floor: 1,227 square feet
Total: 2,496 square feet

L

● A most popular feature of the Victorian house has always been its covered porches. The two finely detailed outdoor living spaces found on this home add much to formal and informal entertaining options. However, in addition to its wonderful Victorian facade, this home provides a myriad of interior features that cater to the active, growing family. Living and dining areas include a formal living room and dining room, a family room with a fireplace, a study and a kitchen with an attached breakfast nook. The second floor has three family bedrooms and a luxurious master bedroom with a whirlpool spa and His and Hers walk-in closets.

Width 70'
Depth 44'-5"

Design by
Home Planners

QUOTE ONE™

Cost to build? See page 230
to order complete cost estimate
to build this house in your area!

Skylights, Clerestories & Transoms

B. NATHAN

Design 9632

First Floor: 1,756 square feet
Second Floor: 565 square feet
Total: 2,321 square feet

Design by
Donald A.
Gardner,
Architects, Inc.

● A wraparound covered porch at the front and sides of this house and an open deck at the back provide plenty of outside living area. The spacious great room features a fireplace, a cathedral ceiling and a clerestory with an arched window. The first-floor master bedroom contains a generous closet and a master bath with a garden tub, a double-bowl vanity and a shower. The second floor sports two bedrooms and a full bath. Please specify basement or crawlspace foundation when ordering.

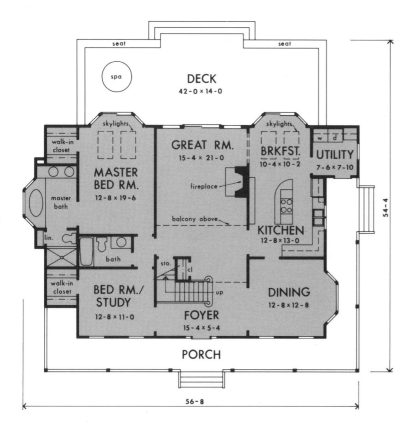

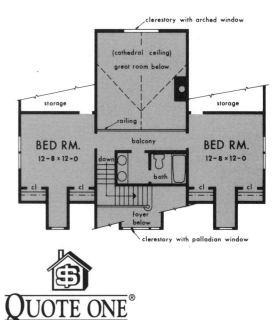

QUOTE ONE®

Cost to build? See page 230
to order complete cost estimate
to build this house in your area!

Design 9673

First Floor: 1,526 square feet
Second Floor: 635 square feet
Total: 2,161 square feet

● This beautiful farmhouse boasts all the extras a three-bedroom design could offer. Clerestory windows with arched tops enhance the exterior both front and back and allow natural light to penetrate into the foyer and great room. A kitchen with island counter and breakfast area is open to the spacious great room through a cased opening with colonnade. The exquisite master suite has a generous bedroom, large walk-in closet and dramatically designed master bath providing emphasis on the whirlpool tub flanked by double columns. Access to the rear deck is possible from the screened porch, master bath and breakfast area. The second level has two bedrooms sharing a full bath and a loft/study area overlooking the great room.

QUOTE ONE®

Cost to build? See page 230 to order complete cost estimate to build this house in your area!

BONUS RM.
27-0 × 12-0
down

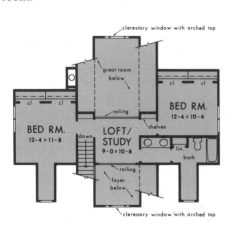

clerestory window with arched top

great room below

cl   cl

BED RM.
12-4 × 10-4

railing

shelves

BED RM.
12-4 × 11-8

down

LOFT/ STUDY
9-0 × 10-8

lin.   bath

railing

foyer below

clerestory window with arched top

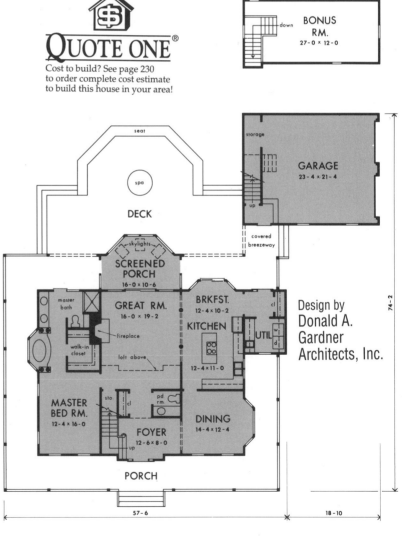

Design by
Donald A. Gardner Architects, Inc.

B. NATHAN

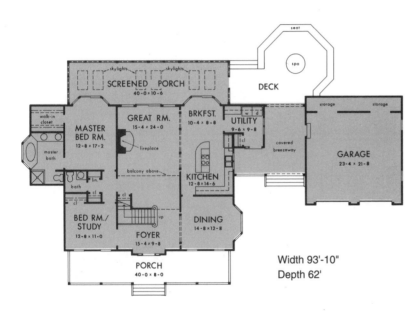

Width 93'-10"
Depth 62'

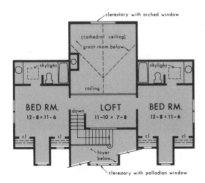

Design by
Donald A.
Gardner,
Architects, Inc.

Design 9712

First Floor: 1,766 square feet
Second Floor: 670 square feet
Total: 2,436 square feet

● With a casually elegant exterior, this four-bedroom farmhouse celebrates sunlight with a Palladian window dormer, skylit screened porch and rear arched window. The clerestory window in the two-story foyer throws natural light across the loft to the great room with fireplace and cathedral ceiling. The center island kitchen and breakfast area open to the great room through an elegant colonnade. The first-floor master suite is a calm retreat opening to the screened porch through a bay area. A garden tub, dual lavatories and a separate shower are touches of luxury in the master bath. The second floor provides two bedrooms with private baths and a loft area.

Cost to build? See page 230
to order complete cost estimate
to build this house in your area!

73

Design 9733

First Floor: 1,871 square feet
Second Floor: 731 square feet
Total: 2,602 square feet
Bonus Room: 402 square feet

● This fetching four-bedroom country home with porches and dormers at both front and rear offers a welcoming touch to an open floor plan. A sloped ceiling and a Palladian clerestory window allow the foyer to fill with natural light. The spacious great room enjoys a large fireplace, a cathedral ceiling and a clerestory with an arched window. An efficient kitchen is centrally located to the dining room and bayed breakfast area for maximum convenience. The expansive master suite is located on the first floor with a generous walk-in closet and includes a luxurious master bath which boasts a whirlpool tub. The second bedroom may be used as a study if desired. The second floor holds two bedrooms that share a full bath.

Design by
Donald A.
Gardner,
Architects, Inc.

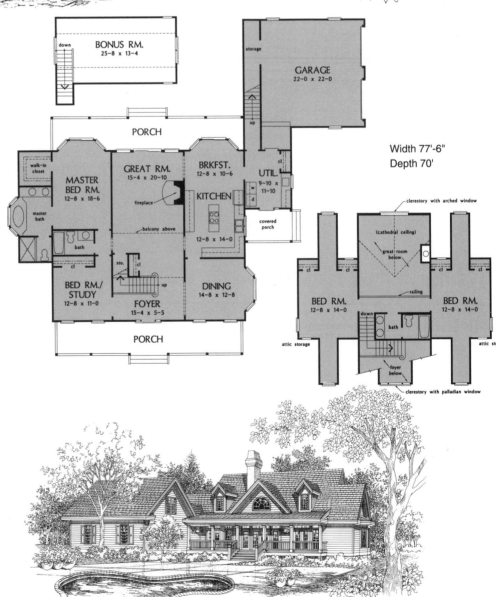

Width 77'-6"
Depth 70'

Design 9621

First Floor: 1,325 square feet
Second Floor: 453 square feet
Total: 1,778 square feet

● This compact design has all the amenities available in larger plans with little wasted space. In addition, a front Palladian window, dormers and rear arched windows provide exciting visual elements to the exterior. The spacious great room has a fireplace, a cathedral ceiling and clerestory windows. A second-level balcony overlooks this gathering area. The kitchen is centrally located for maximum flexibility in layout and features a pass-through to the great room. Besides the generous master suite with its well-appointed full bath, there are two family bedrooms located on the second level sharing a full bath with a double vanity. Please specify basement or crawlspace foundation when ordering.

FRONT

REAR

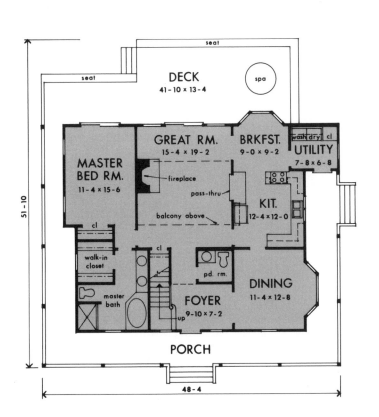

MASTER BED RM.
11-4 x 15-6

GREAT RM.
15-4 x 19-2

BRKFST.
9-0 x 9-2

UTILITY
7-8 x 6-8

wash dry cl

KIT.
12-4 x 12-0

fireplace

pass-thru

balcony above

walk-in closet

cl

master bath

pd. rm.

FOYER
9-10 x 7-2

DINING
11-4 x 12-8

up

DECK
41-10 x 13-4

seat

seat

spa

PORCH

51-10

48-4

Design by
Donald A. Gardner, Architects, Inc.

Quote One®

Cost to build? See page 230 to order complete cost estimate to build this house in your area!

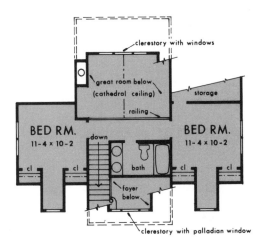

clerestory with windows

great room below
(cathedral ceiling)

storage

railing

BED RM.
11-4 x 10-2

BED RM.
11-4 x 10-2

down

bath

foyer below

cl

cl

clerestory with palladian window

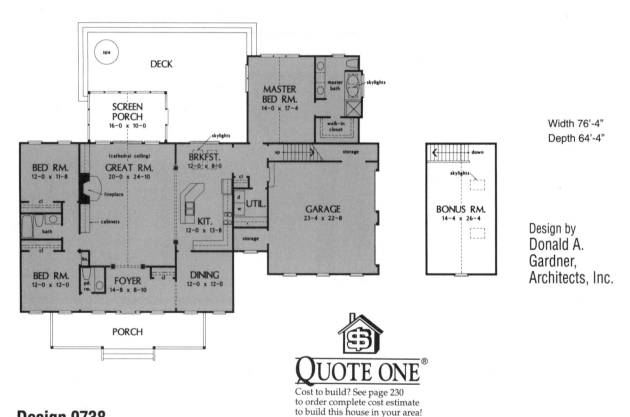

Width 76'-4"
Depth 64'-4"

Design by
Donald A.
Gardner,
Architects, Inc.

Design 9738

Square Footage: 2,136
Bonus Room: 405 square feet

● This exciting three-bedroom country home overflows with amenities. Traditional details such as columns, cathedral ceilings and open living areas combine to create the ideal floor plan for today's active family lifestyle. The spacious great room features built-in cabinets and a fireplace and a cathedral ceiling which continues into the adjoining screened porch. An efficient kitchen with a food prepara-

tion island is conveniently grouped with the great room, the dining room and the skylit breakfast area for the cook who enjoys visiting while preparing meals. A private master bedroom features a cathedral ceiling, a large walk-in closet and a relaxing master bath with a skylit whirlpool tub and a separate shower. Two secondary bedrooms share a full bath at the opposite end of the home.

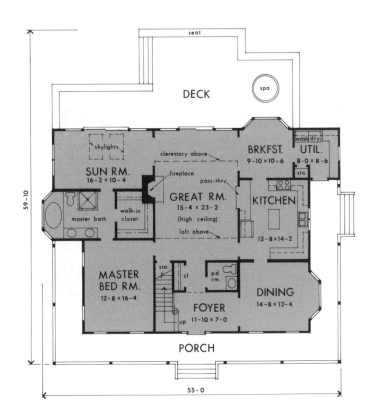

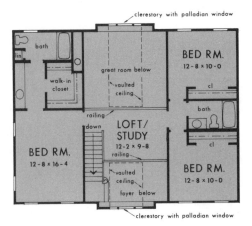

Design 9616

First Floor: 1,734 square feet
Second Floor: 958 square feet
Total: 2,692 square feet

● A wraparound covered porch at the front and sides of this home and the open deck with spa and seating provide plenty of outside living area. A central great room features a vaulted ceiling, fireplace and clerestory windows above. The loft/study on the second floor overlooks this gathering area. Besides a formal dining room, kitchen, breakfast room and sun room on the first floor, there is also a generous master suite with garden tub. Three second-floor bedrooms complete sleeping accommodations. The plan includes a crawl-space foundation.

Design by
Donald A.
Gardner,
Architects, Inc.

FRONT

REAR

Design 9734

Square Footage: 1,977
Bonus Room: 430 square feet

● A two-story foyer with a Palladian window above sets the tone for this sunlit home. Columns mark the passage from the foyer to the great room, where a centered fireplace and built-in cabinets are found. A screened porch with four skylights above and a wet bar provides a pleasant place to start the day or wind down after work. The kitchen is flanked by the formal dining room and the breakfast room with sliding glass doors to the large, rear deck. Hidden quietly in the rear, the master suite includes a bath with dual vanities and skylights. Two family bedrooms (one an optional study) share a bath with twin sinks.

QUOTE ONE®

Cost to build? See page 230 to order complete cost estimate to build this house in your area!

Design by
Donald A. Gardner, Architects, Inc.

attic storage

BONUS RM.
18-0 x 19-0

skylights
down

DECK

seat
spa

SCREEN PORCH
16-0 x 11-0

skylights

MASTER BED RM.
13-4 x 18-8

master bath

skylights

walk-in closet

wet bar

BED RM.
12-4 x 11-8

cl

bath

lin.

GREAT RM.
16-0 x 17-4

fireplace

cabinets

cl

BRKFST.
12-0 x 8-6

KITCHEN
12-0 x 12-8

up

UTIL.

d w

lin.

storage

GARAGE
22-0 x 20-4

FOYER
12-4 x 5-6

PORCH

DINING
12-0 x 13-8

storage

BED RM./ STUDY
12-0 x 12-0

WIDTH 69'-8"
DEPTH 67'-6"

Design 9764

Square Footage: 1,815
Bonus Room: 336 square feet

● Dormers, arched windows and covered porches lend this home its country appeal. Inside, the foyer opens to the dining room on the right and leads through a columned entrance to the great room warmed by a fireplace. Access is provided to the covered, skylit rear porch for outdoor livability. The open kitchen easily serves the great room, the bayed breakfast area and the dining room. A cathedral ceiling graces the master bedroom with its walk-in closet and private bath with a dual vanity and a whirlpool tub. Two additional bedrooms share a full bath. A detached garage with a skylit bonus room is connected to the rear covered porch.

Width 70'-8"
Depth 70'-2"

Design by
Donald A.
Gardner
Architects, Inc.

Design 9748

Square Footage: 1,737

● Inviting porches are just the
beginning of this lovely country
home. Notice the massive great
room with a cathedral ceiling,
built-in bookshelves and a fireplace. It leads through graceful
arches to an octagonal dining room
with a tray ceiling. The breakfast
area is just a step away. The
kitchen includes an island cooktop
and built-in pantry. The master
bedroom, separated by the walk-in
closet and utility room, offers privacy and comfort.

Design by
Donald A.
Gardner,
Architects, Inc.

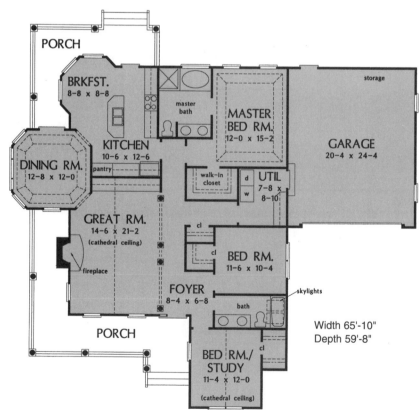

PORCH

BRKFST.
8-8 x 8-8

master
bath

MASTER
BED RM.
12-0 x 15-2

storage

GARAGE
20-4 x 24-4

KITCHEN
10-6 x 12-6

pantry

DINING RM.
12-8 x 12-0

walk-in
closet

UTIL
7-8 x
8-10

d
w

GREAT RM.
14-6 x 21-2
(cathedral ceiling)

cl

cl

BED RM.
11-6 x 10-4

fireplace

FOYER
8-4 x 6-8

skylights

bath

PORCH

Width 65'-10"
Depth 59'-8"

BED RM./
STUDY
11-4 x 12-0

cl

(cathedral ceiling)

B. NATHAN

Design 9750

Square Footage: 1,575
Bonus Room: 276 square feet

● A covered porch and dormers combine to create the inviting exterior on this three-bedroom country home. The foyer leads through columns to an expansive great room with a cozy fireplace, built-in bookshelves and access to the rear covered porch. To the right, an open kitchen is conveniently situated to easily serve the bay-windowed breakfast area and the formal dining room. Sleeping quarters are located on the left, where the master suite enjoys access to the covered porch, a walk-in closet and a relaxing master bath complete with double-bowl vanities, a whirlpool tub and a separate shower. A utility room, two secondary bedrooms and a full bath complete the plan. A bonus room over the garage provides room for future growth.

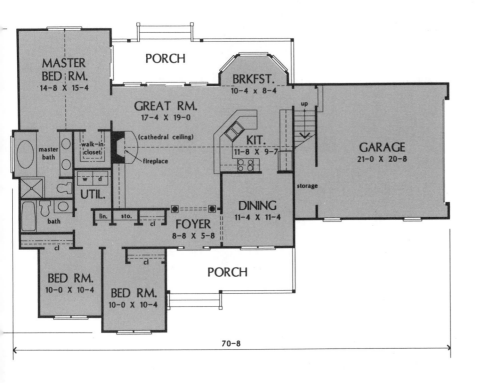

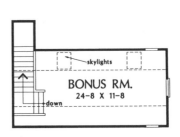

Design by
Donald A.
Gardner,
Architects, Inc.

Design 8144

First Floor: 1,482 square feet
Second Floor: 631 square feet
Total: 2,113 square feet

● Interesting texture, porches and a balcony lend special appeal to this charming two-story home. Inside, the foyer opens through archways to the formal dining room and the living room. Here, clerestory windows flood the area with natural light. The breakfast room and kitchen are located nearby with an angled sink, a serving ledge and a pass-through for convenience. A side porch opening from the breakfast room provides a touch of bygone charm and handy access to the outdoors. The master bedroom is filled with amenities that include a relaxing master bath with His and Hers walk-in closets. The second floor contains two family bedrooms—one with a balcony—and a full bath. Blueprints for this home include a two-car detached garage. Please specify slab or crawlspace foundation when ordering.

Design by
Larry E. Belk
Designs

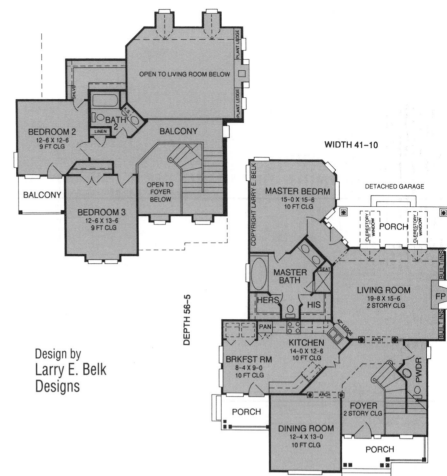

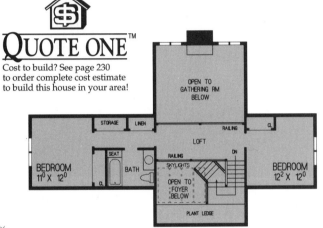

QUOTE ONE™

Cost to build? See page 230
to order complete cost estimate
to build this house in your area!

OPEN TO GATHERING RM BELOW

STORAGE | LINEN

RAILING | CL

LOFT

BEDROOM
11⁰ X 12⁰

SEAT

CL

BATH

RAILING

SKYLIGHTS

OPEN TO FOYER BELOW

PLANT LEDGE

DN

BEDROOM
12² X 12⁰

Design 3321

First Floor: 1,636 square feet
Second Floor: 572 square feet
Total: 2,208 square feet

L D

● Cozy and completely functional, this 1½-story
bungalow has many amenities not often found in
homes its size. The covered porch at the front opens
at the entry to a foyer with an angled staircase. To
the left is a media room. To the rear is the gathering
room with its central fireplace. Attached to the gathering room is a formal dining room with rear terrace
access. The kitchen features a curved casual eating
area and an island work station. The right side of
the first floor is dominated by the master suite. It
has access to the rear terrace and a luxurious bath.
Upstairs are two family bedrooms connected by a
loft area overlooking the gathering room and foyer.

Design by
Home Planners

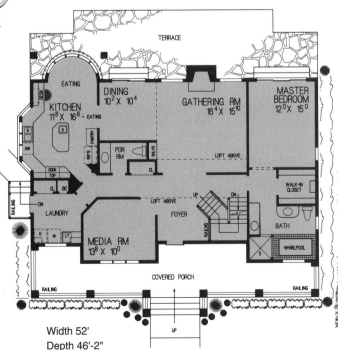

TERRACE

EATING

DESK

KITCHEN
11⁸ X 16⁸ • EATING

DINING
10² X 10⁴

GATHERING RM
16⁴ X 15¹⁰

MASTER BEDROOM
12⁰ X 15⁰

PANTRY

REF'G

PDR RM

CL

SNKS

LOFT ABOVE

COOK TOP

CL

BC

WALK-IN CLOSET

DN

LAUNDRY

LOFT ABOVE

FOYER

UP

DN

BATH

D W LT

MEDIA RM
13⁸ X 10⁰

RAILING

WHIRLPOOL

COVERED PORCH

RAILING

RAILING

UP

Width 52'
Depth 46'-2"

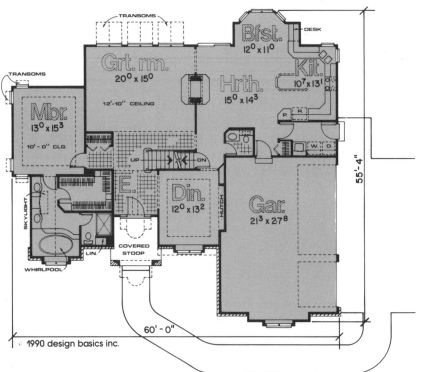

1990 design basics inc.

Design 9249

First Floor: 1,733 square feet
Second Floor: 672 square feet
Total: 2,405 square feet

● Split-bedroom floor planning highlights this volume-look home. The master suite on the first floor is completely private and perfectly pampering. Notice the huge walk-in closet, double vanity and separate tub and shower. The great room and hearth room share a through-fireplace and are complemented by a breakfast area and island kitchen. Formal entertaining is enhanced by the dining room with hutch space and boxed window. A guest half-bath just off the hearth room will be appreciated by visitors. Family bedrooms upstairs share a full bath with double vanity.

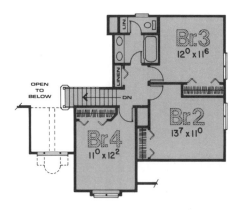

Design by
Design Basics, Inc.

Design 9272

First Floor: 1,520 square feet
Second Floor: 1,334 square feet
Total: 2,854 square feet

● Dramatic details and nine-foot main-level walls make this home worthy of building consideration. An enormous great room with spider-beamed ceiling, built-in bookcases and fireplace connects directly to the sun room with attached wet bar. This skylit area leads to the breakfast room and island kitchen. Complementing these informal gathering areas are the formal living room and dining room. A luxurious master suite features His and Hers walk-in closets and a volume dressing area with angled, oval whirlpool. Generous bath arrangements are made for the three secondary bedrooms.

Design by
Design Basics, Inc.

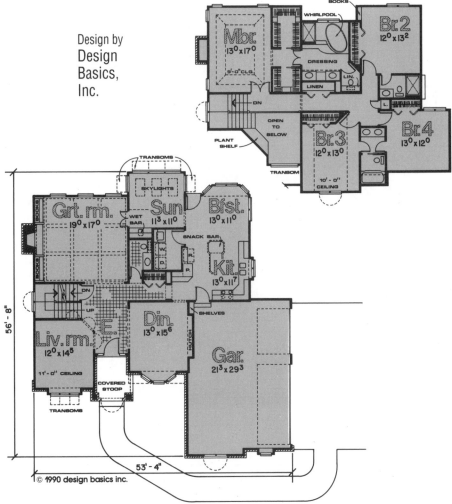

© 1990 design basics inc.

Design by
**Design
Basics,
Inc.**

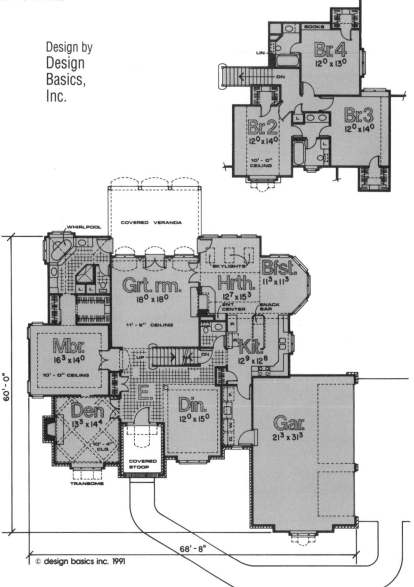

Design 9370

First Floor: 2,084 square feet
Second Floor: 848 square feet
Total: 2,932 square feet

● The combination of brick, stucco and elegant detail provides this home with instant curb appeal. The entry is flanked by the formal dining room and the den with a fireplace and an intriguing ceiling. The great room offers a through-fireplace to the hearth room and French doors to a covered veranda. A sunny breakfast room and kitchen feature an island with a snack bar, wrapping counters and a pantry. The first-floor master suite affords luxury accommodations with two closets, a whirlpool tub, His and Hers vanities and access to the covered veranda. Three secondary bedrooms on the second floor offer walk-in closets and access to bathroom space.

This home, as shown in the photograph, may differ from the actual blueprints. For more detailed information, please check the floor plans carefully.

Design 9228

First Floor: 1,733 square feet
Second Floor: 1,586 square feet
Total: 3,319 square feet

● The creator of this gracious plan seems to have thought of everything. The two-story entry opens into the formal dining room with detailed ceiling and living room. Note the interesting window treatments. Double doors lead from the living room to the beamed-ceiling family room with fireplace and built-in bookshelves. One step down is a cheery sun room with wet bar and pass-through to the kitchen. The kitchen's work area is well-planned with island work center, built-ins and pantry. The sunny bayed windows in the breakfast area overlook the rear yard. The spacious upstairs features three secondary bedrooms and an enormous master suite which includes a sitting area with fireplace, walk-in closet and whirlpool bath.

Design by
Design
Basics,
Inc.

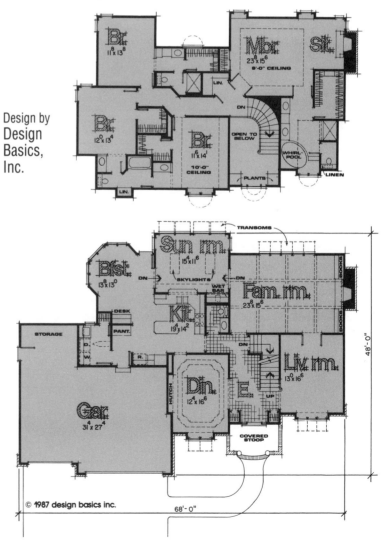

© 1987 design basics inc.

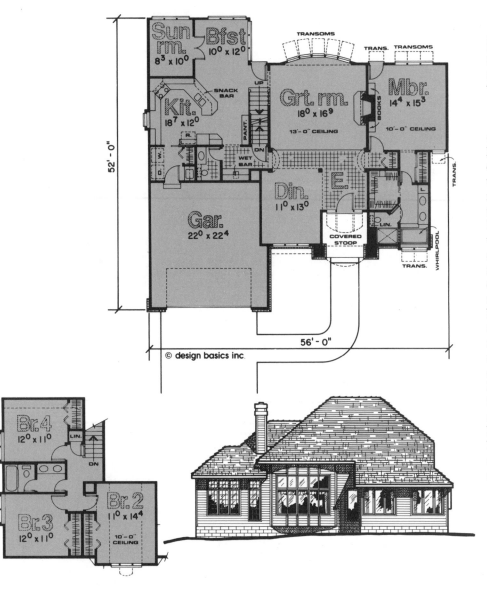

Design 7217

First Floor: 1,654 square feet
Second Floor: 654 square feet
Total: 2,308 square feet

● Brick accents and bright windows highlight this appealing home. After crossing the covered stoop, the entry provides a wide, dramatic view of the formal dining room on the left and the spacious great room ahead. Extra-tall bowed windows provide for a stunning panorama and complement the great room's thirteen-foot ceiling. The efficient kitchen provides a snack bar pass-through to the breakfast area while French doors lead to the connecting sun room. The pantry, the wet bar and the powder room are all conveniently placed to serve the kitchen, the dining room and the great room with ease. A dramatic master suite with dual bookcases features a deluxe bath, abundant windows, outdoor access and generous closet space.

Design by
**Design
Basics,
Inc.**

Design 9305

Square Footage: 2,015

● Romantic appeal radiates from the elegant covered porch and gracious features of this ranch home. A formal dining room with bright windows is viewed from the entry. In the great room, featuring an entertainment center and bookcases, warmth emanates from the three-sided through-fireplace. Homeowners will enjoy the cozy retreat of the bay-windowed hearth room with 10-foot ceiling. Near the hearth is an open breakfast area and kitchen with snack bar, pantry and ample counter space. A window seat framed by closets highlights secondary Bedroom 2. The third bedroom easily converts to an optional den for quiet study. Designed for privacy, the master suite enjoys a boxed ceiling, skylit dressing area with His and Hers lavs, corner whirlpool and large walk-in closet. With many dramatic elements, this will be the home of your dreams!

Design by
Design Basics, Inc.

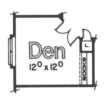

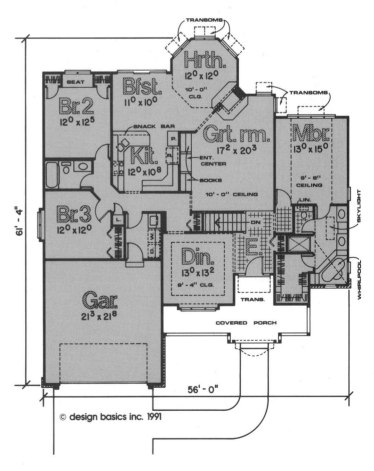

© design basics inc. 1991

Design 7214

Square Footage: 1,658

● The prominent entry of this home enhances a captivating elevation. Inside, the entry captures fantastic views from the great room to the sun room with its arched windows. A peninsula kitchen features a corner sink and a snack bar that opens to the breakfast area. The sun room offers access to the breakfast area, the great room and the master suite. Or use it as a lovely dining room. The spacious master suite includes a whirlpool bath with dual lavs and a walk-in closet. The den off the entry can be used as a bedroom.

Design by
**Design
Basics,
Inc.**

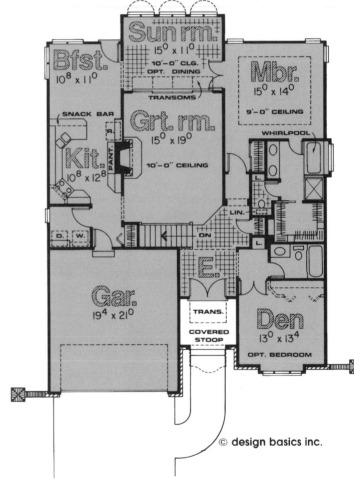

WIDTH 42'
DEPTH 56'

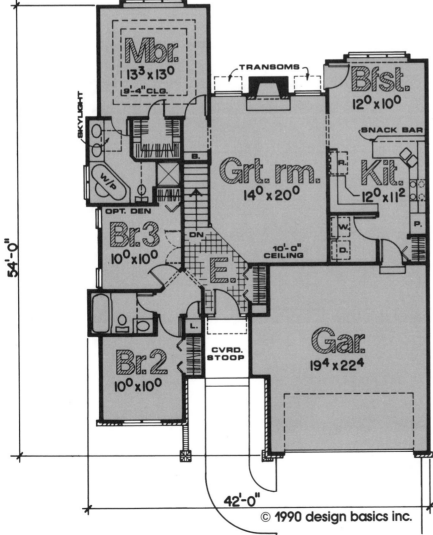

Design 9256

Square Footage: 1,347

● Though it may appear oversized, this plan is really quite compact and economical. From the ten-foot ceiling in the entry to the spacious great room with fireplace, it has an open feeling. A snack bar and pantry in the kitchen complement the work area. Bright windows light up the entire breakfast area. To the left side of the plan are three bedrooms, two of which share a full bath. The master suite has a boxed window, built-in bookcase and tiered ceiling. The skylit dressing area features a double vanity and there's a whirlpool in the bath.

Design by
Design
Basics,
Inc.

91

Design 9377

Square Footage: 2,716

● This traditional, brick ranch
home is designed with the most
discriminating home buyer in
mind. The arched porch creates a
stunning prelude to the double-
door entry. Once inside, the spacious great room is graced by elegant arches leading into the formal
dining area. The combination of the
gathering room and the efficient
U-shaped kitchen provides an ideal
space for informal gatherings. The
three-bedroom sleeping zone
includes a luxurious master suite
with two walk-in closets and a
master bath with a relaxing
whirlpool tub.

Design by
**Design
Basics,
Inc.**

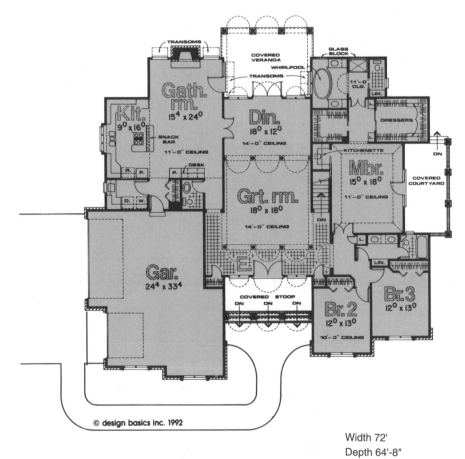

© design basics inc. 1992

Width 72'
Depth 64'-8"

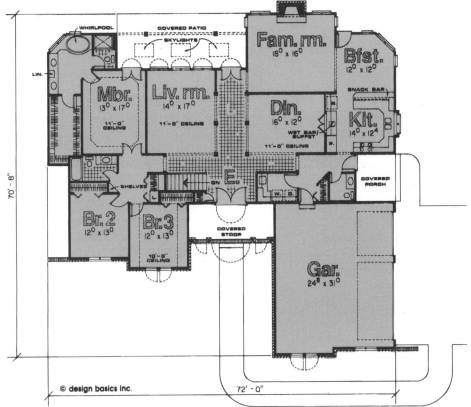

Design 7276
Square Footage: 2,598

● A grand double-door entry leads to a stunning interior. Columns define the formal living areas; living room to the left and dining room to the right. The adjacent kitchen is U-shaped for maximum efficiency and features a pass-through to the dining room and a snack bar which separates it from the breakfast room. A fireplace flanked by windows warms the family room nearby. The luxurious trend continues in the master suite which provides a private retreat and invites relaxation in the exceptional master bath. It features an oval whirlpool bath and a large walk-in closet. Two secondary bedrooms share a hall bath.

Design by
Design
Basics,
Inc.

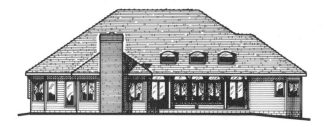

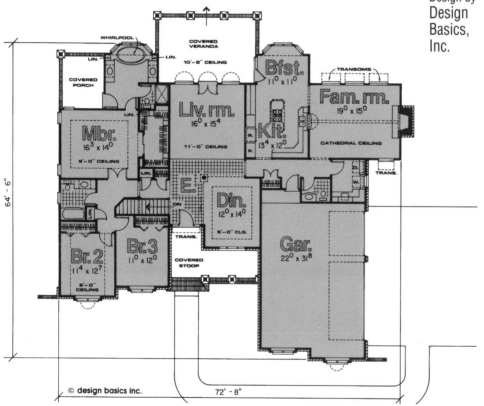

Design by
Design Basics, Inc.

Design 7274
Square Footage: 2,399

● Interesting window treatments and a charming porch extend the attention-getting nature of this brick ranch home. Beyond the covered porch, the entry showcases the formal dining room to the right and the multi-windowed living room straight ahead. The L-shaped kitchen features an island cooktop and blends with the bay-windowed breakfast room and welcoming family room to create a comfortable area for family gatherings. Located for privacy, the master suite includes a huge walk-in closet. A covered porch accessed from the master bath offers a wonderful outdoor retreat. The amenity-filled master bath contains twin vanities and an oval whirlpool tub. Two secondary bedrooms share a full bath.

Design by
Larry W.
Garnett &
Associates, Inc.

Design 9124

First Floor: 2,317 square feet
Second Floor: 400 square feet
Total: 2,717 square feet

● One-story living makes the most of a high roofline in this delightful plan. The family room dominates the center of the design and has easy access to the formal dining room, the breakfast room with a window seat and the island kitchen. The bedrooms are to the right of the plan with the master suite holding space to the rear. It features a hexagonal sitting area with a gazebo ceiling and a skylit bath. Upstairs is a large loft with ½-bath and wet bar that makes a grand game room, studio or hobby room.

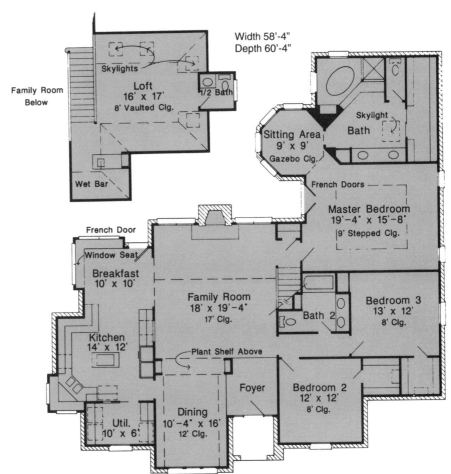

Width 58'-4"
Depth 60'-4"

Skylights

Family Room Below

Loft
16' x 17'
8' Vaulted Clg.

½ Bath

Wet Bar

Sitting Area
9' x 9'
Gazebo Clg.

Skylight
Bath

French Doors

Master Bedroom
19'-4" x 15'-8"
9' Stepped Clg.

French Door

Window Seat

Breakfast
10' x 10'

Family Room
18' x 19'-4"
17' Clg.

Bath 2

Bedroom 3
13' x 12'
8' Clg.

Kitchen
14' x 12'

Plant Shelf Above

Foyer

Bedroom 2
12' x 12'
8' Clg.

Util.
10' x 6'

Dining
10'-4" x 16'
12' Clg.

Design 7245

First Floor: 2,804 square feet
Second Floor: 961 square feet
Total: 3,765 square feet

● This captivating exterior is accentuated by handsome stone columns and a dramatic cantilevered bay. Inside, formal elegance is captured in the stunning living room which features a volume ceiling, bowed windows and an impressive fireplace. For the family gourmet, the kitchen is enhanced with a butcher block island, a snack bar and a pantry. Informal gatherings will be enjoyed in the open breakfast area and light-filled sunroom nearby. Double doors open into the secluded master suite and its adjoining sitting room. The master bath boasts an arched transom window, a walk-in closet with a dresser and access to a covered deck. Upstairs, at landing level is a den complete with a spider-beam ceiling, bookcases and bayed windows. The second floor contains three family bedrooms and two full baths.

Design by
Design Basics, Inc.

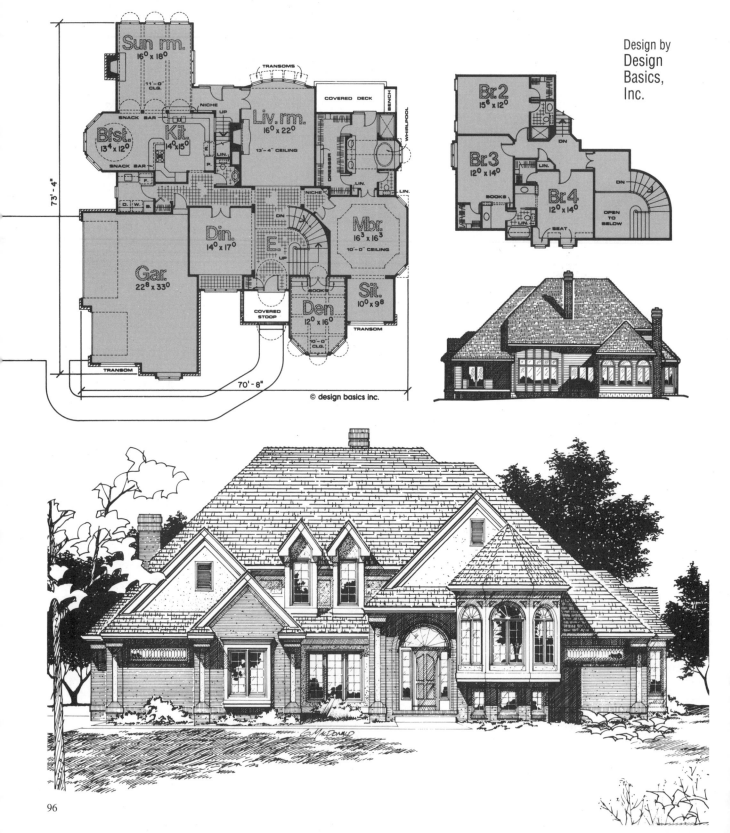

© design basics inc.

Panoramic Windows & Glass Walls

Design 9898

First Floor: 2,070 square feet
Second Floor: 790 square feet
Total: 2,860 square feet

● Wood shingles add a cozy touch to the exterior of this home; the arched covered front porch adds its own bit of warmth. Interior rooms include a great room with a bay window and a fireplace, a formal dining room and a study with another fireplace. A guest room on the first floor contains a full bath and a walk-in closet. The relaxing master suite is also on the first floor and features a pampering master bath with His and Hers walk-in closets, dual vanities, a separate shower and a whirlpool tub just waiting to soothe and rejuvenate. The second floor holds two additional bedrooms, a loft area and a gallery which overlooks the central hall. This home is designed with a basement foundation.

Design by
Design Traditions

Width 57'-6"
Depth 54'

Copyright 1992 Stephen S. Fuller, Inc.

Design 9854

Square Footage: 2,770

● This English cottage with its cedar shake exterior displays the best qualities of a traditional design. With the bay window and recessed entry, visitors will feel welcomed. The foyer opens to both the dining room and the great room with its fireplace and built-in cabinetry. Surrounded by windows, the breakfast room opens to a gourmet kitchen and a laundry room conveniently located near the garage entrance. To the right of the foyer is a hall powder room. Two bedrooms with large closets are joined by a full bath with individual vanities and a window seat. Through double doors at the end of a short hall, the master suite awaits with a tray ceiling and an adjoining sunlit sitting room. The master bath has His and Hers walk-in closets, separate vanities, an individual shower and a garden tub with a bay window. This home is designed with a basement foundation.

Design by
Design Traditions

DECK

SITTING
12'-0"x 12'-0"

W.I.C.

MASTER
BATH

BREAKFAST
12'-0"x 13'-6"

DN.

GREAT ROOM
20'-6"x 18'-6"

MASTER SUITE
16'-6"x 15'-0"

W.I.C.

KITCHEN
14'-3"x 13'-6"

POWDER

BEDROOM NO.3
12'-0"x 12'-0"

LAUNDRY
9'-0" X 8'-6"

DINING ROOM
13'-6" X 14'-6"

FOYER

BATH

STORAGE

BEDROOM NO.2
12'-3"x 14'-0"

STOOP

TWO CAR GARAGE
21'-6"x 27'-6"

Width 73'-6"
Depth 78'

BEDROOM NO. 2
12'-0" X 12'-0"

OPEN TO BELOW

SITTING

MASTER BEDROOM
19'-8" X 13'-6"

BALCONY

W.I.C.   W.I.C.

DN.

MASTER BATH

BATH

BEDROOM NO. 3
12'-0" X 12'-6"

OPEN TO BELOW

W.I.C.

UNFIN. BONUS
12'-0" X 11'-4"

Design 9864

First Floor: 1,395 square feet
Second Floor: 1,210 square feet
Total: 2,605 square feet
Bonus Room: 225 square feet

Cost to build? See page 230
to order complete cost estimate
to build this house in your area!

● The well-balanced use of stucco and stone combined with box-bay window treatments make this English country home especially inviting. The two-story foyer opens on the right to the attractive living and dining rooms with large windows. The step-saving kitchen and breakfast areas flow easily into the two-story great room and a media room with a see-through fireplace. The second floor offers a pleasing combination of open design and privacy. The master bedroom has a modified tray ceiling and is complete with a sitting area. The master bath leads to a large walk-in closet. Bedrooms 2 and 3 are ample in size and feature walk-in closets. This home is designed with a basement foundation.

Design by
Design Traditions

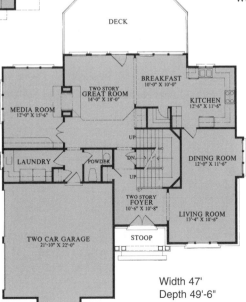

DECK

TWO STORY
GREAT ROOM
14'-0" X 18'-0"

BREAKFAST
10'-0" X 10'-0"

MEDIA ROOM
12'-0" X 15'-6"

KITCHEN
12'-6" X 11'-6"

LAUNDRY

POWDER

DN.   UP

DINING ROOM
12'-0" X 11'-6"

UP

TWO STORY
FOYER
10'-6" X 10'-8"

LIVING ROOM
13'-4" X 10'-6"

TWO CAR GARAGE
21'-10" X 22'-0"

STOOP

Width 47'
Depth 49'-6"

Design 8092

First Floor: 2,092 square feet
Second Floor: 811 square feet
Total: 2,903 square feet
Bonus Room: 242 square feet

● The combination of siding and brick gives this elevation a distinctly homey feeling. Elegant arched openings welcome you upon entering. An open concept is used in the design of the kitchen, breakfast room and keeping room to give the feel of one large area. The master suite has all the extras demanded by today's owner with a sitting area, His and Hers closets and a master bath with a whirlpool tub and a separate shower. Upstairs, Bedroom 3 features its own sitting area. Two other bedrooms and a bath with private dressing/vanity areas are also upstairs. A large expandable area is allocated for flexible space. This plan is available with either a crawlspace or slab foundation. Please specify when ordering.

Design by
Larry E. Belk
Designs

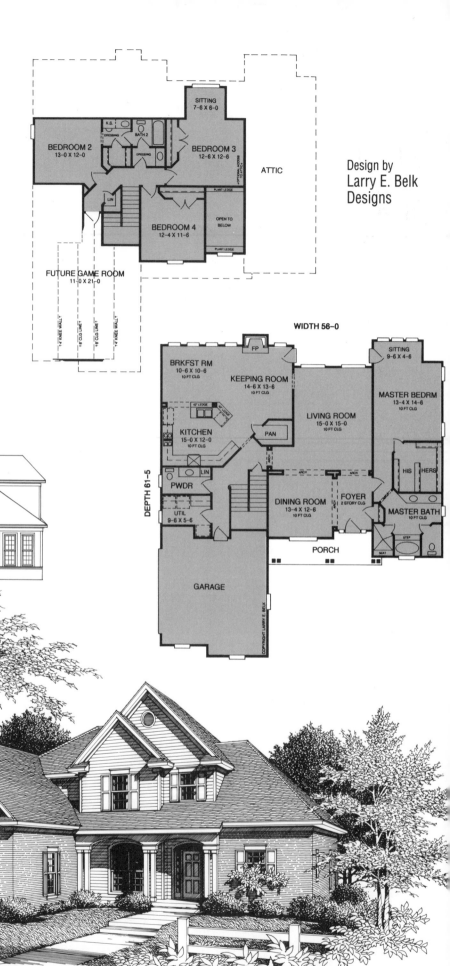

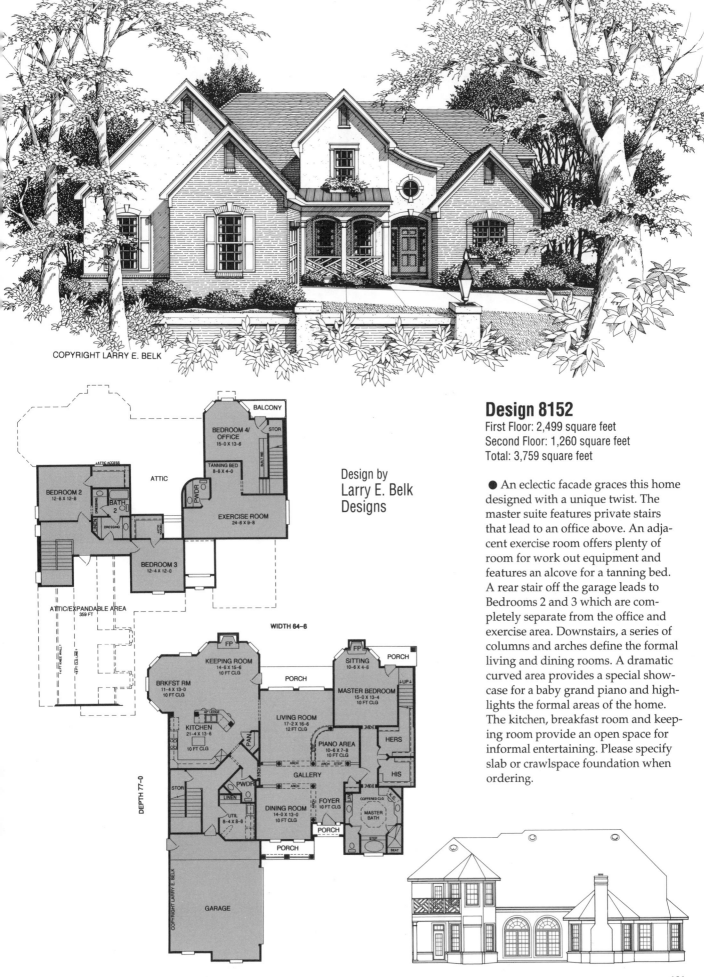

COPYRIGHT LARRY E. BELK

BALCONY

BEDROOM 4/
OFFICE
15-0 X 13-6

STOR

TANNING BED
8-6 X 4-0

ATTIC ACCESS

ATTIC

BEDROOM 2
12-6 X 12-6

BATH
2

DRESSING

PWDR

LINEN

EXERCISE ROOM
24-6 X 9-8

DRESSING

BEDROOM 3
12-4 X 12-0

ATTIC/EXPANDABLE AREA
359 FT

Design by
Larry E. Belk
Designs

WIDTH 64-6

FP

KEEPING ROOM
14-6 X 15-6
10 FT CLG

PORCH

FP

SITTING
10-6 X 4-6

PORCH

BRKFST RM
11-4 X 13-0
10 FT CLG

PORCH

MASTER BEDROOM
15-0 X 13-4
10 FT CLG

UP

KITCHEN
21-4 X 13-6

10 FT CLG

LIVING ROOM
17-2 X 16-6
12 FT CLG

HERS

PAN

PIANO AREA
10-6 X 7-8
10 FT CLG

ARCH STEP

GALLERY

ARCH

HIS

DEPTH 77-0

STOR

PWDR

LINEN

DINING ROOM
14-0 X 13-0
10 FT CLG

FOYER
10 FT CLG

COFFERED CLG

UTIL
8-4 X 8-8

MASTER
BATH

PORCH

PORCH

STEP

SEAT

COPYRIGHT LARRY E. BELK

GARAGE

Design 8152

First Floor: 2,499 square feet
Second Floor: 1,260 square feet
Total: 3,759 square feet

● An eclectic facade graces this home designed with a unique twist. The master suite features private stairs that lead to an office above. An adjacent exercise room offers plenty of room for work out equipment and features an alcove for a tanning bed. A rear stair off the garage leads to Bedrooms 2 and 3 which are completely separate from the office and exercise area. Downstairs, a series of columns and arches define the formal living and dining rooms. A dramatic curved area provides a special showcase for a baby grand piano and highlights the formal areas of the home. The kitchen, breakfast room and keeping room provide an open space for informal entertaining. Please specify slab or crawlspace foundation when ordering.

Copyright 1992 Stephen S. Fuller, Inc.

Design 9869 First Floor: 1,475 square feet
Second Floor: 1,460 square feet; Total: 2,935 square feet

● This country home of stucco and stone features elliptical keystone fetailing and a covered entranceway. Through
the columned entry, the two-story foyer opens to the living
room with wet bar. The media room features a fireplace
and is accessed from both the main hall and great room. A
hall powder room and coat closet are located to the rear of
the foyer. The two-story great room with a fireplace is
open to the breakfast area, kitchen and rear staircase, making entertaining a pleasure. The kitchen design is ideal
with a breakfast bar and a preparation island and is conveniently located near the laundry room. The dining room
with its elliptical window is ideal for formal entertaining.
The upper level begins with the balcony landing overlok-
ing the great room. The master bedroom features a bay-
windowed sitting area and a tray ceiling. The master bath
has dual vanities, a corner garden tub, a separate shower, a
large walk-in closet and an optional secret room. Across
the balcony, Bedroohare a bath. Bedroom 4 in the front of
the home has a pricate bath. This home is designed with a
basement foundation.

QUOTE ONE®
Cost to build? See page 230
to order complete cost estimate
to build this house in your area!

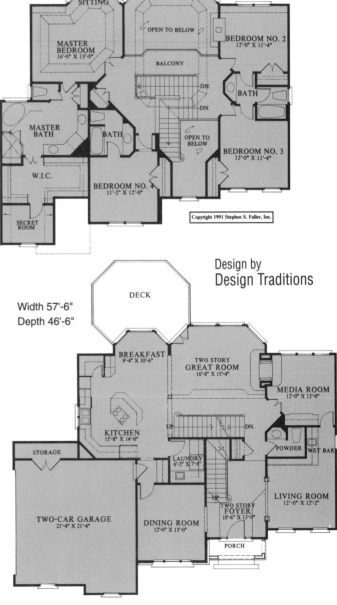

SITTING

MASTER
BEDROOM
16'-0" X 13'-0"

OPEN TO BELOW

BEDROOM NO. 2
12'-0" X 11'-4"

BALCONY

BATH

MASTER
BATH

BATH

DN.

DN.

OPEN TO
BELOW

OPEN TO
BELOW

W.I.C.

BEDROOM NO. 3
12'-0" X 11'-4"

BEDROOM NO. 4
11'-2" X 12'-0"

SECRET
ROOM

Copyright 1991 Stephen S. Fuller, Inc.

Design by
Design Traditions

Width 57'-6"
Depth 46'-6"

DECK

BREAKFAST
9'-4" X 10'-6"

TWO STORY
GREAT ROOM
16'-8" X 15'-4"

MEDIA ROOM
12'-0" X 12'-0"

KITCHEN
15'-8" X 14'-0"

UP

DN.

POWDER

WET BAR

STORAGE

LAUNDRY
6'-2" X 7'-6"

LIVING ROOM
12'-0" X 12'-2"

TWO-CAR GARAGE
21'-4" X 21'-4"

DINING ROOM
12'-0" X 13'-0"

TWO STORY
FOYER
10'-6" X 13'-0"

PORCH

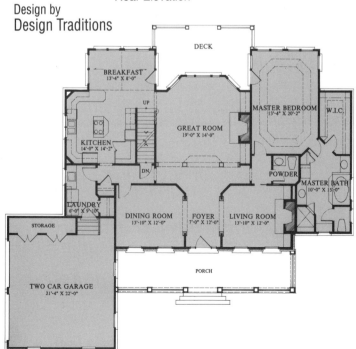

Width 69'-9"
Depth 65'

Rear Elevation

Design by
Design Traditions

Design 9850

First Floor: 2,078 square feet
Second Floor: 896 square feet
Total: 2,974 square feet

QUOTE ONE®
Cost to build? See page 230
to order complete cost estimate
to build this house in your area!

● This Georgian country-style home displays an impressive appearance. Textures of brick and wood are used to reflect this architectural period perfectly. Georgian symmetry balances the living room and dining room to the right and left of the foyer. Both are framed by columns, while the living room features its own fireplace. The foyer opens onto the two-story great room with built-in cabinetry, a fireplace and a large bay window that overlooks the rear deck. A dramatic tray ceiling, a wall of glass and access to the rear deck complete the master bedroom. The master bath features a large walk-in closet. Upstairs are three bedrooms and an open railing overlooking the great room below. Each bedroom features ample closet space and direct access to a bathroom. This home is designed with a basement foundation.

COPYRIGHT 1994 LARRY E. BELK

Design 8028

First Floor: 2,270 square feet
Second Floor: 1,100 square feet
Total: 3,370 square feet

L

● A combination of stacked stone, brick and wood siding make this Southern traditional home a real beauty from the front curb. Designed for a golf course lot, the foyer steps up into a large great room with a view to the rear grounds. On the other side, steps lead down into the dining room with access to a side porch. The master suite includes a fabulous master bath—really two baths in one—with a His and Hers dressing area and a shared shower between. Up a short flight of stairs, a curved landing with windows to the rear is the perfect place for a piano. Continuing up the stairs, a large circular loft overlooks the great room and provides stunning views through high windows in the great room to the rear beyond. Three bedrooms and two baths are included in the upstairs layout. A permanent staircase located in the garage provides access to floored attic space.

Design by
**Larry E. Belk
Designs**

Width 76'-6"
Depth 69'-4"

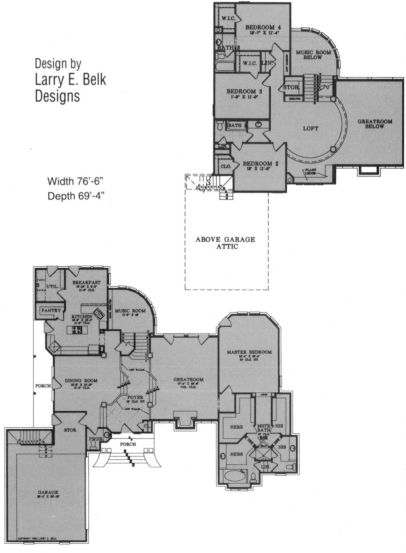

Design 8099

First Floor: 2,374 square feet
Second Floor: 940 square feet
Total: 3,314 square feet
Bonus Room: 360 square feet

L

● The enduring qualities of brick and stucco are hallmarks of this stylish home. Inside, a large kitchen, a family room and a breakfast room are open to one another. The living room and the dining room provide space for formal entertaining. The master suite features a sitting area, a His and Hers walk-in closet and an amenity-filled master bath. Bedroom 2, perfect for a nursery or elderly guests, is conveniently located downstairs. Two bedrooms and a bath with separate dressing areas are located upstairs. Please specify crawlspace or slab foundation when ordering.

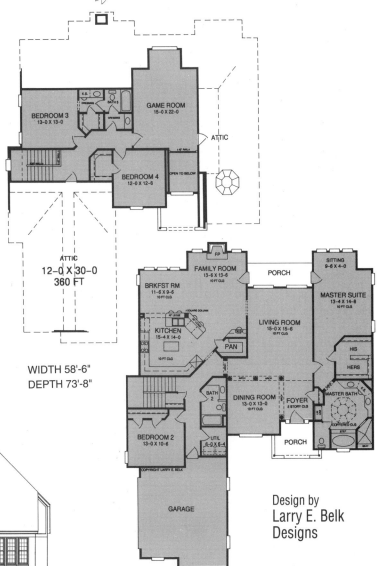

WIDTH 58'-6"
DEPTH 73'-8"

Design by
Larry E. Belk
Designs

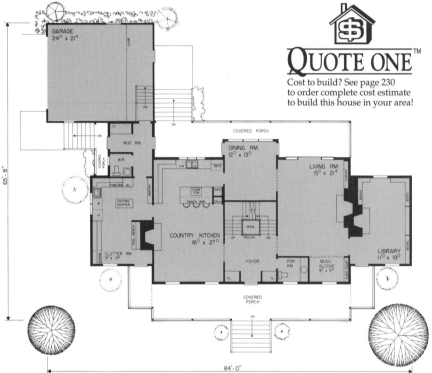

Quote One™

Cost to build? See page 230
to order complete cost estimate
to build this house in your area!

GARAGE 24⁰ x 21⁴

COVERED PORCH

MUD RM.

W.R

COVERED PORCH

FREEZER BC.

SORTING COUNTER

CLUTTER RM.

PANTRY

DW

REF'S

COOK TOP

OVEN

SNACK BAR

COUNTRY KITCHEN 16⁰ x 27⁰

TOOL BENCH

DINING RM. 12⁰ x 13⁰

LIVING RM. 15⁰ x 21⁴

FOYER

POR RM

MUSIC ALCOVE 9⁰ x 5⁵

LIBRARY 11⁰ x 19⁰

CL

CL

CL

OPEN

UP RAILING DN

COVERED PORCH

DN

65'-8"

84'-0"

Design 2694

First Floor: 2,026 square feet
Second Floor: 1,386 square feet
Total: 3,412 square feet

L

SEAT SEAT

DRESSING RM

BATH

WHIRLPOOL

WALK-IN CLOSET

CL

CL

CL

S

OPEN

DN RAILING

LINEN

BATH

MASTER BEDROOM 16⁰ x 17⁴

BEDROOM 16⁰ x 13⁴

BEDROOM 12⁰ x 15⁰

● This two-story design faithfully recalls
the 18th-Century homestead of Secretary of
Foreign Affairs John Jay. Features include a
grand living room, a library, a country
kitchen and three sizable bedrooms, including a master suite.

Design by
Home Planners

106

Design 9771

Square Footage: 1,927

● Sunlight takes center stage in this delightful country home. Each room has at least two windows to add warmth and radiance, and a clerestory window brightens the foyer. Two bedrooms and a full bath are to the left of the foyer. To the right is the dining room, which leads into the L-shaped kitchen with its penninsular cooktop and connecting bay-windowed breakfast area. The central great room offers a cathedral ceiling, a fireplace and access to the rear porch. The master suite is separated for privacy and features two walls of windows, a large walk-in closet and a luxurious whirlpool bath with sky-lights.

Design by
Donald A.
Gardner,
Architects, Inc.

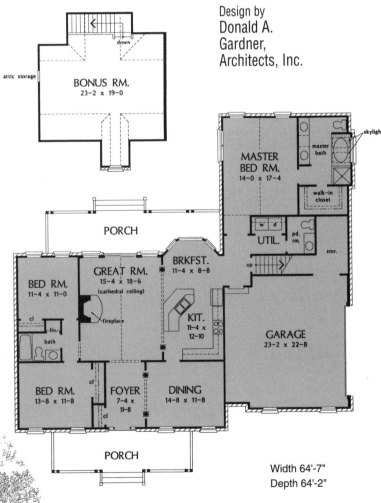

BONUS RM.
23-2 x 19-0

attic storage

down

MASTER BED RM.
14-0 x 17-4

master bath

skylights

walk-in closet

w d

pd. rm.

UTIL.

stor.

up

PORCH

BRKFST.
11-4 x 8-8

GREAT RM.
15-4 x 18-6
(cathedral ceiling)

KIT.
11-4 x 12-10

GARAGE
23-2 x 22-8

BED RM.
11-4 x 11-0

fireplace

cl

lin.

bath

BED RM.
13-8 x 11-8

cl

FOYER
7-4 x 11-8

cl

DINING
14-8 x 11-8

PORCH

Width 64'-7"
Depth 64'-2"

Design 9756

Square Footage: 2,207
Bonus Room: 435 square feet

● This quaint four-bedroom home with front and rear porches reinforces its beauty with arched windows and dormers. The pillared dining room opens on your right while a study that could double as a guest room is available on your left. Straight ahead lies the massive great room with its cathedral ceiling, fireplace and access to the private rear porch. Within steps of the dining room is the efficient kitchen and the sunny breakfast nook. The master suite enjoys rear deck access and a master bath with a skylit whirlpool tub and a walk-in closet. Two additional bedrooms are located at the opposite end of the house.

QUOTE ONE®

Cost to build? See page 230 to order complete cost estimate to build this house in your area!

Design by
Donald A. Gardner, Architects, Inc.

BONUS RM.
14-4 x 24-8

down

seat

spa

DECK

PORCH

arched window above door

BED RM.
11-0 x 12-0

cl

lin.

bath

BRKFST.
11-4 x 9-4

(cathedral ceiling)

MASTER BED RM.
14-0 x 17-4

master bath

skylights

walk-in closet

up

storage

BED RM.
13-5 x 11-0

fireplace

GREAT RM.
15-4 x 19-8

11-4 x 12-9

KITCHEN

d
w

UTIL.

pd. rm.

GARAGE
23-4 x 24-8

cl

STUDY/ BED RM.
13-8 x 11-8

FOYER
7-4 x 11-8

cl

DINING
14-8 x 11-8

PORCH

Width 76'-1"
Depth 50'

Design 9753

Square Footage: 1,346

● A great room that stretches into the dining room makes this design perfect for entertaining. A fireplace and built-ins, as well as a cathedral ceiling, further the atmosphere. A rear deck extends livability. The ample kitchen features lots of counter and cabinet space as well as an angled cooktop. Three bedrooms include the master suite with its sloped ceiling, private bath and deck access.

Design by
Donald A.
Gardner,
Architects, Inc.

QUOTE ONE®

Cost to build? See page 230
to order complete cost estimate
to build this house in your area!

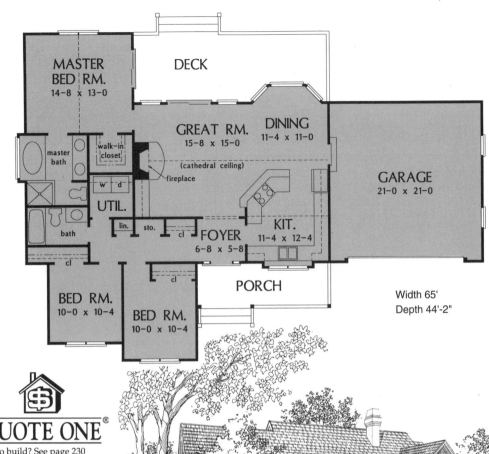

MASTER BED RM.
14-8 x 13-0

DECK

master bath

walk-in closet

w d

UTIL.

GREAT RM.
15-8 x 15-0

DINING
11-4 x 11-0

(cathedral ceiling)

fireplace

GARAGE
21-0 x 21-0

lin.   sto.   cl

bath

cl

BED RM.
10-0 x 10-4

cl

BED RM.
10-0 x 10-4

KIT.
11-4 x 12-4

FOYER
6-8 x 5-8

PORCH

Width 65'
Depth 44'-2"

PORCH

arched window above door

BED RM.
11-4 x 10-0

cl | lin.
bath

BED RM.
11-4 x 11-8

cl
FOYER
5-4 x
11-8
cl

GREAT RM.
15-4 x 17-8
(cathedral ceiling)

fireplace

KITCHEN
11-8 x
11-2

DINING
12-0 x 11-8

BRKFST.
9-6 x 9-8

UTIL.
w | d
cl

MASTER
BED RM.
13-4 x 13-4
(cathedral ceiling)

master
bath

walk-in
closet

lin.

stor.

GARAGE
20-0 x 20-4

51-6

PORCH

60-10

© 1995 Donald A Gardner Architects, Inc.

Design 9780
Square Footage: 1,561

● This country farmhouse embraces a big heart in a cozy package. Special touches such as interior columns, a bay window and dormers add their own special brand of charm. The centrally located great room features a cathedral ceiling, a fireplace and a clerestory window that fills the room with natural light. The adjoining kitchen, designed to save steps, easily services the bay-windowed breakfast room and the dining room nearby. Split for privacy, the master suite boasts amenities found in much larger homes. Efficient use of space in the master bath allows room for a whirlpool tub, a separate shower and a walk-in closet. Two additional bedrooms share a full bath.

Design by
Donald A.
Gardner,
Architects, Inc.

QUOTE ONE®
Cost to build? See page 230
to order complete cost estimate
to build this house in your area!

DECK
35-0 × 10-10

spa

DINING
12-8 × 12-0

KITCHEN
16-8 × 11-2

BRKFST.
10-4 × 6-6

skylights

fireplace

GREAT RM.
15-4 × 20-0
(cathedral ceiling)

FOYER
7-4 × 8-0

BED RM./
STUDY
11-2 × 10-8

whirlpool

master bath

lin.

walk-in closet

COVERED DECK
11-0 × 7-0

MASTER BED RM.
16-6 × 14-2

lin.

bath

wash
dry

UTIL.

BED RM.
11-0 × 10-6

GARAGE
19-8 × 20-0

62-8

58-10

Design 9611

Square Footage: 1,817

● This inviting ranch offers many special features uncommon to the typical house this size. A large entrance foyer leads to the spacious great room with cathedral ceiling, fireplace, and operable skylights that allow for natural ventilation. A bedroom just off the foyer doubles nicely as a study. The large master suite contains a walk-in closet and a pampering master bath with double-bowl vanity, shower and whirlpool tub. For outdoor living, look to the open deck with spa at the great room and kitchen, as well as the covered deck at the master suite.

Design by
Donald A.
Gardner,
Architects, Inc.

REAR

Design by
Home Planners

Design 3366

Main Level: 1,638 square feet
Upper Level: 650 square feet
Lower Level: 934 square feet
Total: 3,222 square feet

L

● There is much more to this design than
meets the eye. While it may look like a 1½-story
plan, bonus recreation and hobby space in the
walk-out basement adds almost 1,000 square
feet. The first floor holds living and dining
areas as well as the master bedroom suite. Two
family bedrooms on the second floor are connected by a balcony area that overlooks the
gathering room below. Notice the covered
porch beyond the breakfast and dining rooms.

QUOTE ONE™

Cost to build? See page 230
to order complete cost estimate
to build this house in your area!

This home, as shown in the photograph, may differ from the actual blueprints. For more detailed information, please check the floor plans carefully.

Photos by Andrew D. Lautman

Design 2947

Square Footage: 1,830

L **D**

● This charming, one-story traditional home greets visitors with a covered porch. A galley-style kitchen shares a snack bar with the spacious gathering room where a fireplace is the focal point. An ample master suite includes a luxury bath with a whirlpool tub and a separate dressing room. Two additional bedrooms, with one that could double as a study, are located at the front of the home.

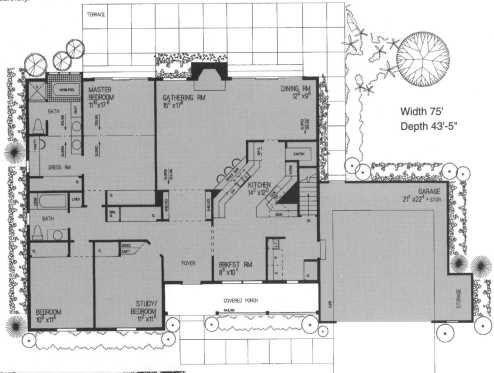

Width 75'
Depth 43'-5"

Cost to build? See page 230 to order complete cost estimate to build this house in your area!

Design by
Home Planners

Design 3455

First Floor: 1,408 square feet
Second Floor: 667 square feet
Total: 2,075 square feet

L **D**

● Whether you're just starting out or looking to retire, this 1½-story, sun-country design will make an excellent home. The focal point of the first floor, the two-story living room utilizes a central fireplace and columns for comfort and elegance. Open to the living room, the dining room complements this space with its influx of natural light. The kitchen services this room easily and also enjoys a cozy breakfast nook. An island work counter in the kitchen guarantees ease in food preparation. Note the service entry to the garage; a full washer/dryer set-up adds convenience to laundry chores. On the second floor you'll find a skylit balcony—a dramatic yet purposeful design feature—leading to two bedrooms.

Design by
Home Planners

Quote One™

Cost to build? See page 230
to order complete cost estimate
to build this house in your area!

114

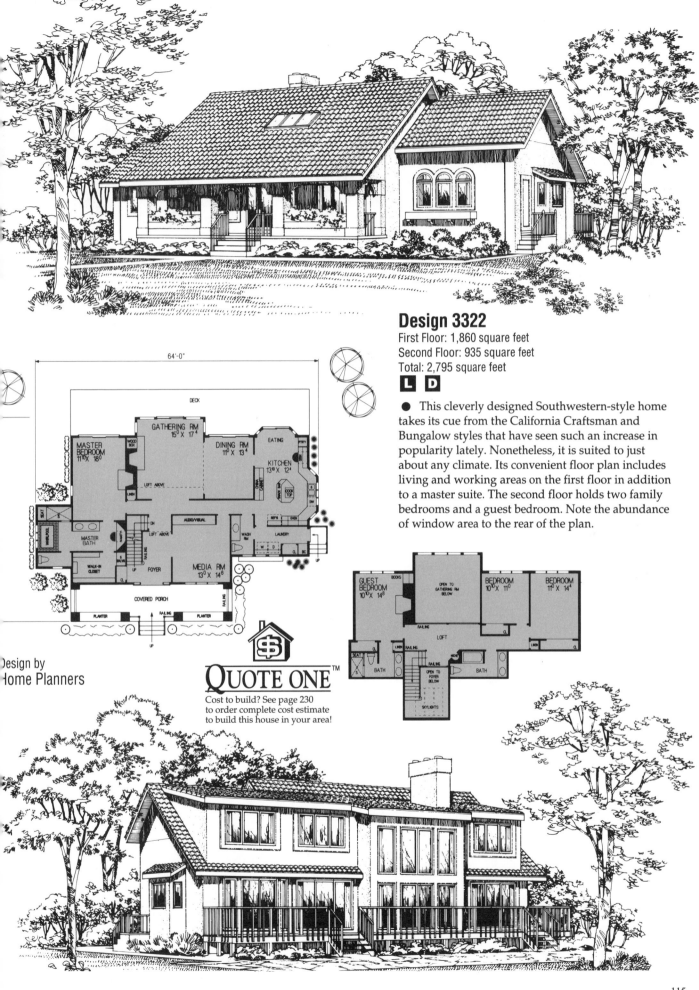

Design 3322

First Floor: 1,860 square feet
Second Floor: 935 square feet
Total: 2,795 square feet

L **D**

● This cleverly designed Southwestern-style home takes its cue from the California Craftsman and Bungalow styles that have seen such an increase in popularity lately. Nonetheless, it is suited to just about any climate. Its convenient floor plan includes living and working areas on the first floor in addition to a master suite. The second floor holds two family bedrooms and a guest bedroom. Note the abundance of window area to the rear of the plan.

Design by
Home Planners

QUOTE ONE™

Cost to build? See page 230
to order complete cost estimate
to build this house in your area!

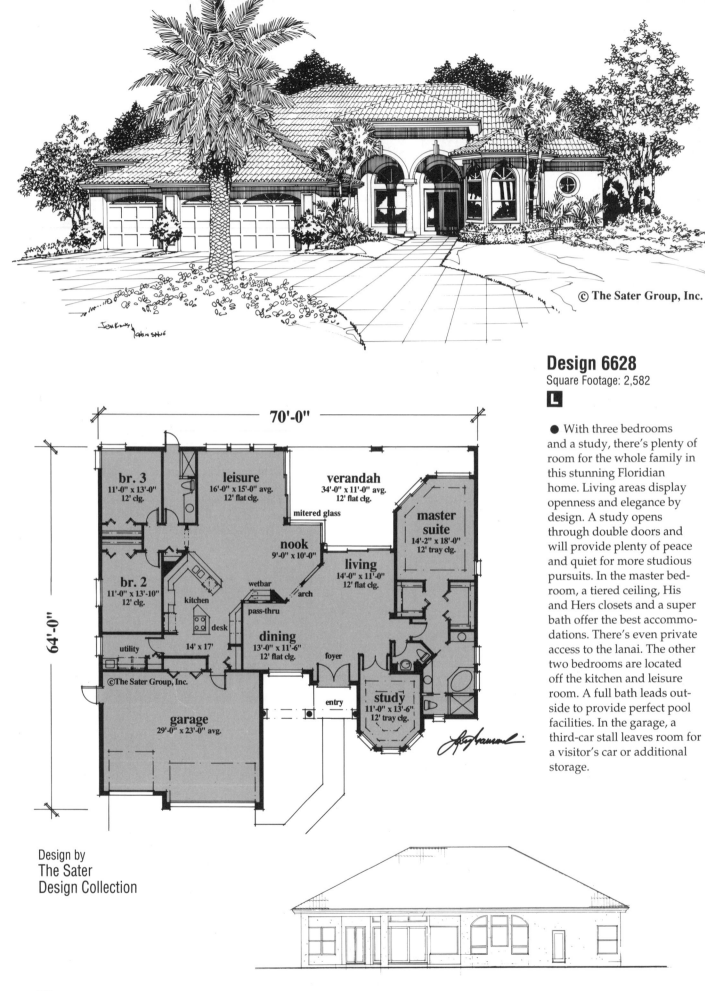

© The Sater Group, Inc.

Design 6628
Square Footage: 2,582

L

● With three bedrooms and a study, there's plenty of room for the whole family in this stunning Floridian home. Living areas display openness and elegance by design. A study opens through double doors and will provide plenty of peace and quiet for more studious pursuits. In the master bedroom, a tiered ceiling, His and Hers closets and a super bath offer the best accommodations. There's even private access to the lanai. The other two bedrooms are located off the kitchen and leisure room. A full bath leads outside to provide perfect pool facilities. In the garage, a third-car stall leaves room for a visitor's car or additional storage.

70'-0"

64'-0"

br. 3
11'-0" x 13'-0"
12' clg.

leisure
16'-0" x 15'-0" avg.
12' flat clg.

verandah
34'-0" x 11'-0" avg.
12' flat clg.

mitered glass

master suite
14'-2" x 18'-0"
12' tray clg.

nook
9'-0" x 10'-0"

living
14'-0" x 11'-0"
12' flat clg.

wetbar

arch

pass-thru

kitchen

desk

br. 2
11'-0" x 13'-10"
12' clg.

utility

dining
13'-0" x 11'-6"
12' flat clg.

14' x 17'

foyer

© The Sater Group, Inc.

entry

study
11'-0" x 13'-6"
12' tray clg.

garage
29'-0" x 23'-0" avg.

Design by
The Sater
Design Collection

© The Sater Group, Inc.

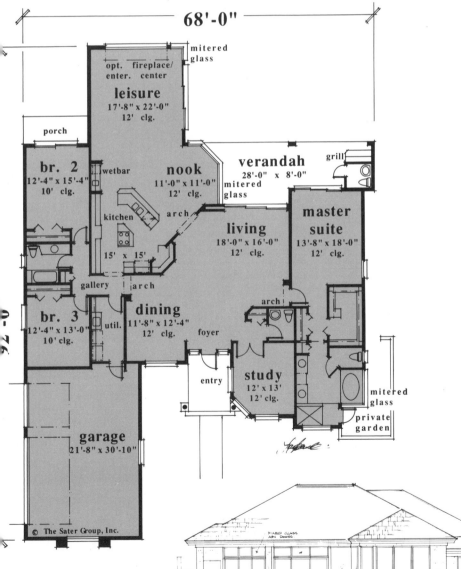

© The Sater Group, Inc.

68'-0"

mitered glass

opt. fireplace/ enter. center

leisure
17'-8" x 22'-0"
12' clg.

porch

wetbar

nook
11'-0" x 11'-0"
12' clg.

verandah
28'-0" x 8'-0"
mitered glass

grill

br. 2
12'-4" x 15'-4"
10' clg.

kitchen

arch

living
18'-0" x 16'-0"
12' clg.

master suite
13'-8" x 18'-0"
12' clg.

15' x 15'

gallery

arch

arch

br. 3
12'-4" x 13'-0"
10' clg.

util.

dining
11'-8" x 12'-4"
12' clg.

foyer

arch

study
12' x 13'
12' clg.

entry

mitered glass

private garden

garage
21'-8" x 30'-10"

72'-0"

© The Sater Group, Inc.

Design 6606

Square Footage: 2,984

L

● Glass surrounds the entry of this appealing stucco home. Arched doorways lead from the formal living and dining rooms to the sleeping zones and the informal living area. The study is situated to the right of the entry and will make a wonderful home office. Ideally suited for informal entertaining, the gourmet kitchen shares space with a sunny breakfast nook and a spacious leisure room which offers access to the rear grounds and a covered veranda. The leisure room provides optional space for a fireplace and entertainment center. The master suite sports two closets: an oversized walk-in closet and a smaller closet nearby. Treat yourself to a relaxing soak in the garden tub or enter the private garden through an adjacent door. A separate shower, dual vanities and a compartmented toilet complete the master sleeping quarters. On the opposite side of the plan, two secondary bedrooms share a full bath.

Design by
**The Sater
Design Collection**

117

Design 6615

First Floor: 1,736 square feet
Second Floor: 640 square feet
Total: 2,376 square feet
Lower Floor: 840 square feet

L

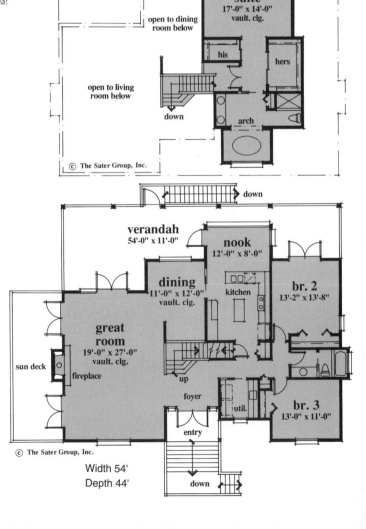

QUOTE ONE®

Cost to build? See page 230
to order complete cost estimate
to build this house in your area!

● Lattice panels, shutters, a balustrade and a metal roof
add character to this delightful coastal home. Double doors
flanking a fireplace open to the sun deck from the spacious
great room sporting a vaulted ceiling. Access to the veranda is provided from this room also. An adjacent dining
room provides views of the rear grounds and space for formal and informal entertaining. The glassed-in nook shares
space with the L-shaped kitchen and a center work island.
Bedrooms 2 and 3, a full bath and a utility room complete
this floor. Upstairs, a sumptuous master suite awaits.
Double doors extend to a private deck from the master bedroom. His and Hers walk-in closets lead the way to a grand
master bath featuring an arched whirlpool tub, a double-
bowl vanity and a separate shower.

Design by
The Sater
Design Collection

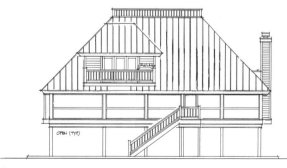

© The Sater Group, Inc.

Design 6618

First Floor: 1,944 square feet
Second Floor: 1,196 square feet
Total: 3,335 square feet
Island Basement: 195 square feet

L

● In the grand room of this home, family and friends will enjoy the ambience created by arches and access to a veranda. Two guest rooms flank a full bath—one of the guest rooms also sports a private deck. The kitchen services a circular breakfast nook. Upstairs, a balcony overlook furthers the drama of the great room. The master suite, with a deck and a private bath opening through a pocket door, will be a pleasure to occupy. Another bedroom—or use this room for a study—sits at the other side of this floor. It extends a curved bay window, an expansive deck, built-ins and a full bath. This home is designed with an island basement.

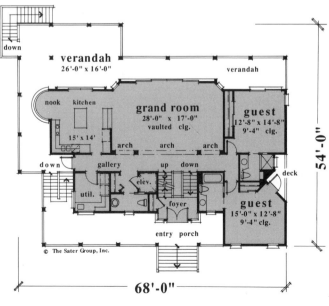

Design by
**The Sater
Design Collection**

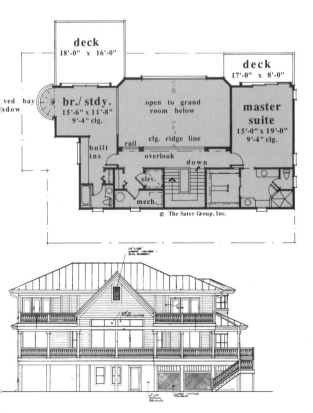

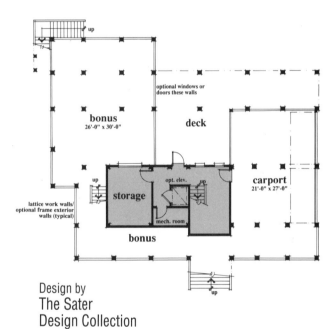

© The Sater Group, Inc.

This home, as shown in the photograph, may differ from the actual blueprints. For more detailed information, please check the floor plans carefully.

Design by
Home Planners

Design 2488

First Floor: 1,113 square feet
Second Floor: 543 square feet
Total: 1,656 square feet

D

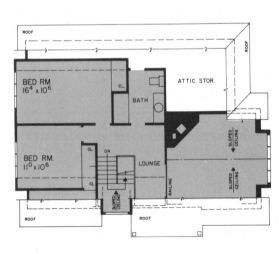

QUOTE ONE®

Cost to build? See page 230
to order complete cost estimate
to build this house in your area!

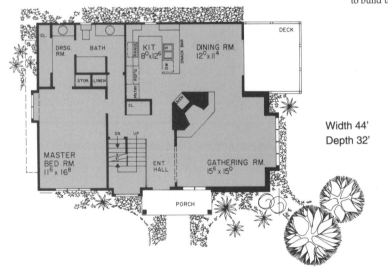

Width 44'
Depth 32'

● A cozy cottage filled with versatility! The upstairs, with its two sizable bedrooms, full bath and lounge area looking down into the gathering room below, will ideally accommodate the younger members of the household. If functioning as a retirement home, the second floor caters to visiting family members and friends. Other uses for the second floor may include an office, a study, a sewing room, a music room or a hobby room—the choices are many.

This home, as shown in the photograph, may differ from the actual blueprints. For more detailed information, please check the floor plans carefully.

Photos by Bob Greenspan

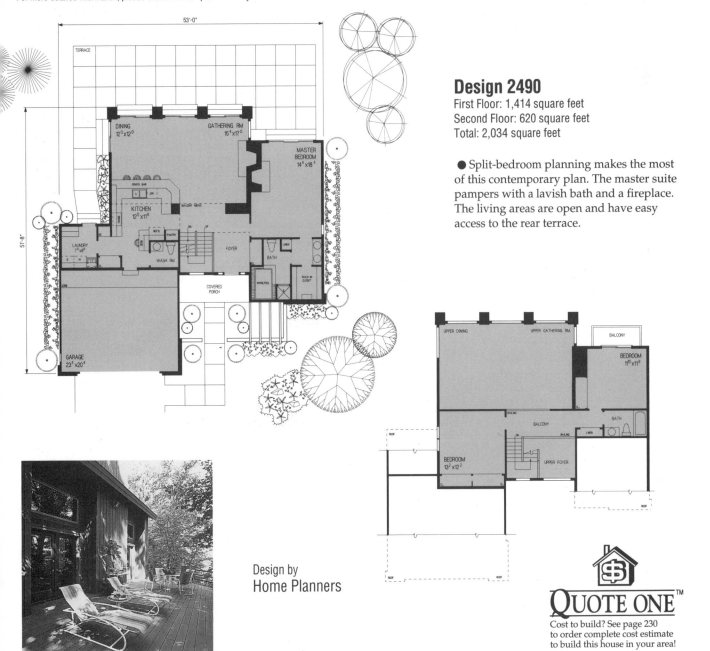

Design 2490

First Floor: 1,414 square feet
Second Floor: 620 square feet
Total: 2,034 square feet

● Split-bedroom planning makes the most of this contemporary plan. The master suite pampers with a lavish bath and a fireplace. The living areas are open and have easy access to the rear terrace.

Design by
Home Planners

QUOTE ONE™
Cost to build? See page 230
to order complete cost estimate
to build this house in your area!

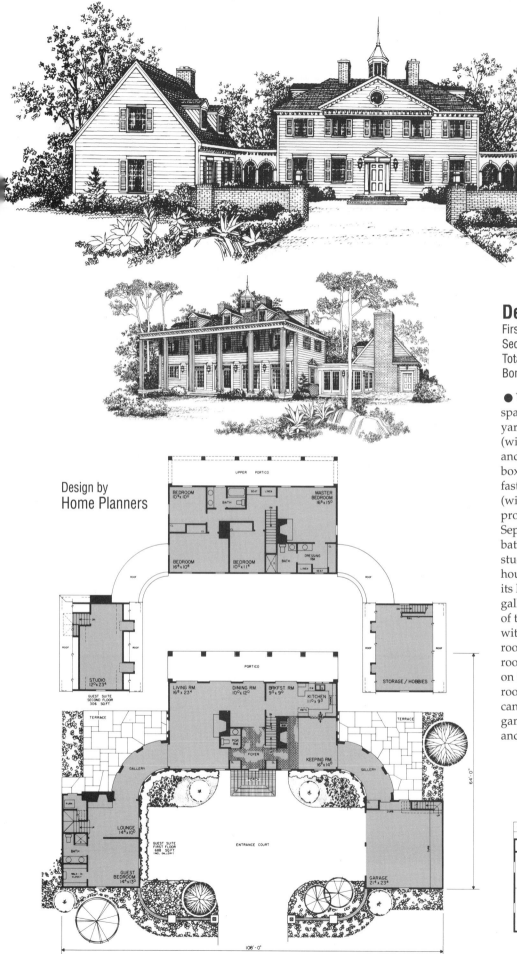

Design by Home Planners

Design 2665

First Floor: 1,992 square feet
Second Floor: 1,458 square feet
Total: 3,450 square feet
Bonus Space: 380 square feet

● Versatility and planned use of space are key factors in this courtyard mini-estate. A keeping room (with a pass-through to the kitchen and a fireplace with built-in wood box), a formal dining room, a breakfast room and a formal living room (with a fireplace) on the first floor provide plenty of social areas. Separate guest quarters with a full bath, a lounge area and an upstairs studio (connected to the main house by a gallery) further enhance its livability. A complementary gallery is located on the other side of the house and leads to the garage with a storage room or hobbies room situated above. Four bedrooms with two full baths are found on the second floor. The guest bedroom/lounge with upstairs study can be optionally designed as a game room with a spiral staircase and loft area.

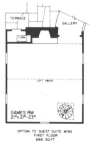

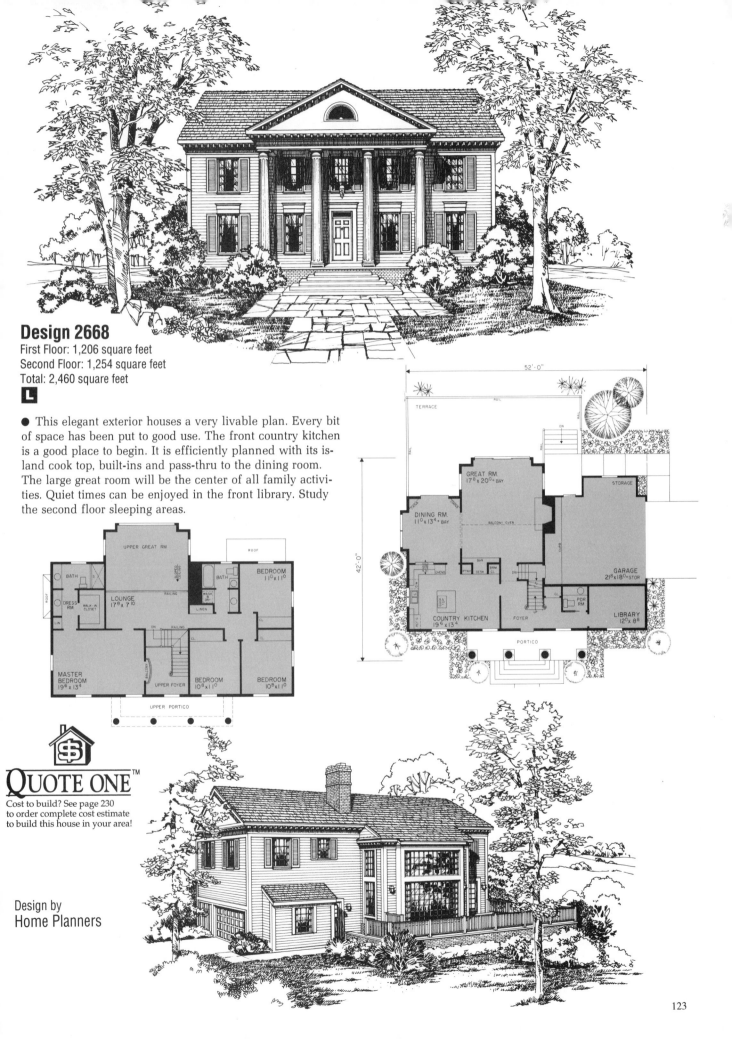

Design 2668

First Floor: 1,206 square feet
Second Floor: 1,254 square feet
Total: 2,460 square feet

L

● This elegant exterior houses a very livable plan. Every bit of space has been put to good use. The front country kitchen is a good place to begin. It is efficiently planned with its island cook top, built-ins and pass-thru to the dining room. The large great room will be the center of all family activities. Quiet times can be enjoyed in the front library. Study the second floor sleeping areas.

QUOTE ONE™

Cost to build? See page 230 to order complete cost estimate to build this house in your area!

Design by
Home Planners

123

Design 9203

Square Footage: 2,422

● You can't help but feel spoiled by this amenity-filled plan. A tiled entry and open stairwell with dome ceiling greet visitors to this unusual home. Just off the entry is a den or optional bedroom, an open dining room with hutch space and an enormous great room with arched windows. An open-hearth fireplace serves both the great room and kitchen, creating a hearth room on the kitchen side. A large work area in the kitchen caters to serious cooks. The spacious master suite includes ten-foot ceilings, a whirlpool with dome ceiling and an enormous walk-in closet.

Design by
**Design
Basics,
Inc.**

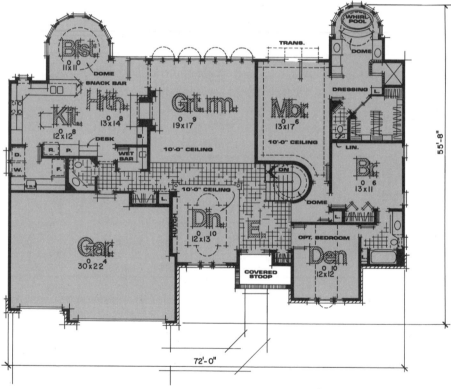

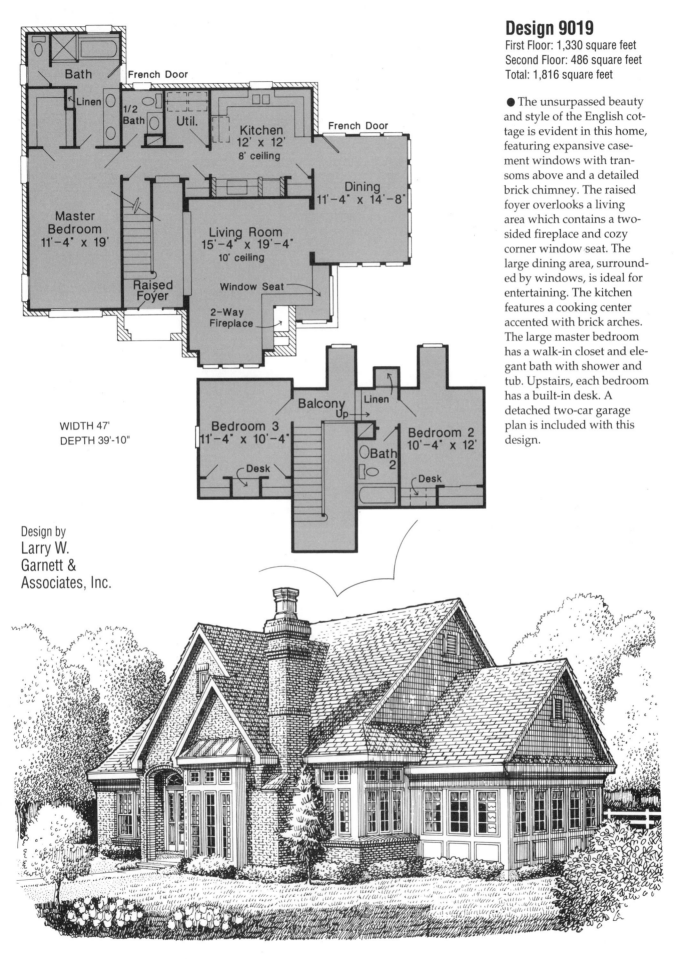

Bath

Linen

French Door

1/2
Bath

Util.

Kitchen
12' x 12'
8' ceiling

French Door

Master
Bedroom
11'-4" x 19'

Raised
Foyer

Living Room
15'-4" x 19'-4"
10' ceiling

Dining
11'-4" x 14'-8"

Window Seat

2-Way
Fireplace

WIDTH 47'
DEPTH 39'-10"

Balcony

Linen

Up

Bedroom 3
11'-4" x 10'-4"

Desk

Bath
2

Bedroom 2
10'-4" x 12'

Desk

Design by
Larry W.
Garnett &
Associates, Inc.

Design 9019

First Floor: 1,330 square feet
Second Floor: 486 square feet
Total: 1,816 square feet

● The unsurpassed beauty and style of the English cottage is evident in this home, featuring expansive casement windows with transoms above and a detailed brick chimney. The raised foyer overlooks a living area which contains a two-sided fireplace and cozy corner window seat. The large dining area, surrounded by windows, is ideal for entertaining. The kitchen features a cooking center accented with brick arches. The large master bedroom has a walk-in closet and elegant bath with shower and tub. Upstairs, each bedroom has a built-in desk. A detached two-car garage plan is included with this design.

This home, as shown in photograph, may differ from the actual blueprints.
For more detailed information, please check the floor plans carefully.

Photo by Dave Dawson

Design 9838 First Floor: 1,896 square feet; Second Floor: 1,500 square feet; Total: 3,396 square feet

● This magnificent home reflects architectural elegance at its finest, executed in stucco and stone. Perhaps its most distinctive feature is the octagonal living room which forms the focal point. Its attached dining room is bathed in natural light from a bay window. The island kitchen is nearby and has an attached octagonal breakfast room. The family room contains two sets of French doors and a fireplace. An optional room may be used for a guest room, music room or study. The second floor holds two family bedrooms and an owners suite with sitting room. Additional storage space is located over the garage. This home is designed with a basement foundation.

Width 132'
Depth 53'-6"

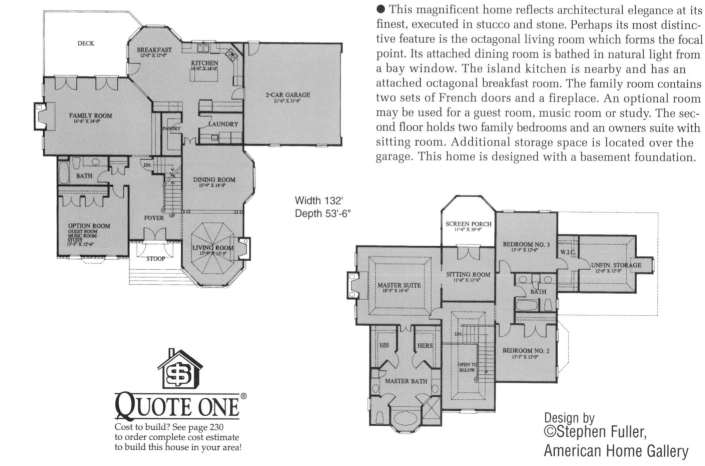

QUOTE ONE®

Cost to build? See page 230
to order complete cost estimate
to build this house in your area!

Design by
©Stephen Fuller,
American Home Gallery

126

BEDROOM NO. 4
13'-0" X 11'-0"

OPEN TO BELOW

BEDROOM NO. 3
15'-0" X 12'-0"

BATH

BEDROOM NO. 2
12'-0" X 13'-0"

OPEN TO BELOW

Design by
Design Traditions

DECK

BREAKFAST
11'-0" X 10'-0"

KITCHEN
13'-0" X 16'-0"

GREAT ROOM
14'-0" X 18'-0"

MASTER BEDROOM
13'-0" X 17'-10"

LAUNDRY
8'-0" X 9'-0"

W.I.C.

MASTER BATH
10'-0" X 16'-0"

TWO CAR GARAGE
21'-0" X 21'-0"

DINING ROOM
12'-0" X 16'-0"

FOYER
7'-0" X 13'-0"

STUDY
11'-0" X 15'-0"

W.I.C.

QUOTE ONE®

Cost to build? See page 230
to order complete cost estimate
to build this house in your area!

Design 9824

First Floor: 1,900 square feet
Second Floor: 800 square feet
Total: 2,700 square feet

● Stucco and stacked stone give this Country French
home classic European styling. The foyer is flanked
by a dining room and study. Adjacent to the great
room is the breakfast area which acts like a sun room
extension for the kitchen. The master suite of this
home is located on the main level. The second floor
holds three bedrooms and a shared bath. This home
is designed with a basement foundation.

Width 63'
Depth 51'

Rear Elevation

Design 9823

First Floor: 1,960 square feet; Second Floor: 905 square feet
Total: 2,865 square feet; Bonus Room: 297 square feet

● The classical styling of this Colonial home will be appreciated by traditionalists. The foyer opens to both a banquet-sized dining room and formal living room with fireplace. Just beyond is the two-story great room. The entire right side of the main level is taken up by the master suite. The other side of the main level includes a large kitchen and breakfast room just steps away from the detached garage. Upstairs, each bedroom features ample closet space and direct access to bathrooms. The detached garage features an unfinished office or studio on its second level. This home is designed with a walk-out basement.

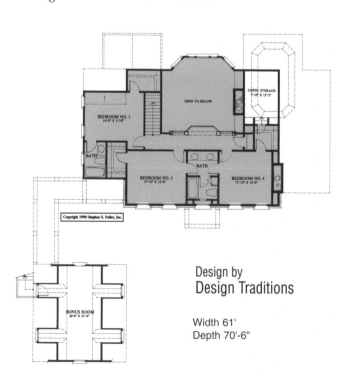

Design by
Design Traditions

Width 61'
Depth 70'-6"

Quote One®

Cost to build? See page 230 to order complete cost estimate to build this house in your area!

Quote One™

Cost to build? See page 230
to order complete cost estimate
to build this house in your area!

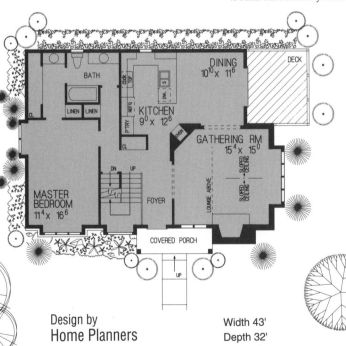

Design by
Home Planners

Width 43'
Depth 32'

Design 3331

First Floor: 1,115 square feet
Second Floor: 690 square feet
Total: 1,805 square feet

L

● Who could guess that this compact design contains three bedrooms and two full baths? The kitchen has indoor eating space in the dining room and outdoor eating space on an attached deck. A fireplace in the two-story gathering room welcomes company.

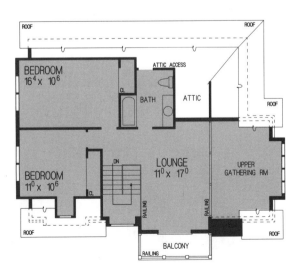

Design 2699

First Floor: 2,188 square feet
Second Floor: 858 square feet
Total: 3,046 square feet

L

Design by
Home Planners

QUOTE ONE™

Cost to build? See page 230
to order complete cost estimate
to build this house in your area!

Width 106'-8"
Depth 32'

Floor plan labels (second floor):
ROOF
UPPER LIVING RM.
BEDROOM 11⁰ x 15⁸
BEDROOM 11⁰ x 12⁰
LOUNGE
RAILING
VANITY
BATH
SHELVES
CL.
BATH
ACCESS PANEL
ATTIC
CL.
CL.
BALCONY
LINEN
UPPER FOYER
DN
ROOF

Floor plan labels (first floor):
TERRACE
TERRACE
LIVING RM. 18⁴ x 15⁰
DINING RM. 12⁰ x 13⁰
EATING
WHIRLPOOL
MASTER BEDROOM 15⁰ x 18⁰
LOUNGE ABOVE
BATH
COUNTRY KITCHEN 15⁸ x 21⁰
COOK TOP
MUD AREA
W.R.
CL.
VANITY
LAUNDRY 11⁸ x 6⁰
WALK-IN CLOSET
LOUNGE 12⁰ x 8⁸
BALCONY ABOVE
FOYER
CL.
PDR. RM.
MEDIA RM. 12⁰ x 10⁰
DN
PORCH
GARAGE 21⁴ x 29⁴

Photos by Andrew D. Lautman

This home, as shown in the photograph, may differ from the actual blueprints. For more detailed information, please check the floor plans carefully.

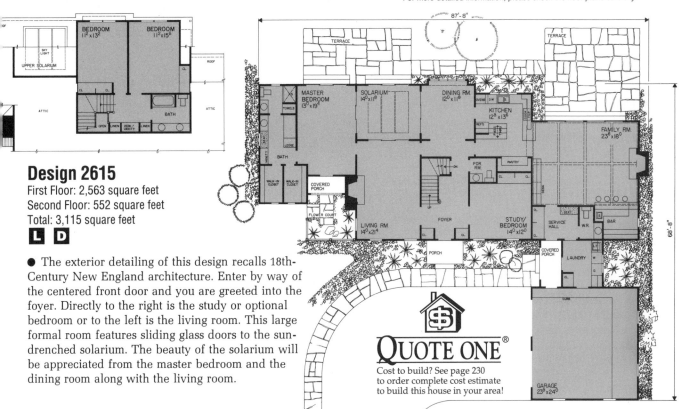

Design 2615

First Floor: 2,563 square feet
Second Floor: 552 square feet
Total: 3,115 square feet

L **D**

● The exterior detailing of this design recalls 18th-Century New England architecture. Enter by way of the centered front door and you are greeted into the foyer. Directly to the right is the study or optional bedroom or to the left is the living room. This large formal room features sliding glass doors to the sun-drenched solarium. The beauty of the solarium will be appreciated from the master bedroom and the dining room along with the living room.

QUOTE ONE®

Cost to build? See page 230 to order complete cost estimate to build this house in your area!

Design by
Home Planners

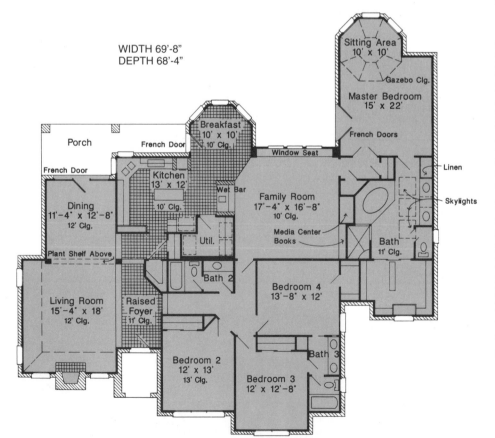

Design by
Larry W.
Garnett &
Associates, Inc.

Design 9156

Square Footage: 2,885

● An entire wing on the right side of this house is dedicated to making the owners feel at home. The master bedroom includes an octagonal sitting area with gazebo ceiling and French doors to the rear yard. Three skylights illuminate a lavish master bath with tub, shower, and dual vanities, as well as abundant closet space. Three family bedrooms and two full baths complete the sleeping areas. A large family room features a wet bar and built-in media center and bookshelves. A breakfast bay is adjacent to the island kitchen. To the left of the home, formal areas include the dining room with French door and the living room with fireplace and plant shelf.

WIDTH 69'-8"
DEPTH 68'-4"

Sliding Glass & French Doors

Photo by Bob Greenspan

This home, as shown in the photograph, may differ from the actual blueprints. For more detailed information, please check the floor plans carefully.

Design 3309

First Floor: 1,375 square feet
Second Floor: 1,016 square feet
Total: 2,391 square feet

L

● Covered porches, front and back, are a fine preview to the livable nature of this Victorian. Living areas are defined in a family room with a fireplace, formal living and dining rooms and a kitchen with a breakfast room. An ample laundry room, a garage with storage space and a powder room round out the first floor. Three second floor bedrooms are joined by a study and two full baths.

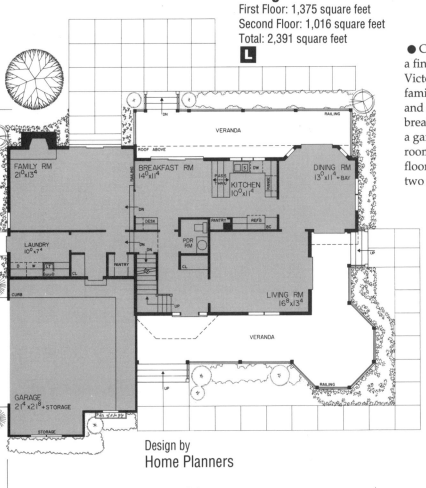

Design by
Home Planners

62'-7"

QUOTE ONE™
Cost to build? See page 230
to order complete cost estimate
to build this house in your area!

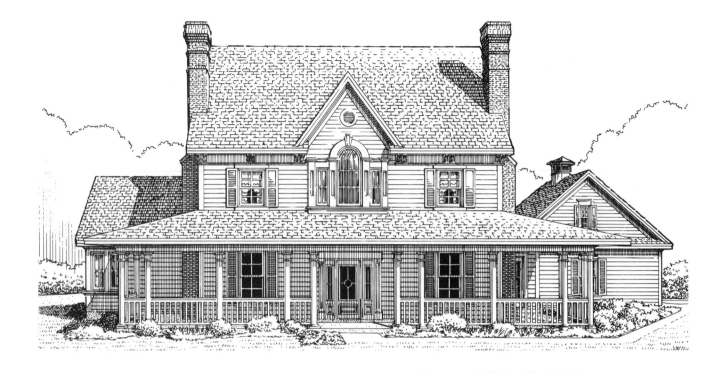

Design 9067

First Floor: 1,999 square feet
Second Floor: 933 square feet
Total: 2,932 square feet

● The wraparound veranda and simple lines give this home an unassuming elegance that is characteristic of its Folk Victorian heritage. Opening directly to the formal dining room, the two-story foyer offers extra space for large dinner parties. Double French doors lead to the study with raised paneling and a cozy fireplace. Built-in bookcases conceal a hidden security vault. The private master suite features a corner garden tub, glass-enclosed shower and a walk-in closet. Overlooking the family room and built-in breakfast nook is the central kitchen. A rear staircase provides convenient access to the second floor from the family room. The balcony provides a view of the foyer below and the Palladian window. Three additional bedrooms complete this exquisite home.

Design by
Larry W. Garnett & Associates, Inc.

Width 80'
Depth 59'

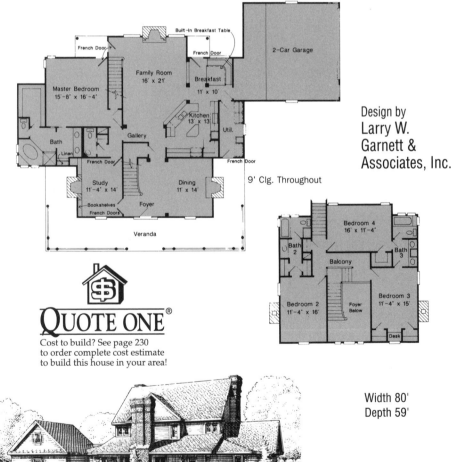

Cost to build? See page 230 to order complete cost estimate to build this house in your area!

REAR VIEW

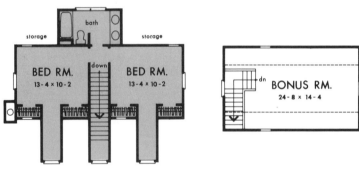

storage · storage

bath

BED RM.
13-4 × 10-2

down

BED RM.
13-4 × 10-2

dn

BONUS RM.
24-8 × 14-4

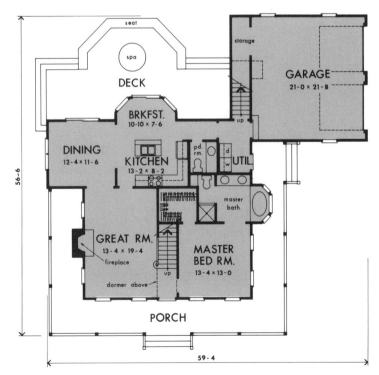

seat

spa

DECK

storage

GARAGE
21-0 × 21-8

BRKFST.
10-10 × 7-6

DINING
12-4 × 11-6

KITCHEN
13-2 × 8-2

pd.
rm.

UTIL

up

56-6

master
bath

GREAT RM.
13-4 × 19-4

fireplace

MASTER
BED RM.
13-4 × 13-0

dormer above

up

PORCH

59-4

Design 9690

First Floor: 1,145 square feet
Second Floor: 518 square feet
Total: 1,663 square feet
Bonus Room: 380 square feet

● Look this plan over and you'll
be amazed at how much livability
can be found in less than 2,000
square feet. A wraparound porch
welcomes visitors to the home.
Inside lies an enormous great room
with fireplace. To the rear of the
home, the breakfast and dining
rooms have sliding glass doors to a
large deck with room for a spa.
The master bedroom contains a
walk-in closet and airy bath with a
whirlpool tub. Two bedrooms are
found on the second floor, as well
as a bonus room over the garage.

Design by
Donald A.
Gardner,
Architects, Inc.

QUOTE ONE®

Cost to build? See page 230
to order complete cost estimate
to build this house in your area!

Design 3461

First Floor: 1,391 square feet
Second Floor: 611 square feet
Total: 2,002 square feet

L

● A Palladian window set in a dormer provides a nice introduction to this 1½-story country home. The two-story foyer draws on natural light and a pair of columns to set a comfortable, yet elegant mood. The living room, to the left, presents a grand space for entertaining. From full-course dinners to family suppers, the dining room serves its purpose well. The kitchen delights with an island work station and openness to the family room. Here, a raised-hearth fireplace provides added comfort. Sleeping accommodations are comprised of four bedrooms, one a first-floor master suite. With a luxurious private bath, including dual lavatories, this room will surely be a favorite retreat. Upstairs, three secondary bedrooms meet the needs of the growing family.

QUOTE ONE™

Cost to build? See page 230
to order complete cost estimate
to build this house in your area!

Design by
Home Planners

Design 3608

First Floor: 2,347 square feet
Second Floor: 1,087 square feet
Total: 3,434 square feet

L

● Dutch gable roof lines and a gabled wraparound porch with star-burst trim matching the star-burst clerestory window on the center dormer make this a farmhouse with style! The clerestory window sheds radiant light on the U-shaped stairway leading from the foyer to the upstairs family bedrooms and loft. Downstairs, the foyer opens to all areas of the home, from the study or guest bedroom on the left that leads to the master suite, to the formal dining room on the right and to the massive great room in the center of the home. A large fireplace in the great room provides a cozy centerpiece for gathering and entertaining. The kitchen is convenient to the great room, the breakfast nook and the dining room and features an island cooktop and an interesting snack bar and work area combination. The luxurious master suite includes access to the covered patio, a spacious walk-in closet and a master bath with a whirlpool tub, a separate shower, a compartmented toilet and a double-bowl vanity.

Design by
Home Planners

Quote One™

Cost to build? See page 230 to order complete cost estimate to build this house in your area!

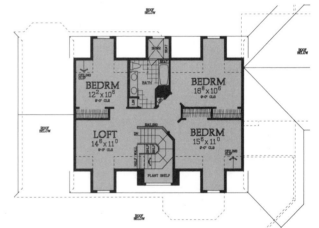

Width 93'-6"
Depth 61'

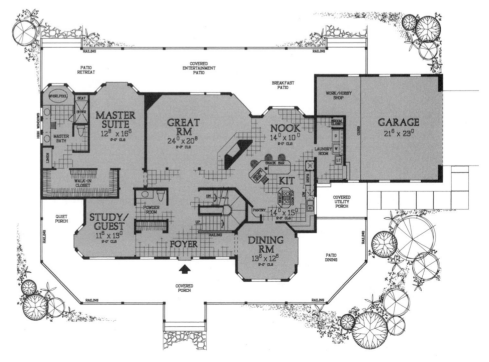

This home, as shown in the photograph, may differ from the actual blueprints. For more detailed information, please check the floor plans carefully.

Photo by Andrew D. Lautman

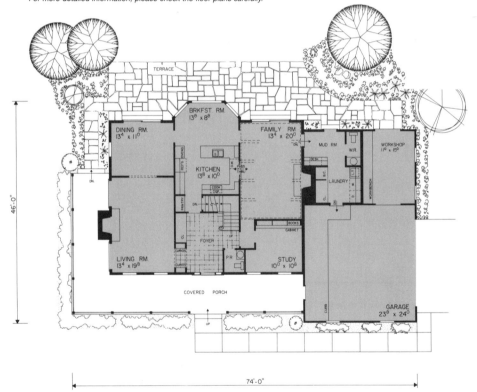

Design by
Home Planners

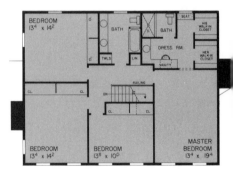

QUOTE ONE™
Cost to build? See page 230
to order complete cost estimate
to build this house in your area!

Design 2946 First Floor: 1,581 square feet; Second Floor: 1,344 square feet; Total: 2,925 square feet
L **D**

● Here's a traditional design that's made for down-home hospitality, the pleasures of casual conversation, and the good grace of pleasant company. The star attractions are the large covered porch and terrace, perfectly relaxing gathering points for family and friends. Inside, though, the design is truly a hard worker; separate living room and family room, each with its own fireplace; formal dining room; large kitchen and breakfast area with bay windows; separate study; workshop with plenty of room to maneuver; mud room; and four bedrooms up, including a master suite. Not to be overlooked are the curio niches, the powder room, the built-in bookshelves, the kitchen pass-through, the pantry, the planning desk, the workbench, and the stairs to the basement.

This home, as shown in the photograph, may differ from the actual blueprints.
For more detailed information, please check the floor plans carefully.

Photo by Carl Socolow

Design 2774 First Floor: 1,366 square feet; Second Floor: 969 square feet; Total: 2,335 square feet

L D

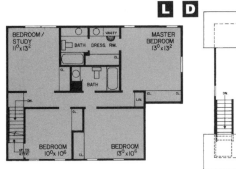

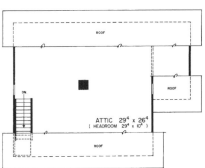

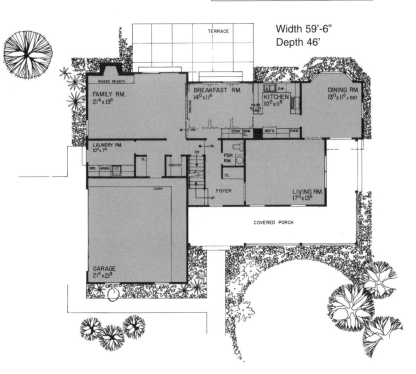

Width 59'-6"
Depth 46'

● This design offers pleasures for the entire family. There is a quiet corner living room which has an opening to the sizable dining room. This room will enjoy plenty of natural light from the delightful bay window overlooking the rear yard and is conveniently located next to the efficient U-shaped kitchen. The kitchen features many built-ins with a pass-through to the beam-ceilinged breakfast room. Sliding glass doors to the terrace are fine attractions in both the sunken family room and breakfast room. The service entrance to the garage is flanked by a clothes closet and a large, walk-in pantry. Recreational activities and hobbies can be pursued in the basement area. Four bedrooms and two bathrooms are upstairs.

Cost to build? See page 230
to order complete cost estimate
to build this house in your area!

Design by
Home Planners

Design 9557

First Floor: 1,371 square feet
Second Floor: 916 square feet
Total: 2,287 square feet

● The decorative pillars and the wraparound porch are just the beginning of this comfortable home. Inside, an angled, U-shaped stairway leads to the second-floor sleeping zone. On the first floor, French doors lead to a bay-windowed den that shares a see-through fireplace with the two-story family room. The large island kitchen includes a writing desk, a corner sink, a breakfast nook and access to the laundry room, the powder room and the two-car garage. The master suite is a real treat with its French-door access, vaulted ceiling and luxurious bath. Two other bedrooms and a full bath complete the second floor.

Quote One®
Cost to build? See page 230 to order complete cost estimate to build this house in your area!

Design by
Alan Mascord
Design Associates, Inc.

WIDTH 43'
DEPTH 69'

Design 9536

First Floor: 1,200 square feet
Second Floor: 1,339 square feet
Total: 2,539 square feet

L

● A covered front porch introduces this home's comfortable living pattern. The two-story foyer opens to a living room with a fireplace and lots of natural light. The formal dining room looks out over the living room. In the kitchen, an island cooktop, a pantry, a built-in planning desk and a nook with double doors to outside livability aims to please. A spacious family room with another fireplace will accommodate casual living. Upstairs, five bedrooms—or four and a den— make room for all family members and guests. The master bedroom suite exudes elegance with an elegant ceiling and a pampering spa bath. A full hall bath with a skylight and dual lavatories serves the secondary bedrooms.

Design by
**Alan Mascord
Design Associates, Inc.**

◄ 56' ►

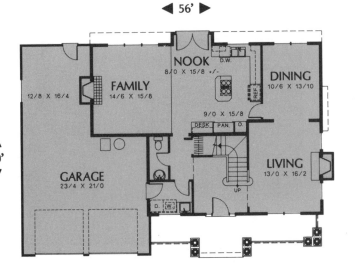

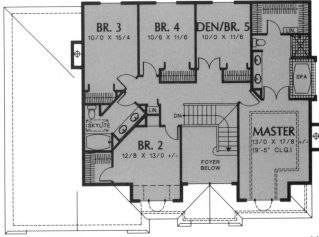

Design 9908 First Floor: 1,944 square feet
Second Floor: 1,055 square feet, Total: 2,999 square feet

● Interesting rooflines, multi-level eaves and a two-story double-bay window create a unique cottage farmhouse appearance for this charming home. A combination of columns and stone create a cozy and inviting porch. The grand foyer leads to the formal dining room and large great room, both graced with columns. The great room features a cozy fireplace and opens to the deck through French door. The breakfast room, divided from the great room by an open staircase, shares space with an efficient L-shaped kitchen and nearby laundry room, making domestic endeavors easy to accomplish. The right wing is devoted to a sumptuous, amenity-filled master suite with convenient access to the study for after-hours research or quiet reading. The second floor contains three secondary bedrooms and two baths for family and guests. This home is designed with a basement foundation.

Width 51'-6"
Depth 72'

Design by
Design Traditions

Design 3495

First Floor: 1,457 square feet
Second Floor: 1,288 square feet
Total: 2,745 square feet

L D

● The very best in modern design comes into play with this extraordinary two-story home. Columns and half walls define the formal living and dining rooms—a curved niche adds appeal to the latter. Beyond the centrally located stair-case, the family room extends to its occupants a sloped ceiling, and an angled corner fireplace. At the other side of the house, the bright breakfast area—adjacent to the kitchen—enjoys the use of a patio. In the kitchen, an abundance of counter and storage space sets the stage for convenient food preparation. Notice, too, the powder room nestled between the kitchen and the laundry room. Two full bathrooms grace the upstairs: one in the master suite includes a soaking tub and separate shower; one in the hallway serves the three secondary bedrooms.

Width 42'
Depth 63'-4"

Design by
Home Planners

QUOTE ONE™

Cost to build? See page 230 to order complete cost estimate to build this house in your area!

Design 9666

First Floor: 1,027 square feet
Second Floor: 580 square feet
Total: 1,607 square feet

Cost to build? See page 230 to order complete cost estimate to build this house in your area!

● This economical, rustic three-bedroom plan sports a relaxing country image with both front and back covered porches. The openness of the expansive great room to kitchen/dining areas and loft/study areas is reinforced with a shared cathedral ceiling for impressive space. The first level allows for two bedrooms, a full bath and a utility area. The master suite on the second level has a walk-in closet and a master bath with whirlpool tub, shower and double-bowl vanity. The plan is available with a crawl-space foundation.

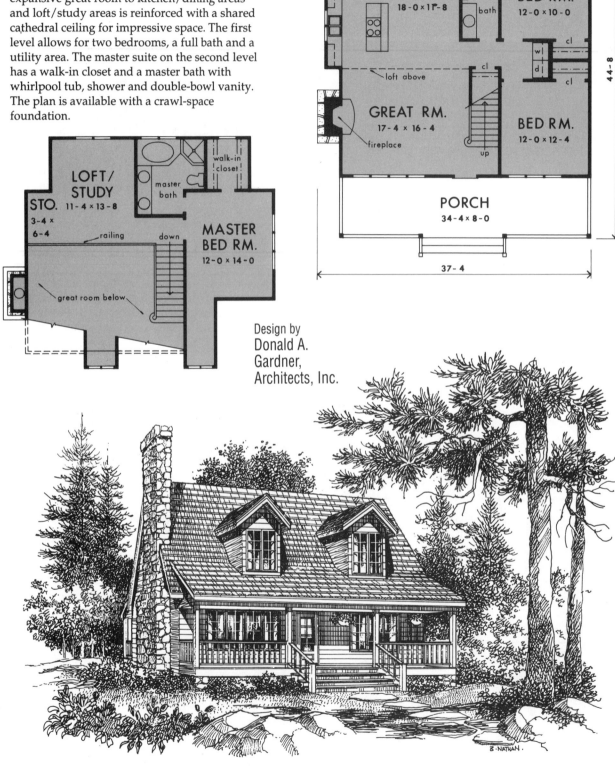

PORCH
34-4 × 8-0

KIT./DINING
18-0 × 11-8

bath

BED RM.
12-0 × 10-0

wl
d
cl
cl

loft above

cl

GREAT RM.
17-4 × 16-4

up

fireplace

BED RM.
12-0 × 12-4

PORCH
34-4 × 8-0

44-8

37-4

LOFT/
STUDY
11-4 × 13-8

STO.
3-4 × 6-4

master bath

walk-in closet

railing

down

great room below

MASTER
BED RM.
12-0 × 14-0

Design by
Donald A.
Gardner,
Architects, Inc.

B·NATHAN.

Design 2682

First Floor (Basic Plan): 1,016 square feet
First Floor (Expanded Plan): 1,272 square feet
Second Floor (Both Plans): 766 square feet
Total (Basic Plan): 1,782 square feet: Total (Expanded Plan): 2,038 square feet

L **D**

Width 33'
Depth 32'

● Here is an expandable Colonial with a full measure of Cape Cod charm. For those who wish to build the basic house, there is an abundance of low-budget livability. Twin fireplaces serve the formal living room and the informal country kitchen. A dining room and powder room are also on the first floor of the basic plan. The second floor contains three bedrooms and two full baths. The expanded version provides for the addition of wings to accommodate a large study, a garage and an upstairs attic.

Design by
Home Planners

Cost to build? See page 230
to order complete cost estimate
to build this house in your area!

145

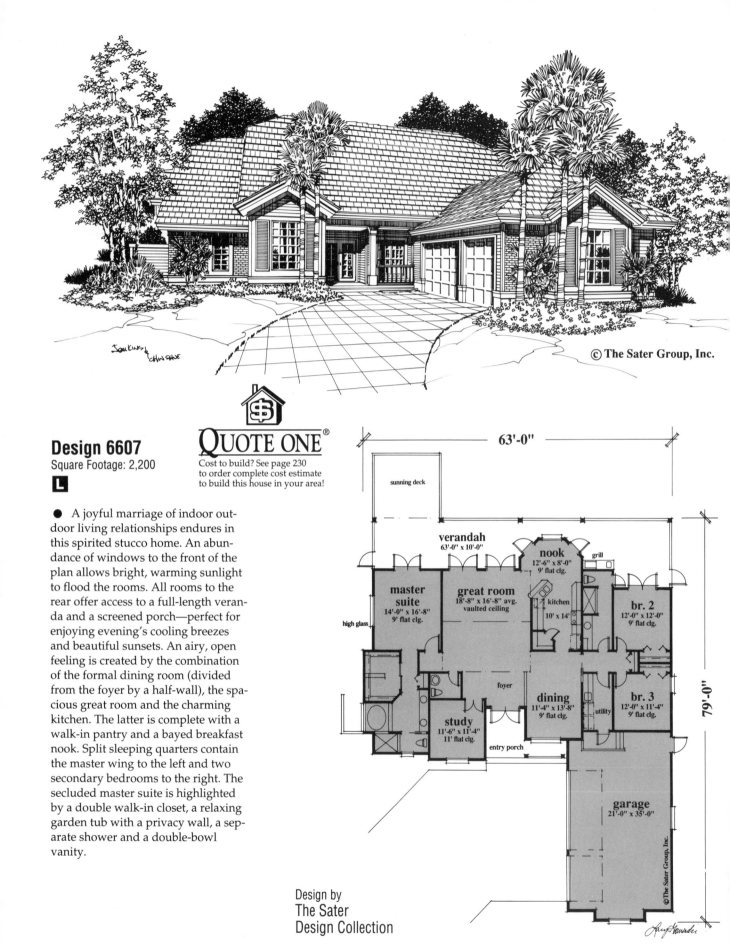

Design 6607
Square Footage: 2,200

L

Quote One®

Cost to build? See page 230 to order complete cost estimate to build this house in your area!

● A joyful marriage of indoor out-door living relationships endures in this spirited stucco home. An abundance of windows to the front of the plan allows bright, warming sunlight to flood the rooms. All rooms to the rear offer access to a full-length veranda and a screened porch—perfect for enjoying evening's cooling breezes and beautiful sunsets. An airy, open feeling is created by the combination of the formal dining room (divided from the foyer by a half-wall), the spacious great room and the charming kitchen. The latter is complete with a walk-in pantry and a bayed breakfast nook. Split sleeping quarters contain the master wing to the left and two secondary bedrooms to the right. The secluded master suite is highlighted by a double walk-in closet, a relaxing garden tub with a privacy wall, a separate shower and a double-bowl vanity.

Design by
**The Sater
Design Collection**

© The Sater Group, Inc.

63'-0"

sunning deck

verandah
63'-0" x 10'-0"

nook
12'-6" x 8'-0"
9' flat clg.

grill

master suite
14'-0" x 16'-8"
9' flat clg.

great room
18'-8" x 16'-8" avg.
vaulted ceiling

kitchen
10' x 14'

br. 2
12'-0" x 12'-0"
9' flat clg.

high glass

foyer

dining
11'-4" x 13'-8"
9' flat clg.

br. 3
12'-0" x 11'-4"
9' flat clg.

utility

study
11'-6" x 11'-4"
11' flat clg.

entry porch

garage
21'-0" x 35'-0"

79'-0"

Design 3560

Square Footage: 2,189

● Simplicity is the key to the stylish good looks of this home's facade. A walled garden entry and large window areas appeal to outdoor enthusiasts. Inside, the kitchen forms the hub of the plan. It opens directly off the foyer and contains an island counter and a work counter with eating space on the living area side. A sloped ceiling, a fireplace and sliding glass doors to a rear terrace are highlights in the living area. The master bedroom also sports sliding glass doors to the terrace. Its dressing area is enhanced with double walk-in closets and lavatories. A whirlpool tub and seated shower are additional amenities. Two family bedrooms are found on the opposite side of the house. They share a full bath with twin lavatories.

Cost to build? See page 230 to order complete cost estimate to build this house in your area!

Design by
Home Planners

Design 3458

First Floor: 1,617 square feet
Second Floor: 725 square feet
Total: 2,342 square feet

L **D**

● With end gables, and five front gables, this design becomes an updated "house of seven gables." Meanwhile, brick veneer, horizontal siding, radial head windows and an interesting roof add an extra measure of charm. Designed for a growing family with a modest building budget, the floor plan incorporates four bedrooms and both formal and informal living areas. The central foyer, with its open staircase to the second floor, looks up to the balcony. The spacious family room has a high ceiling and a dramatic view of the rear grounds. In the U-shaped kitchen, a snack bar caters to quick, on-the-run meals. A pantry facilitates stocking-up on foodstuffs. A basement allows for bonus space should development of recreational, hobby or storage space come into play.

Design by
Home Planners

QUOTE ONE™

Cost to build? See page 230
to order complete cost estimate
to build this house in your area!

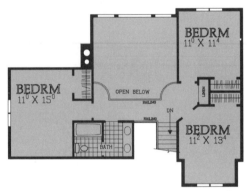

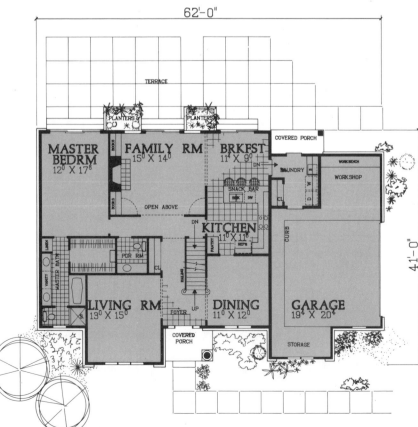

This home, as shown in the photograph, may differ from the actual blueprints. For more detailed information, please check the floor plans carefully.

Photo by Andrew D. Lautman

Design by
Home Planners

QUOTE ONE®

Cost to build? See page 230
to order complete cost estimate
to build this house in your area!

Design 2927

First Floor: 1,425 square feet
Second Floor: 704 square feet
Total: 2,129 square feet

D

● This charming Early American design is just as warm on the inside. The first floor features a convenient kitchen with a pass-through to the breakfast room. There's also a formal dining room just steps away in the rear of the house. An adjacent rear living room enjoys its own fireplace.

Other features include a rear media room (or optional third bedroom) and a complete second-floor master suite. A downstairs bedroom enjoys an excellent front view. Other highlights include a garden court, a covered porch and a large garage with extra storage.

Design 3327

Square Footage: 2,881

L **D**

● The high, massive hipped roof of this home creates an imposing facade while varying roof planes and projecting gables enhance appeal. A central, high-ceilinged foyer routes traffic efficiently to the sleeping, formal and informal zones of the house. Note the sliding glass doors that provide access to outdoor living facilities. A built-in china cabinet and planter unit are fine decor features. In the angular kitchen, a high ceiling and efficient work patterning set the pace. The conversation room may act as a multi-purpose room. For TV time, a media room caters to audio-visual activities. Sleeping quarters take off with the spacious master bedroom; here you'll find a tray ceiling and sliding doors to the rear yard. An abundance of wall space for effective and flexible furniture arrangement further characterizes the room. Two sizable bedrooms serve the children.

Width 77'-11"
Depth 73'-11"

Design by
Home Planners

Cost to build? See page 230 to order complete cost estimate to build this house in your area!

Design 3498
Square Footage: 2,135

● You'll savor the timeless style of this charming bungalow design. With pleasing proportions, it welcomes all onto its expansive front porch—perfect for quiet conversations. Inside, livability excels with a side-facing family kitchen. Here, an interesting bumped-out nook facilitates a built-in table and bench seats. A formal dining room rests to the rear of the plan and enjoys direct access to a back porch. The parlor, with a central fireplace, also has access to this outdoor living area. The master bedroom is just a step away from the parlor. It offers large dimensions and a private bath with a walk-in closet, dual lavs and a bumped-out tub. An additional bedroom may also serve as a study.

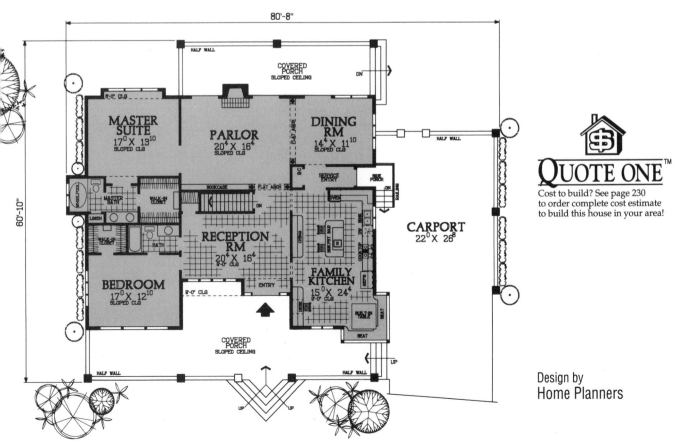

QUOTE ONE™

Cost to build? See page 230 to order complete cost estimate to build this house in your area!

Design by
Home Planners

Design 9483

First Floor: 1,697 square feet
Second Floor: 433 square feet
Total: 2,130 square feet

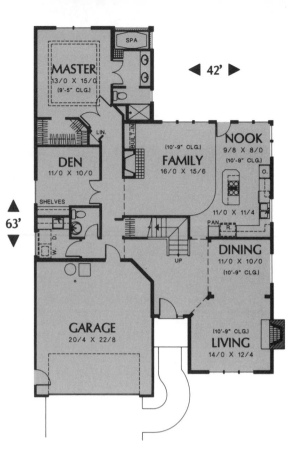

Design by
Alan Mascord
Design Associates, Inc.

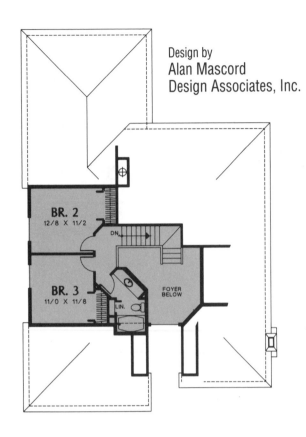

● High, sloping rooflines allow for a volume look with expansive windows in this two-story plan. The living areas are clustered on the first floor along with a private master suite tucked privately to the rear. The living room and family room both have fireplaces. Two family bedrooms are found on the second floor along with a full bath.

Design 9403/9403A

Square Footage: 1,565

L

● If you're looking for a traditional home with front-facing gables and cedar shingles, Design 9403 may be just right for you. If however, you prefer the formal look of a hip roof and a brick exterior, then Design 9403A should be your choice. The floor plan is basically the same for both designs. The difference is found in the living room. While Design 9403 features a Palladian window, Design 9403A is graced with a bay window. The remainder of the floor plan is the same. Highlights include a family room with an angled fireplace, formal and informal eating areas, and a private master suite with a pampering master bath. From the entry, French doors open onto a den that easily converts to a third bedroom. Please specify design number when ordering.

SPA

NOOK
8/8 X 9/8

VAULTED
MASTER
12/0 X 14/0

VAULTED
FAMILY
12/0 X 14/0

11/2 X 12/0

PAN. REF.

DINING

BR. 2
12/0 X 10/0

D.W. LIN.

VAULTED
LIVING
13/0 X 20/8

DEN/BR. 3
10/6 X 10/8

GARAGE
19/4 X 21/8

WIDTH 50'
DEPTH 52'-10"

Design by
**Alan Mascord
Design Associates, Inc.**

Design 9403A

153

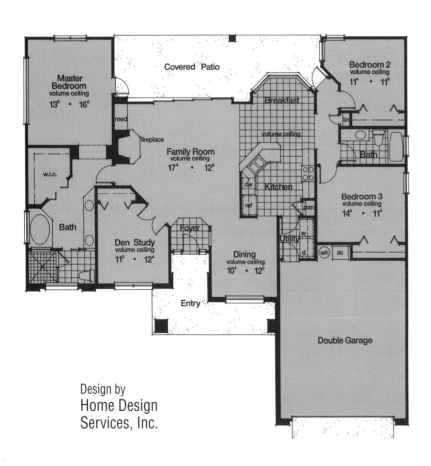

Master Bedroom
volume ceiling
13⁰ · 16⁰

w.i.c.

Bath

med

fireplace

Family Room
volume ceiling
17⁴ · 12⁸

Den Study
volume ceiling
11⁰ · 12⁴

Foyer

Covered Patio

Breakfast

volume ceiling

Kitchen

dw

ref

Dining
volume ceiling
10⁴ · 12⁰

Entry

Utility

w

d

wh

ac

pan

Bedroom 2
volume ceiling
11⁴ · 11⁰

lin

Bath

Bedroom 3
volume ceiling
14⁰ · 11⁴

Double Garage

Design by
**Home Design
Services, Inc.**

Design 8684
Square Footage: 1,898

● Family living is at the core of this brick one-story home inspired by the design of Frank Lloyd Wright. To the left of the foyer, double doors open onto a den/study which easily converts for use as a nursery. The master suite is conveniently located nearby. Split away from family bedrooms for privacy, it features a spacious bedroom and a pampering bath with a large walk-in closet, a separate shower and a relaxing tub. Centrally located, the family room with its cozy fireplace combines well with the kitchen and the bay-windowed breakfast nook for casual family get-togethers. The sleeping wing to the right contains two secondary bedrooms that share a full bath and patio access via a "kids" door.

Width 60'
Depth 59'-4"

Design 8685

Square Footage: 1,951

● The brick exterior of this one-story home extends a warm welcome that is nice to come home to. Upon entering the foyer, you can look directly ahead into the generous living room and beyond for views of the back yard. An adjacent dining room completes the formal living area. The family room is situated to the rear and combines with the U-shaped kitchen with its walk-in pantry and the breakfast area for informal occasions. Two family bedrooms share an oversize bath just off the kitchen. The master suite has a grand arched entry and the potential for a sitting area. A well-appointed master bath features dual vanities, a soaking tub, a separate shower and a large walk-in closet.

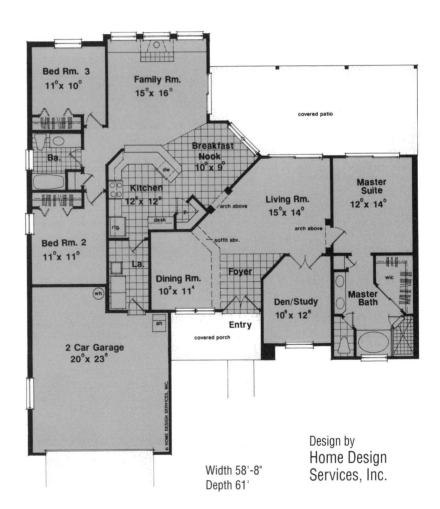

Width 58'-8"
Depth 61'

Design by
Home Design
Services, Inc.

155

Design 8600

Square Footage: 2,041

● The striking facade of this house is only the beginning to a very livable design. A dramatic foyer with columns branches off into the living room on one side, the dining room on the other. A spacious family room graces the center of the house—a true focal point. Beyond the kitchen and breakfast nook you'll find the master bedroom with private access to the covered patio. Three family bedrooms occupy the other side of the house.

Width 60'
Depth 56'

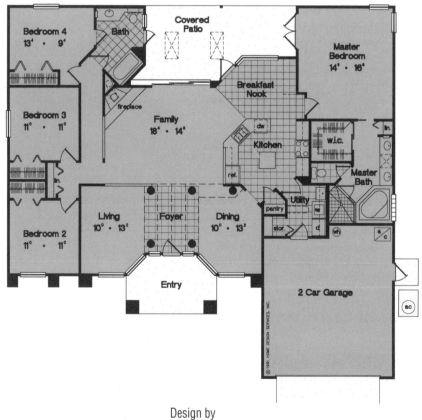

Design by
Home Design
Services, Inc.

Design 3638

Square Footage: 2,861

● Double columns and an arched entry create a grand entrance to this elegant one-story home. Inside, arched colonnades add grace and definition to the formal living and dining rooms as well as the family room. The master suite occupies a separate wing, providing a private retreat. Treat yourself to luxury in the master bath which includes a bumped-out whirlpool tub, a separate shower and twin vanities. An office/den located nearby easily converts to a nursery. A snack bar provides space for meals on-the-go and separates the island kitchen from the bay-windowed morning room. Three additional bedrooms—one a guest room with an adjacent bath—share two baths.

Design by
Home Planners

Width 93'-4"
Depth 66'-6"

Quote One™

Cost to build? See page 230 to order complete cost estimate to build this house in your area!

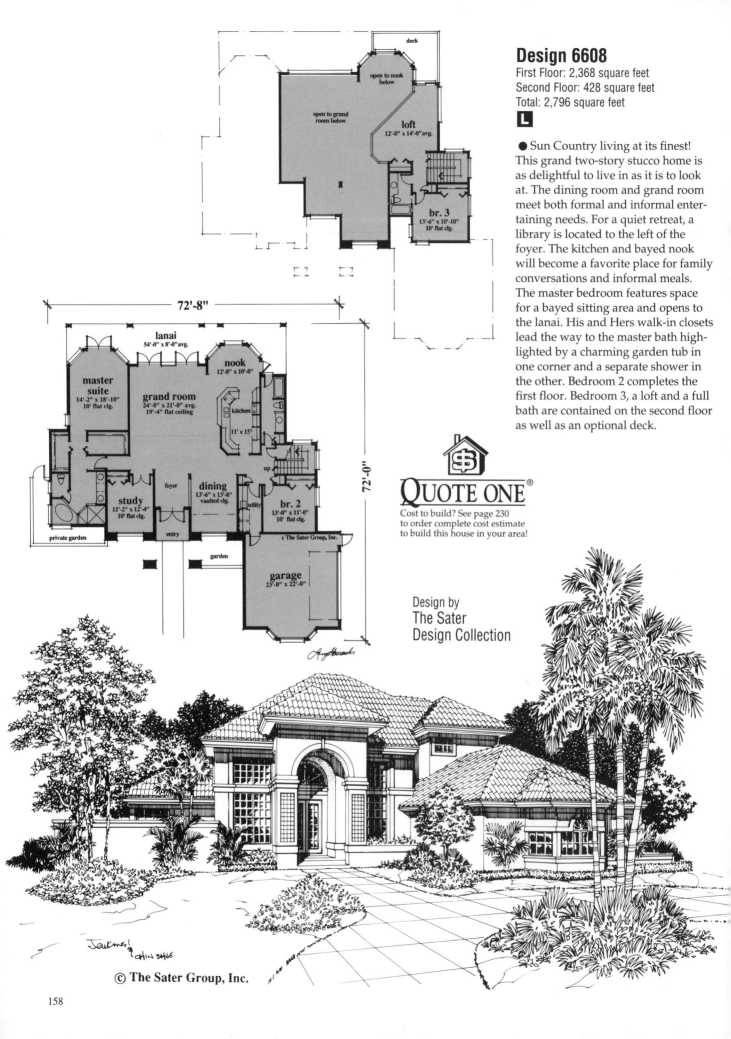

deck

open to nook below

open to grand room below

loft
12'-0" x 14'-0" avg.

br. 3
13'-6" x 10'-10"
10' flat clg.

72'-8"

72'-0"

lanai
54'-0" x 8'-0" avg.

nook
12'-8" x 10'-0"

master suite
14'-2" x 18'-10"
10' flat clg.

grand room
24'-0" x 21'-0" avg.
19'-4" flat ceiling

kitchen

11' x 15'

study
11'-2" x 12'-4"
10' flat clg.

foyer

dining
13'-6" x 13'-8"
vaulted clg.

utility

up

br. 2
13'-0" x 11'-0"
10' flat clg.

private garden

entry

garden

c The Sater Group, Inc.

garage
23'-0" x 22'-0"

Design 6608

First Floor: 2,368 square feet
Second Floor: 428 square feet
Total: 2,796 square feet

L

● Sun Country living at its finest! This grand two-story stucco home is as delightful to live in as it is to look at. The dining room and grand room meet both formal and informal entertaining needs. For a quiet retreat, a library is located to the left of the foyer. The kitchen and bayed nook will become a favorite place for family conversations and informal meals. The master bedroom features space for a bayed sitting area and opens to the lanai. His and Hers walk-in closets lead the way to the master bath highlighted by a charming garden tub in one corner and a separate shower in the other. Bedroom 2 completes the first floor. Bedroom 3, a loft and a full bath are contained on the second floor as well as an optional deck.

Quote One®

Cost to build? See page 230 to order complete cost estimate to build this house in your area!

Design by
The Sater
Design Collection

© The Sater Group, Inc.

© The Sater Group, Inc.

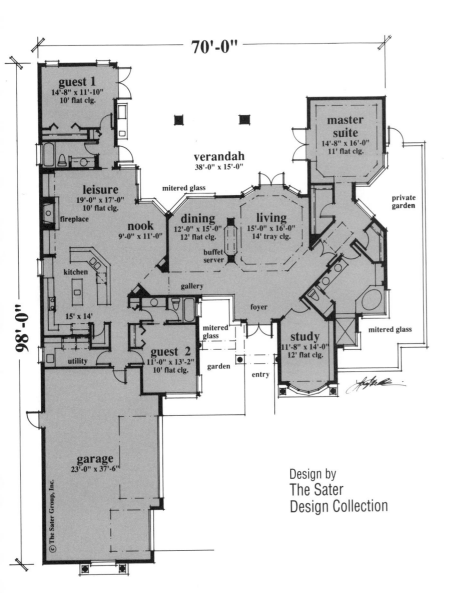

70'-0"

guest 1
14'-8" x 11'-10"
10' flat clg.

verandah
38'-0" x 15'-0"

master
suite
14'-8" x 16'-0"
11' flat clg.

leisure
19'-0" x 17'-0"
10' flat clg.

mitered glass

fireplace

nook
9'-0" x 11'-0"

dining
12'-0" x 15'-0"
12' flat clg.

living
15'-0" x 16'-0"
14' tray clg.

private
garden

buffet
server

kitchen

15' x 14'

gallery

98'-0"

foyer

utility

guest 2
11'-0" x 13'-2"
10' flat clg.

mitered
glass

garden

entry

study
11'-8" x 14'-0"
12' flat clg.

mitered glass

garage
23'-0" x 37'-6"

Design by
The Sater
Design Collection

© The Sater Group, Inc.

Design 6602

Square Footage: 2,794

L

● Classic columns, circle-head windows and a bay-windowed study give this stucco home a wonderful street presence. The foyer leads into the formal living and dining areas. An arched buffet server separates these rooms and contributes an open feeling. The kitchen, nook and leisure room are grouped for informal living. A desk/message center in the island kitchen, art niches in the nook and a fireplace with an entertainment center and shelves add custom touches. Two secondary suites have guest baths and offer full privacy from the master wing. The master suite hosts a private garden area, while the master bath features a walk-in shower that overlooks the garden, and a water closet room with space for books or a television. Large His and Hers walk-in closets complete these private quarters.

QUOTE ONE®

Cost to build? See page 230
to order complete cost estimate
to build this house in your area!

Design by
Home Planners

Width 92'-7"
Depth 79'

Design 3433

Square Footage: 2,350

L

● Santa Fe styling creates interesting angles in this one-story home. A grand entrance leads through a courtyard into the foyer with circular skylight, closet space and niches, and convenient powder room. Turn right to the master suite with deluxe bath and a bedroom close at hand, perfect for a nursery, home office or exercise room. Two more family bedrooms are placed quietly in the far wing of the house. Fireplaces in the living room, dining room and covered porch create various shapes. Make note of the island range in the kitchen, extra storage in the garage, and covered porches on two sides.

QUOTE ONE™

Cost to build? See page 230
to order complete cost estimate
to build this house in your area!

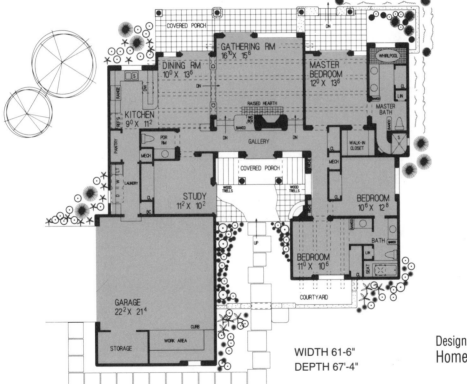

WIDTH 61-6"
DEPTH 67'-4"

Design by
Home Planners

Design 3431

Square Footage: 1,907

● Graceful curves welcome you into the courtyard of this Santa Fe home. Inside, a gallery directs traffic to the work zone on the left or the sleeping zone on the right. Straight ahead lies a sunken gathering room with a beamed ceiling and a raised-hearth fireplace. A large pantry offers extra storage space for kitchen items. The covered rear porch is accessible from the dining room, the gathering room and the secluded master bedroom. Luxury describes the feeling in the master bath with a whirlpool tub, a separate shower, a double vanity and closet space. Two family bedrooms share a compartmented bath. The study could serve as a guest room, a media room or a home office.

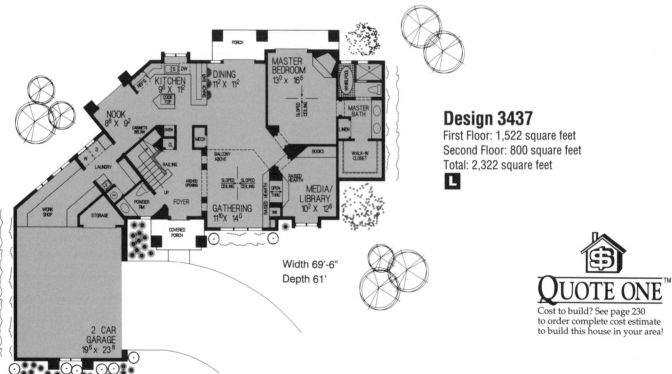

Design 3437

First Floor: 1,522 square feet
Second Floor: 800 square feet
Total: 2,322 square feet

L

QUOTE ONE™

Cost to build? See page 230
to order complete cost estimate
to build this house in your area!

Width 69'-6"
Depth 61'

● This two-story Spanish Mission-style home has character
inside and out. The first-floor master suite features a fireplace and gracious bath with walk-in closet, whirlpool,
shower, dual vanities, and linen storage. A second fireplace
serves both the gathering room and media room or library.
The kitchen with island cook top includes a snack bar and
an adjoining breakfast nook. Three bedrooms and two full
baths occupy the second floor.

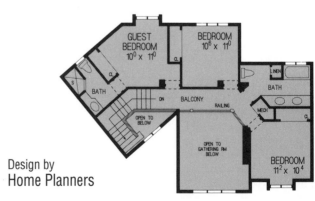

Design by
Home Planners

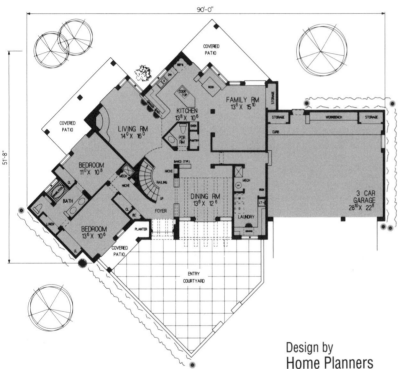

Design by
Home Planners

Design 3432

First Floor: 1,966 square feet
Second Floor: 831 square feet
Total: 2,797 square feet

L

● Unique in nature, this two-story Santa Fe-style home is as practical as it is lovely. The facade is elegantly enhanced by a large entry court, over-looked by windows in the dining room and a covered patio from one of two family bedrooms. The entry foyer leads to living areas at the back of the plan: a living room with corner fire-place and a family room connected to the kitchen via a built-in eating nook. Upstairs, the master suite features a grand bath and large walk-in closet. The guest bedroom has a private bath. Every room in this home has its own outdoor area.

Quote One™

Cost to build? See page 230
to order complete cost estimate
to build this house in your area!

This home, as shown in the photograph, may differ from the actual blueprints.
For more detailed information, please check the floor plans carefully.

Photos by Andrew D. Lautman

Design by Home Planners

Width 54'-8"
Depth 54'

Design 2822

First Floor: 1,363 square feet
Second Floor: 351 square feet
Total: 1,714 square feet

L

● Here is a truly unique house whose interior was designed with the current decade's economies, lifestyles and demographics in mind. While functioning as a one-story home, the second floor provides an extra measure of livability when required. In addition, this two-story section adds to the dramatic appeal of both the exterior and the interior. Within only 1,363 square feet, this contemporary delivers refreshing and outstanding living patterns for those who are buying their first home, those who have raised their family and are looking for a smaller home and those in search of a retirement home.

ALTERNATE SECOND FLOOR

QUOTE ONE™

Cost to build? See page 230 to order complete cost estimate to build this house in your area!

● This volume-look home's angled entry opens to a wealth of living potential with a media room to the right and formal living and dining rooms to the left. Remaining exposed to the dining room, the living room pleases with its marbled hearth and sliding glass doors to the back terrace. A covered porch, accessed from both the dining and breakfast rooms, adds outdoor dining possibilities. The kitchen utilizes a built-in desk and a snack bar pass-through to the breakfast area. A large pantry and closet lead to the laundry area near the garage. Upstairs, four bedrooms accommodate the large family well. In the master suite, amenities such as a sitting area and a balcony add definition. The master bath sports a whirlpool and a walk-in closet.

Design 3456

First Floor: 1,130 square feet
Second Floor: 1,189 square feet
Total: 2,319 square feet

L

Design by
Home Planners

Width 40'-7"
Depth 57'-8"

Design 3459

First Floor: 1,392 square feet
Second Floor: 1,178 square feet
Total: 2,570 square feet

L

Design by
Home Planners

● This innovative, compact plan affords over 2,500 square feet in living space! A central, angled staircase provides an interesting pivot with which to admire the floor plan. To begin with, the living room rises to two stories and even sports a front porch. The dining room, with its bumped-out nook, enjoys the use of a china alcove. The island kitchen finds easy access to the dining room and blends nicely into the airy breakfast room. A large pantry and a built-in desk also grace the kitchen and the breakfast room, respectively. In the family room, relaxed living comes through with the introduction of a fireplace and access to a covered patio and a terrace. The second floor will please all your family members with its four bedrooms, including a master suite with a private bath.

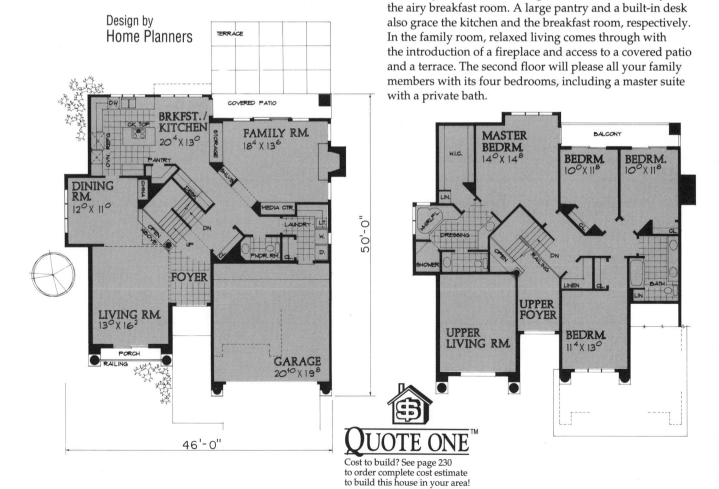

Quote One™

Cost to build? See page 230
to order complete cost estimate
to build this house in your area!

Design 3457

First Floor: 1,252 square feet
Second Floor: 972 square feet
Total: 2,224 square feet

L

Design by
Home Planners

● For family living, this delightful three-bedroom plan scores big. Stretching across the back of the plan, casual living areas take precedence. The family room focuses on a fireplace and enjoys direct access to a covered porch. The breakfast room allows plenty of space for friendly meals—the island kitchen remains open to this room thus providing ease in serving meals and, of course, conversations with the cook. From the two-car garage, a utility area opens to the main-floor living areas. Upstairs, the master suite affords a quiet retreat with its private bath; here you'll find a whirlpool tub set in a sunny nook. A balcony further enhances this bedroom. The two secondary bedrooms share a full hall bath with a double-bowl vanity.

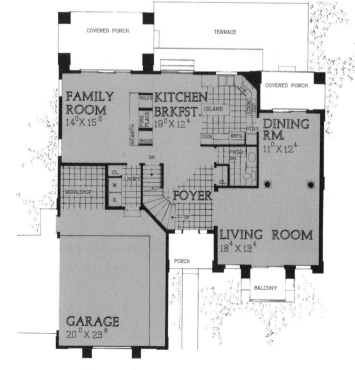

WIDTH 48'
DEPTH 58'

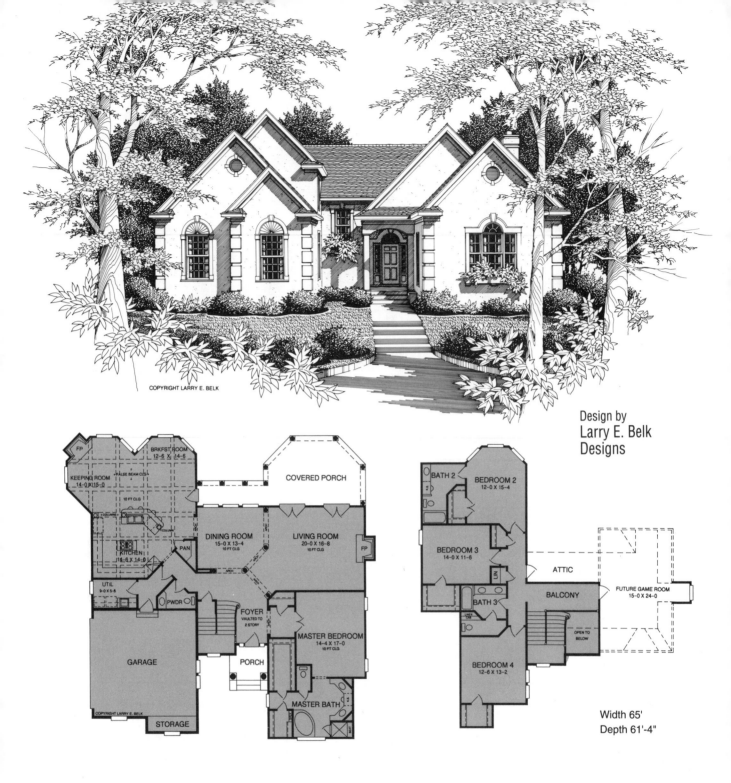

COPYRIGHT LARRY E. BELK

Design by
Larry E. Belk
Designs

First Floor:

FP

BRKFST ROOM
12-6 X 14-6

KEEPING ROOM
14-0 X 15-0

FALSE BEAM CLG

10 FT CLG

COLUMNS

COLUMN

KITCHEN
11-6 X 14-0

PAN

UTIL
9-0 X 5-8

PWDR

COVERED PORCH

DINING ROOM
15-0 X 13-4
10 FT CLG

LIVING ROOM
20-0 X 16-8
10 FT CLG

FP

ARCH

FOYER
VAULTED TO
2 STORY

GARAGE

PORCH

MASTER BEDROOM
14-4 X 17-0
10 FT CLG

COPYRIGHT LARRY E. BELK

STORAGE

MASTER BATH

Second Floor:

BATH 2

BEDROOM 2
12-0 X 15-4

BEDROOM 3
14-0 X 11-6

LIN

ATTIC

BATH 3

LINEN CAB

BALCONY

OPEN TO
BELOW

BEDROOM 4
12-6 X 13-2

FUTURE GAME ROOM
15-0 X 24-0

Width 65'
Depth 61'-4"

Design 8102

First Floor: 2,184 square feet
Second Floor: 1,068 square feet
Total: 3,252 square feet
Bonus Room: 360 square feet

● The front elevation of this home features a vintage stucco finish that evokes an Old World, European charm. The ten-foot false beam ceiling used throughout the kitchen, the keeping room and the breakfast room continues the theme. An angled foyer graced by columns and connecting arches gives the home an elegant, refined feel. The large master suite features a lovely bath with a corner tub and His and Hers walk-in closets. The angled vanity adds interest to the area. Three bedrooms and two baths are located upstairs. Bedroom 2 features a sunny bay window. An area designed for a game room or office is allocated for future expansion. Please specify crawlspace or slab foundation when ordering.

Design 3488
Square Footage: 1,944

L **D**

● The tudor facade of this comfortable home is just the beginning to a truly unique design. As you enter the foyer via a quaint covered porch, you are greeted by the sleeping zone on the right and the living zone on the left, beginning with the breakfast area which faces the front. A large kitchen connects to this room and includes a desk, a walk-in pantry, a spacious counter area with a snack bar that connects to the gathering room and entry to the formal dining room. The massive gathering room features a fireplace, a sloped ceiling and access to the back-yard terrace. The master bedroom also accesses the terrace and revels in a master bath with a whirlpool tub, a separate shower, dual lavs and an individual vanity. A study at the front of the home could be converted into an additional bedroom.

Quote One™

Cost to build? See page 230 to order complete cost estimate to build this house in your area!

Width 72'-8"
Depth 47'-4"

Design by
Home Planners

Design by
Home Planners

Design 2905

First Floor: 1,342 square feet
Second Floor: 619 square feet
Total: 1,961 square feet

L **D**

● All of the livability in this plan is in the back! Each first-floor room, except the kitchen, has access to the rear terrace via sliding glass doors. A great way to capture an excellent view. This plan is also ideal for a narrow lot seeing that its width is less than 50 feet. Two bedrooms and a lounge, overlooking the gathering room, are on the second floor.

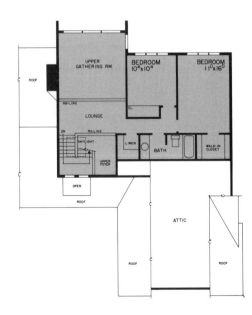

TERRACE

GATHERING RM.
14⁰x17⁸

MASTER
BEDROOM
11⁸x16⁰

DINING RM.
10⁴x12⁰

BRKFST. RM.
11⁰x11⁶

LINE OF BALCONY ABOVE

SNACK BAR

DRESSING
RM.

WALK-IN
CLOSET

DN   UP

FOYER

PDR.
RM.

LAUND.

KITCHEN
12⁰x12⁰

REF'S.

COOK
TOP

DW

BATH

COVERED
PORCH

DISAPPEARING
STAIRS

CURB

GARAGE
21⁸x22⁸

UPPER
GATHERING RM.

BEDROOM
10⁴x10⁴

BEDROOM
11⁰x16⁰

ROOF

RAILING

CL.

LOUNGE

DN   RAILING

SKYLIGHT

LINEN

BATH

WALK-IN
CLOSET

UPPER
FOYER

OPEN

ROOF

ATTIC

ROOF   ROOF

QUOTE ONE™

Cost to build? See page 230
to order complete cost estimate
to build this house in your area!

Width 49'-8"
Depth 55'-8"

170

COPYRIGHT LARRY E. BELK

Design 8109

First Floor: 3,120 square feet
Second Floor: 1,083 square feet
Total: 4,203 square feet

● The blending of natural materials and a nostalgic farmhouse look give this home its unique character. Inside, a sophisticated floor plan includes all the amenities requested by today's homeowner. Three large covered porches, one on the front and two on the rear, provide ample outdoor entertaining areas. The kitchen features a built-in stone fireplace visible from the breakfast and sun rooms. The master suite includes a large sitting area and a luxurious bath. Upstairs, two additional bedrooms and a large sitting area will please family and guests. A three-car garage with a work shop is connected to the home via a breezeway. Please specify crawlspace or slab foundation when ordering.

Design by
Larry E. Belk
Designs

WIDTH 118'-1"
DEPTH 52'-2"

REAR

Design by
Donald A.
Gardner,
Architects, Inc.

GARAGE
20-4 × 20-4

DECK
36-8 × 10-0

covered
breezeway

SUN RM.
15-8 × 7-10

hot tub

GREAT RM.
20-0 × 15-6
(cathedral ceiling)

fireplace

UTILITY
9-0 × 5-4

wash dry

bath

powder rm.

BED RM.
11-4 × 13-8

lin.

walk-in closet

master bath

rail

67-4

FOYER
4-6 × 12-4

DINING
12-0 × 12-0

KITCHEN
14-4 × 12-0

BED RM.
14-8 × 11-0

MASTER
BED RM.
13-4 × 16-8

PORCH
19-2 × 5-0

BRKFST.
13-4 × 7-8

67-6

Design 9619

Square Footage: 2,021

● Multi-pane windows, shutters, dormers, bay windows and a delightful covered porch grace the facade of this country cottage. Inside, the floor plan is no less appealing. Note that the great room has a fireplace, a cathedral ceiling and sliding glass doors with an arched window above to allow for natural illumination of the room. A sun room with a hot tub leads to an adjacent deck. This space can also be reached from the master bath. The generous master bedroom has a walk-in closet and a spacious bath with a double-bowl vanity, a shower and a garden tub. Two additional bedrooms are located at the other end of the house for privacy. The garage is connected to the house by a breezeway. Please specify basement or crawlspace foundation when ordering.

FRONT

seat

seat

DECK

spa

SUN RM.
16-2 × 8-10

skylights

GREAT RM.
15-4 × 21-0
(cathedral ceiling)

fireplace

pass-thru

BRKFST.
9-10 × 9-10

wash dry

UTILITY
8-0 × 7-10

master bath

walk-in closet

balcony above

KITCHEN
12-8 × 13-0

MASTER BED RM.
12-8 × 16-4

sto.

cl

p.d. rm.

FOYER
11-10 × 7-2
(sloped ceiling)

up

DINING
14-8 × 12-8

PORCH

55-0

53-10

Design 9623

First Floor: 1,651 square feet
Second Floor: 567 square feet
Total: 2,218 square feet

● A wonderful wraparound covered porch at the front and sides of this house and the open deck with a spa at the back provide plenty of outside living area. Inside, the spacious great room has a fireplace, a cathedral ceiling and a clerestory with an arched window. The kitchen is centrally located for maximum flexibility in layout and has a food preparation island for convenience. Besides the master bedroom and its access to the sun room, there are two second-level bedrooms that share a full bath. Please specify basement or crawlspace foundation when ordering.

Design by
Donald A. Gardner, Architects, Inc

QUOTE ONE®

Cost to build? See page 230 to order complete cost estimate to build this house in your area!

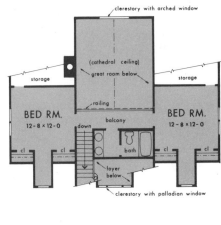

clerestory with arched window

(cathedral ceiling)

great room below

storage

storage

railing

BED RM.
12-8 × 12-0

balcony

BED RM.
12-8 × 12-0

cl

cl

down

bath

cl

cl

foyer below

clerestory with palladian window

B. NATHAN

Copyright 1992 Stephen S. Fuller, Inc.

Design by
Design Traditions

Design 9862
Square Footage: 2,170

● This classic cottage features a stone and wooden exterior with an arch-detailed porch and a box-bay window. From the foyer, double doors open to the den with built-in bookcases and a fireplace. A full bath is situated next to the den, allowing for an optional guest room. The family room is centrally located, just beyond the foyer. Its hearth is framed by windows overlooking the porch at the rear of the home. The master bedroom opens onto the rear porch. The master bath, with a large walk-in closet, double vanities, a corner tub and a separate shower, completes this relaxing retreat. Left of the family room awaits a sun room with access to the covered porch. A breakfast area complements the attractive and efficiently designed kitchen. Two secondary bedrooms with large closets share a full bath featuring double vanities. This home is designed with a basement foundation.

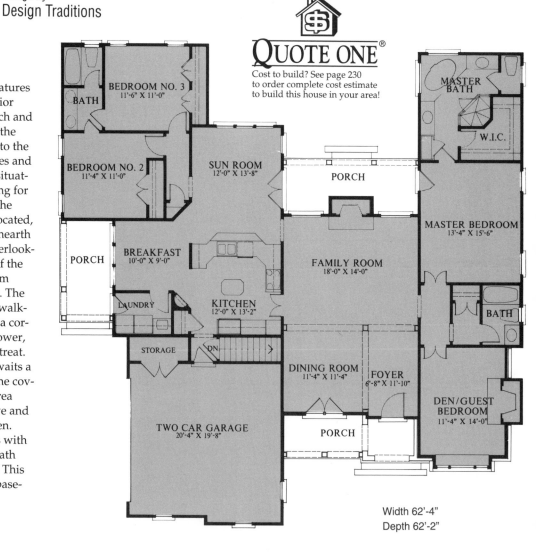

QUOTE ONE®
Cost to build? See page 230 to order complete cost estimate to build this house in your area!

Width 62'-4"
Depth 62'-2"

Design 9966
Square Footage: 2,796

● Country details brighten the exterior of this one-story design and grace it with a warmth and charm that says "home." The floor plan includes a formal dining room and an all-purpose great room that opens to the kitchen and the sun room. A bayed breakfast room is completely enclosed in glass. A master bedroom suite is found to the rear of the plan for privacy. It holds access to the rear covered porch and sports an extra large walk-in closet and detailed bath. The family bedrooms share a full bath but each has its own lavatory. A two-car, side-load garage has extra room for storage. This home is designed with a basement foundation.

Floor plan labels:

Porch

Master Bedroom 17⁰x16⁰

Keeping Room 10⁰x12⁰

Breakfast 10⁰x10⁹

Great Room 18⁰x21⁹

Kitchen 18⁶x10⁰

Bedroom No. 2 12⁰x13⁰

Dining Room 13³x13⁹

Foyer

Two Car Garage 21³x21³

Porch

Bedroom No. 3 12⁰x13⁹

Width 70'-9"
Depth 66'-6"

Design by
Design Traditions

Design by
Design Traditions

Design 9910

First Floor: 2,565 square feet
Second Floor: 1,375 square feet
Total: 3,940 square feet

● A symmetrical facade with twin
chimneys makes a grand statement.
A covered porch welcomes visitors and
provides a pleasant place to spend cool
evenings. The entry foyer is flanked by
formal living areas: a dining room and a
living room, each with a fireplace. A
third fireplace is the highlight of the
expansive great room to the rear. The
deck is accessible through the great
room, the sun room or the master bedroom. The second floor offers three bedrooms, two full baths and plenty of storage space. This home is designed with
a basement foundation.

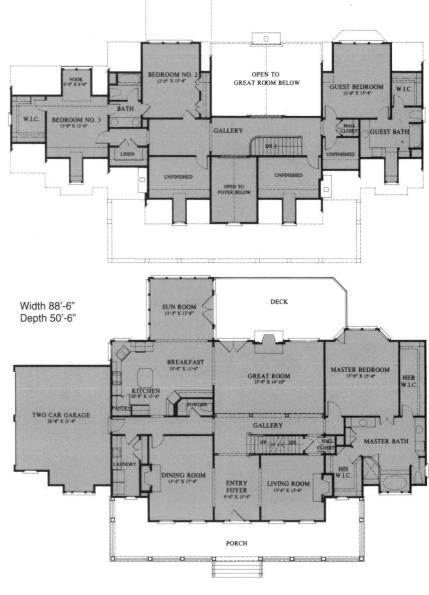

Width 88'-6"
Depth 50'-6"

Design 8932

First Floor: 2,775 square feet
Second Floor: 1,082 square feet
Total: 3,857 square feet
Guest Quarters: 347 square feet

● This design showcases an extensive front porch and a dual-pitched hipped roof—both of which are typical features of the French Colonial style. Step inside to find a central foyer that dissolves into a dining room on one side and, on the other, a living room with a two-way fireplace and French doors to the conservatory and library. The house gourmet will relish the kitchen with its island cooktop and easy access to the dining room, family room and breakfast area. One of the more notable features of this house is the sunroom; it encompasses exposed brick walls, French doors to a back porch and a spiral staircase leading up to the loft which overlooks the breakfast room. Three bedrooms define the upstairs—one has its own bath. A cozy alcove, accessible from Bedrooms 2 and 3, would serve well as a children's hideaway. The master bedroom, with a sitting area, library access and a large master bath, remains on the first floor for privacy. Not to be missed are the guest quarters located over the three-car garage.

WIDTH 108'-10"
DEPTH 58'

Design by
Larry W.
Garnett &
Associates, Inc.

This home, as shown in the photograph, may differ from the actual blueprints. For more detailed information, please check the floor plans carefully.

Photos by Bob Greenspan

Design 2920 First Floor: 3,067 square feet
Second Floor: 648 square feet
Total: 3,715 square feet

L **D**

● This contemporary design also has a great deal to offer. A fireplace opens up to both the living room and country kitchen. Privacy is the key word when describing the sleeping areas. The first floor master bedroom is away from the traffic of the house and features a dressing/exercise room, a whirlpool tub and shower and a spacious walk-in closet. Two more bedrooms and a full bath are on the second floor. The three-car garage is arranged so that the owners have use of a double-garage with an attached single on reserve for guests. The cheerful sun room adds 296 square feet to the total.

Width 97'
Depth 102'-8"

QUOTE ONE™
Cost to build? See page 230 to order complete cost estimate to build this house in your area!

Design by
Home Planners

Photos by Laszlo Regos

Width 97'-8"
Depth 101'-4"

Design by
Home Planners

Design 2921

First Floor: 3,215 square feet
Second Floor: 711 square feet
Total: 3,926 square feet
Sun Room: 296 square feet

L **D**

● Organized zoning by room functions makes this traditional design a comfortable home for living. Quiet areas of the house include a media room and luxurious master bedroom suite with a fitness area, a spacious closet and bath, as well as a lounge or writing area. Informal living areas of the house include a sun room, a large country kitchen and an efficient food preparation area with an island. Formal living areas include a living area and a formal dining room. The second floor holds two bedrooms and a lounge.

Design 9804

First Floor: 2,199 square feet
Second Floor: 1,235 square feet
Total: 3,434 square feet

● The covered front porch of this home warmly welcomes family and visitors. To the right of the foyer is a versatile option room. On the other side is the formal dining room, located just across from the open great room—which also opens into the breakfast room. The kitchen includes a cooking island/breakfast bar. Adjacent to the breakfast room is the sun room. At the rear of the main level is the master suite, which features a lavish bath loaded with features. Just off the bedroom is a private deck. On the second level, three additional bedrooms and two baths are found. This home is designed with a basement foundation.

Width 62'-6"
Depth 54'-3"

Cost to build? See page 230 to order complete cost estimate to build this house in your area!

Design by
Design Traditions

Design 9978

First Floor: 1,615 square feet
Second Floor: 1,510 square feet
Total: 3,125 square feet

● Formal Georgian detailing such as the Tuscan columns that support this full, classically turned balustrade transform a simple porch into an elegant entrance. Inside, the elegance continues with living and dining rooms that open to one another, sized to accommodate any formal occasion. Beyond the dining room is an efficient U-shaped kitchen that also serves the informal living area. This space combines the breakfast room and great room which both open onto the light-filled keeping room/solarium. Sleeping quarters are located on the second floor. The master suite features His and Hers walk-in closets, a deluxe master bath and unfinished bonus space perfect for a nursery, study or library. Three family bedrooms and two full baths complete the plan. This home is designed with a basement foundation.

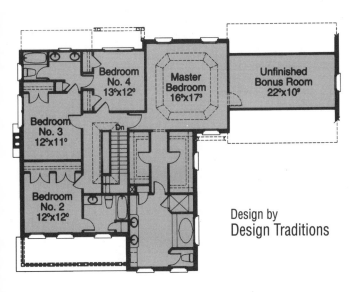

Design by
Design Traditions

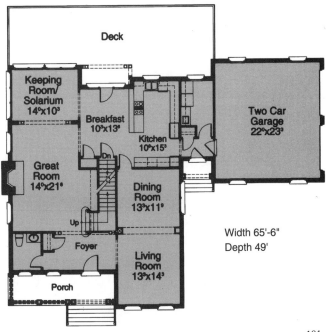

Width 65'-6"
Depth 49'

181

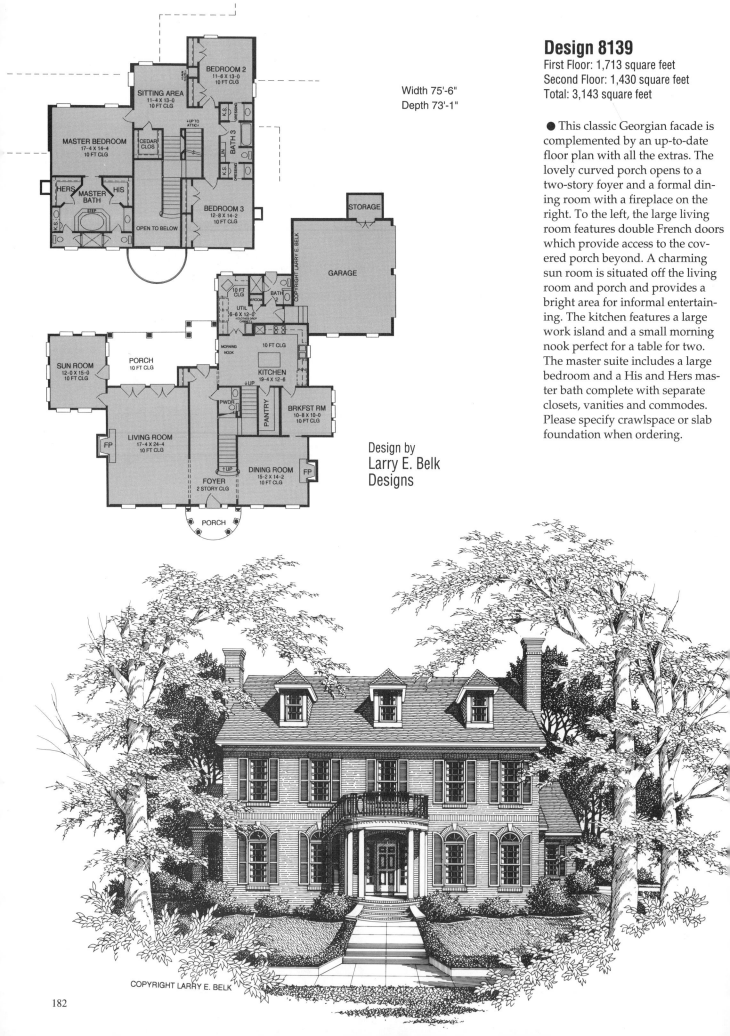

Design 8139

First Floor: 1,713 square feet
Second Floor: 1,430 square feet
Total: 3,143 square feet

● This classic Georgian facade is complemented by an up-to-date floor plan with all the extras. The lovely curved porch opens to a two-story foyer and a formal dining room with a fireplace on the right. To the left, the large living room features double French doors which provide access to the covered porch beyond. A charming sun room is situated off the living room and porch and provides a bright area for informal entertaining. The kitchen features a large work island and a small morning nook perfect for a table for two. The master suite includes a large bedroom and a His and Hers master bath complete with separate closets, vanities and commodes. Please specify crawlspace or slab foundation when ordering.

Width 75'-6"
Depth 73'-1"

Design by
Larry E. Belk
Designs

Second Floor

BEDROOM 2
11-6 X 13-0
10 FT CLG

SITTING AREA
11-4 X 13-0
10 FT CLG

MASTER BEDROOM
17-4 X 14-4
10 FT CLG

CEDAR CLOS

UP TO ATTIC

K.S.

LIN

BATH 3

DRESSING

K.S.

HERS

MASTER BATH

HIS

K.S.

STEP

OPEN TO BELOW

BEDROOM 3
12-8 X 14-2
10 FT CLG

First Floor

STORAGE

GARAGE

10 FT CLG

BATH 2

BROOM

UTIL
16-6 X 12-0
CLOTHES DROP
CABINETS

10 FT CLG

SUN ROOM
12-0 X 15-0
10 FT CLG

PORCH
10 FT CLG

MORNING NOOK

KITCHEN
19-4 X 12-6

UP

PWDR

PANTRY

BRKFST RM
10-8 X 10-0
10 FT CLG

LIVING ROOM
17-4 X 24-4
10 FT CLG

FP

UP

FOYER
2 STORY CLG

DINING ROOM
15-2 X 14-2
10 FT CLG

FP

PORCH

COPYRIGHT LARRY E. BELK

Design 9979

First Floor: 1,698 square feet
Second Floor: 1,542 square feet
Total: 3,240 square feet

● Make your mark with this brick traditional. With a walk-out basement, there's lots of room to grow. On the first floor, such attributes as informal/formal zones, a gourmet kitchen and a solarium, deck and screened porch are immediate attention getters. In the kitchen, meal preparation is a breeze with an island work station and plenty of counter space. Four bedrooms make up the second floor of this plan. One of the family bedrooms possesses a personal bath. The master bedroom has its own bath and a giant walk-in closet.

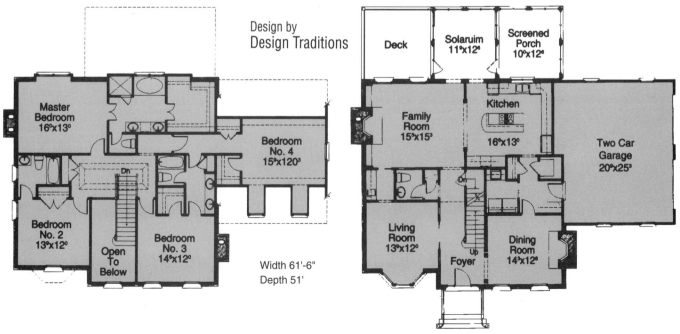

Design by
Design Traditions

Master Bedroom 16⁰x13⁰

Bedroom No. 4 15⁰x120³

Bedroom No. 2 13⁰x12⁰

Open To Below

Bedroom No. 3 14⁰x12⁰

Width 61'-6"
Depth 51'

Deck

Solaruim 11⁰x12⁶

Screened Porch 10⁰x12⁶

Family Room 15³x15³

Kitchen 16⁰x13⁰

Two Car Garage 20⁰x25³

Living Room 13⁰x12⁰

Dining Room 14⁰x12⁶

Foyer

Design 9980

First Floor: 1,448 square feet
Second Floor: 1,491 square feet
Total: 2,939 square feet

● The semi-circular fanlight in the low-pitched gable echoes the one over the door, furthering the symmetry that dignifies the exterior of this impressive traditional home. Formal living areas are entered from the foyer– to the right is the living room and to the left, the dining room. Holiday banquets and dinner parties are simplified with a butler's pantry that links the dining room to the kitchen. Here, an island cooktop aids meal preparation and invites conversation with the family in the adjacent breakfast/sunroom and great room. This is sure to be a favorite place to kick back and relax. The second floor holds a spacious master suite, three secondary bedrooms—Bedroom 4 enjoys its own private bath—and three full baths. This home is designed with a basement foundation.

Design by
Design Traditions

Width 57'
Depth 46'-4"

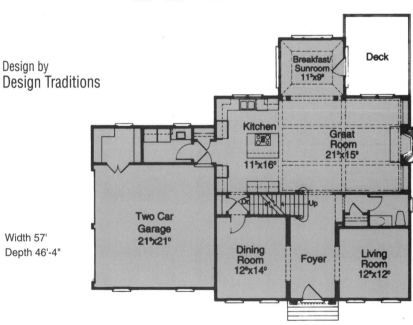

Design 9970

First Floor: 1,980 square feet
Second Floor: 1,317 square feet
Total: 3,297 square feet

● Centuries ago, the center column played a vital role in the support of a double-arched window such as the one that graces this home's exterior. Today's amenities combined with the well-seasoned architecture of Europe offer the best of both worlds. The contemporary floor plan begins with a soaring foyer that opens onto the formal living and dining rooms. Casual living is enjoyed at the rear of the plan in the L-shaped kitchen, the family room and the light-filled breakfast/sunroom. A guest bedroom is tucked behind the family room for privacy. Upstairs, an exquisite master suite features a lavish bath and a huge walk-in closet. Two family bedrooms, a full bath and unfinished bonus space complete the second floor. This home is designed with a basement foundation.

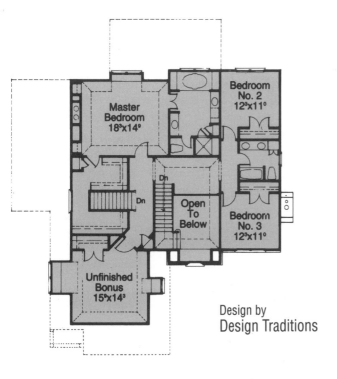

Master Bedroom 18³x14⁹

Bedroom No. 2 12³x11⁰

Open To Below

Bedroom No. 3 12³x11⁰

Dn

Dn

Unfinished Bonus 15³x14³

Design by
Design Traditions

Deck

Breakfast/ Sunroom 22³x11⁹

Guest Bedroom 12³x12⁰

Family Room 14³x16⁰

Kitchen 13³x16³

Dining Room 12³x16³

Up

Foyer

Living Room 12³x16³

Two Car Garage 21³x23³

Up

Width 58'-9"
Depth 66'-9"

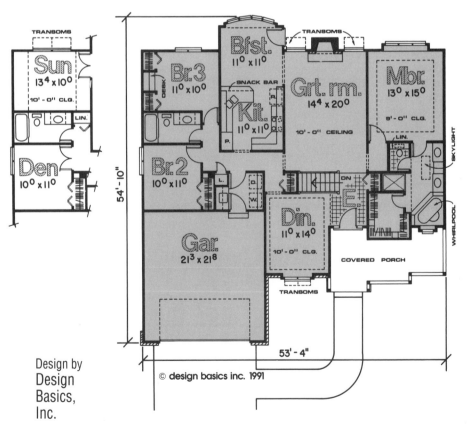

TRANSOMS

Sun
13⁴ x 10⁰
10'-0" CLG.

LIN.

Den
10⁰ x 11⁰

Br. 3
11⁰ x 10⁰

DESK

Bfst.
11⁰ x 11⁰

SNACK BAR

Kit.
11⁰ x 11⁰

P.

TRANSOMS

Grt. rm.
14⁴ x 20⁰

10'-0" CEILING

Mbr.
13⁰ x 15⁰

9'-0" CLG.

LIN.

SKYLIGHT

Br. 2
10⁰ x 11⁰

DN

WHIRLPOOL

Gar.
21³ x 21⁸

Din.
11⁰ x 14⁰

10'-0" CLG.

COVERED PORCH

TRANSOMS

54'-10"

53'-4"

Design by
Design
Basics,
Inc.

© design basics inc. 1991

Design 9321
Square Footage: 1,710

● Comfort awaits you in this appealing ranch home. Notice the repeating rooflines and the covered porch before studying the inside amenities. A formal dining room features elegant ceiling details. In the volume great room, designed for daily family gatherings, pay careful attention to a raised-hearth fireplace flanked by sparkling windows. Outdoor access and a Lazy Susan are thoughtful details designed into the kitchen and bowed dinette. For added flexibility, two secondary bedrooms can be easily converted to a sun room with French doors and an optional den. The secluded master suite is enhanced by a boxed ceiling and deluxe skylit dressing room.

Design by
Design Traditions

Design 9843
Square Footage: 2,120
Lower Level: 1,191 square feet

● As quaint as the European countryside, this charming cottage boasts a unique interior. Living patterns revolve around the central family room—notice the placement of the formal dining room, the kitchen with an attached breakfast nook and the sun room. Family bedrooms are tucked quietly away to the rear, while the master suite maintains privacy at the opposite end of the plan. A den with a fireplace attaches to the master bedroom or can be accessed from the entry foyer. Bonus space in the basement can be developed later.

Width 62'
Depth 62'-6"

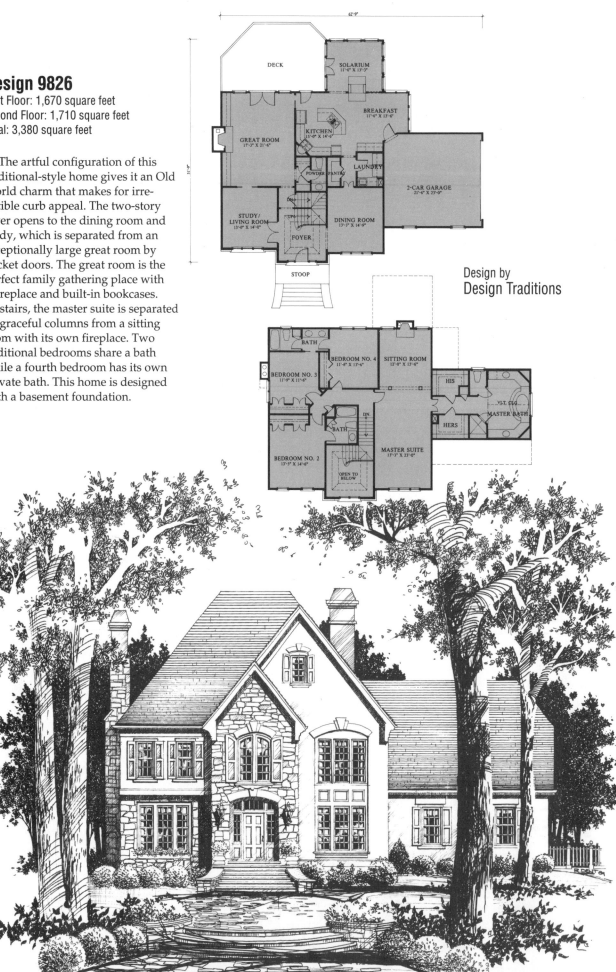

Design 9826

First Floor: 1,670 square feet
Second Floor: 1,710 square feet
Total: 3,380 square feet

● The artful configuration of this traditional-style home gives it an Old World charm that makes for irresistible curb appeal. The two-story foyer opens to the dining room and study, which is separated from an exceptionally large great room by pocket doors. The great room is the perfect family gathering place with a fireplace and built-in bookcases. Upstairs, the master suite is separated by graceful columns from a sitting room with its own fireplace. Two additional bedrooms share a bath while a fourth bedroom has its own private bath. This home is designed with a basement foundation.

Design by
Design Traditions

Design 9801

First Floor: 1,650 square feet
Second Floor: 1,250 square feet
Total: 2,900 square feet

● The roomy sunlit foyer and double bay window tower of this home are equally impressive. An open formal dining/living room combination is divided by classic colonnade detail. Double doors lead from the foyer to the family room with fireplace and French doors. Another French door provides access to and from the breakfast room or solarium just off the kitchen. Upstairs, a comfortable master suite includes a tray ceiling, an accommodating bath and a walk-in closet. Two other bedrooms share access to a bath. This home is designed with a basement foundation.

Design by
Design Traditions

This home, as shown in the photograph, may differ from the actual blueprints. For more detailed information, please check the floor plans carefully.

Photo by Dave Dawson

Design 9990

First Floor: 3,065 square feet
Second Floor: 1,969 square feet
Total: 5,034 square feet

● Elegance and luxury define this stately brick home. Creative design continues inside with a dramatic foyer that leads to the formal living and dining rooms and the casual two-story family room. A butler's pantry links the dining room and kitchen to simplify grand-scale entertaining. Casual gatherings with family and friends will be enjoyed in the family room that connects with the breakfast room and kitchen located at the rear of the plan. Here, a solarium and porch enhance indoor/outdoor relationships. An exquisite master bedroom featuring a unique master bath with a corner tub completes the first floor. Upstairs, space is reserved for two family bedrooms—each with its own bath—a sewing room and a bedroom/office. This home is designed with a basement foundation.

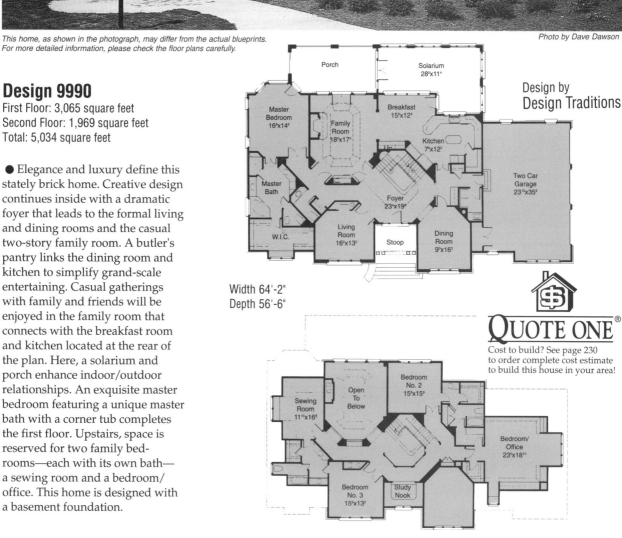

Width 64'-2"
Depth 56'-6"

Design by
Design Traditions

QUOTE ONE®
Cost to build? See page 230 to order complete cost estimate to build this house in your area!

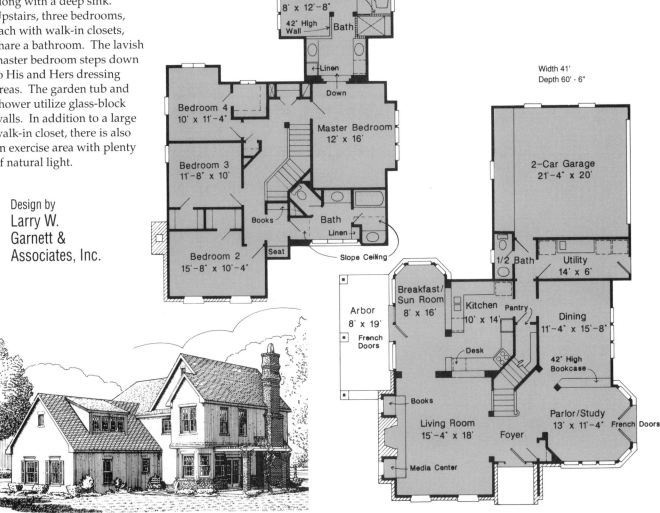

● Brick and stucco combine to create a home reminiscent of the French countryside. A detailed brick archway leads to the front entry with a glass transom above an elegant front door with sidelights. Inside, the living room features a massive fireplace, flanked by built-in bookcases and a media center. The study, with its expansive windows and a forty-two-inch high bookcase is a delightful area for reading or relaxing. Opening directly to the light-filled breakfast/sunroom, the conveniently located kitchen also serves the living area. Adjacent to the two-car garage is a large utility room, with plenty of counter and cabinet space, along with a deep sink. Upstairs, three bedrooms, each with walk-in closets, share a bathroom. The lavish master bedroom steps down to His and Hers dressing areas. The garden tub and shower utilize glass-block walls. In addition to a large walk-in closet, there is also an exercise area with plenty of natural light.

Design by
Larry W.
Garnett &
Associates, Inc.

Design 9018

First Floor: 1,341 square feet
Second Floor: 1,377 square feet
Total: 2,718 square feet

Width 41'
Depth 60' - 6"

Closet

Exercise Area
8' x 12'-8"

Glass Block

Bath

42" High Wall

Linen

Down

Bedroom 4
10' x 11'-4"

Master Bedroom
12' x 16'

Bedroom 3
11'-8" x 10'

Books

Bath

Linen

Seat

Slope Ceiling

Bedroom 2
15'-8" x 10'-4"

2-Car Garage
21'-4" x 20'

1/2 Bath

Utility
14' x 6'

Arbor
8' x 19'

French Doors

Breakfast/Sun Room
8' x 16'

Kitchen
10' x 14'

Pantry

Dining
11'-4" x 15'-8"

Desk

42" High Bookcase

Books

Living Room
15'-4" x 18'

Foyer

Parlor/Study
13' x 11'-4"

French Doors

Media Center

FRONT

Design 9613

First Floor: 1,340 square feet
Second Floor: 504 square feet
Total: 1,844 square feet

● Because this home's sun room is a full two stories high, it acts as a solar collector when oriented to the south. Enjoying the benefits of this warmth are the dining room and great room on the first floor, and the master suite on the second floor. A spacious deck further extends the outdoor living potential. Special features to be found in this house include: a sloped ceiling with exposed wood beams and a fireplace in the great room; a cathedral ceiling, a fireplace, built-in shelves and ample closet space in the master bedroom; clerestory windows and a balcony overlook in the upstairs study; and convenient storage space in the attic over the garage. Please specify basement or crawlspace foundation when ordering.

DECK
27-8 × 12-0

45-4

60-0

balcony above

SUN RM.
13-4 × 8-0

GREAT RM.
13-4 × 25-0

BED RM.
10-4 × 11-4

DINING
11-4 × 12-4

fireplace

study above

storage

cl

window planter

KITCHEN
11-4 × 8-0

down

FOYER
6-0 × 5-0

bath

up

lin.

cl

SERVICE

dry wash

cl

pantry

BED RM.
10-4 × 11-4

cl

GARAGE
20-2 × 21-4

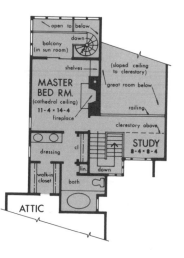

open to below

balcony (in sun room)

down

shelves

MASTER BED RM.
(cathedral ceiling)
11-4 × 14-4
fireplace

(sloped ceiling to clerestory)

great room below

railing

clerestory above

dressing

cl

STUDY
8-4 × 8-4

walk-in closet

lin.

down

bath

ATTIC

Design by
Donald A.
Gardner,
Architects, Inc.

REAR

192

Greenhouse Rooms & Atriums

This home, as shown in the photograph, may differ from the actual blueprints. For more detailed information, please check the floor plans carefully.

Photo by Laszlo Regos

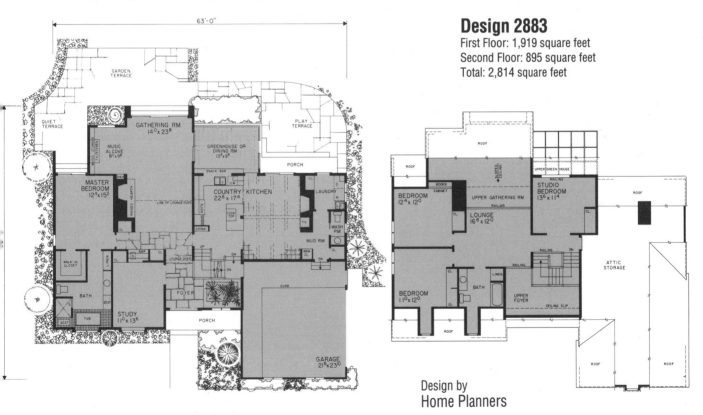

Design 2883

First Floor: 1,919 square feet
Second Floor: 895 square feet
Total: 2,814 square feet

Design by
Home Planners

● A country-style home is part of America's fascination with the rural past. This design's emphasis of the traditional home is in its gambrel roof, dormers and fanlight windows. Having a traditional exterior from the street view, this home also has window walls and a greenhouse, which opens the house to the outdoors in a thoroughly contemporary manner. Like the country houses of the past, it has a gathering room for family get-togethers or entertaining; but the adjacent two-story greenhouse doubles as the dining room and has a pass-through to the country kitchen, which just might be the heart of the house with its work zone and sitting room. There are four bedrooms on the two floors—the master bedroom suite on the first floor and three more on the second floor. A lounge, overlooking the gathering room and front foyer, is also on the second floor.

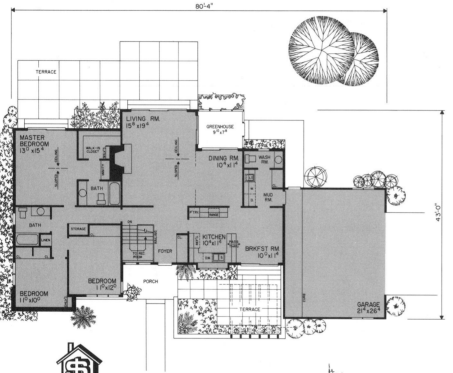

Design 2871

Square Footage: 1,824
Greenhouse: 81 square feet

D

● A greenhouse area off the dining room and living room provides a cheerful focal point for this comfortable three-bedroom Trend Home. The spacious living room features a cozy fireplace and sloped ceiling. In addition to the dining room, there's a less formal breakfast room just off the modern kitchen. Both kitchen and breakfast areas look out into a front terrace. Stairs just off the foyer lead down to a recreation room. The master bedroom suite opens to a terrace. A mud room and washroom off the garage allow rear entry to the house during inclement weather.

Design by
Home Planners

QUOTE ONE™

Cost to build? See page 230 to order complete cost estimate to build this house in your area!

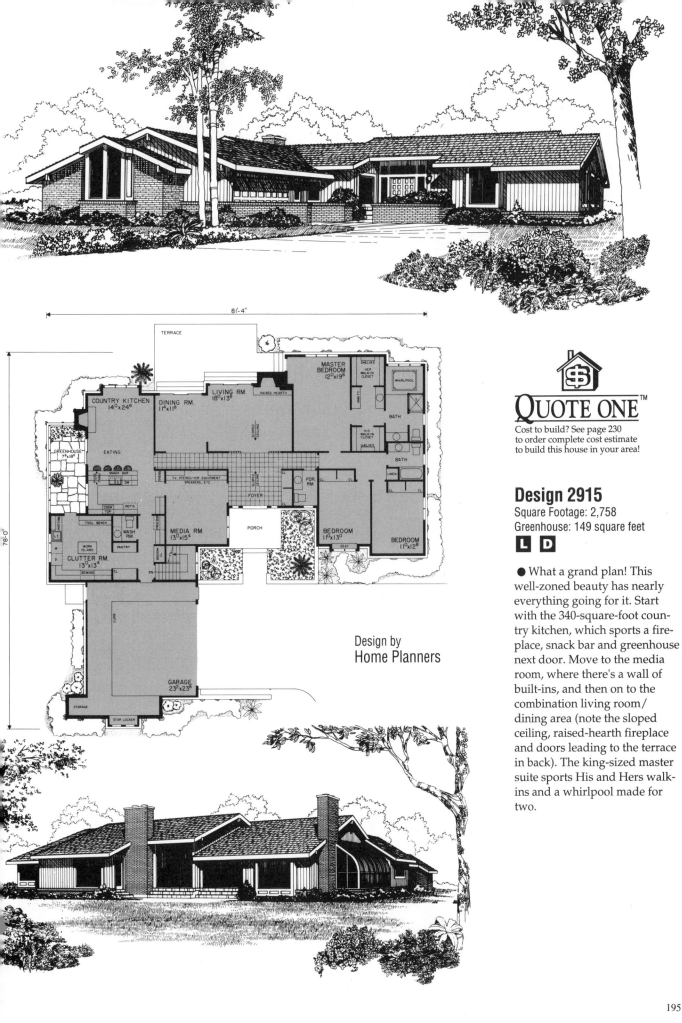

81'-4"

TERRACE

MASTER BEDROOM
12⁰x19⁸

SHELVES

HER WALK-IN CLOSET

WHIRLPOOL

LIVING RM.
18⁰x13⁸

RAISED HEARTH

VANITY

COUNTRY KITCHEN
14⁰x24⁶

DINING RM.
11⁴x11⁸

SLOPED CEILING

BATH

GREENHOUSE
7⁸x18⁰

EATING

HIS WALK-IN CLOSET

SHELVES

SNACK BAR

BATH

T.V. STEREO/VCR EQUIPMENT
SPEAKERS, ETC.

COOK TOP

REF'S

PDR. RM.

LINEN

FOYER

CL

WASH RM

MEDIA RM.
13⁰x15⁴

PORCH

BEDROOM
11⁰x13⁰

BEDROOM
11⁰x12⁸

TOOL BENCH

PANTRY

WORK ISLAND

CLUTTER RM.
13⁰x13⁴

SEWING

CL

SEAT

78'-0"

DN

GARAGE
23²x23⁸

STORAGE

STOP LOCKER

Design by
Home Planners

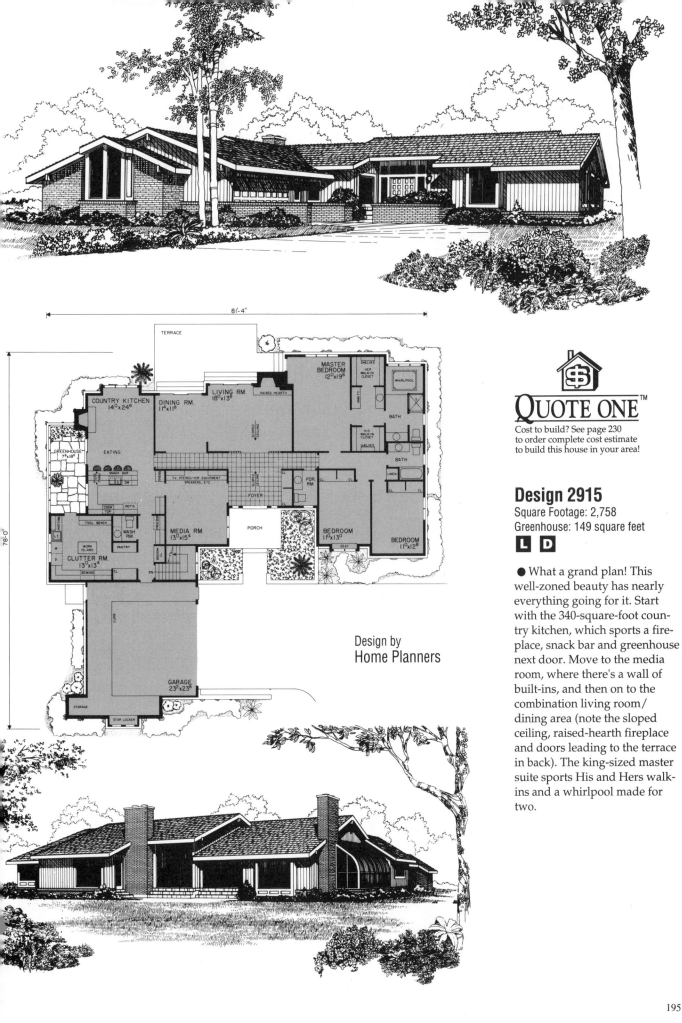

QUOTE ONE™

Cost to build? See page 230
to order complete cost estimate
to build this house in your area!

Design 2915
Square Footage: 2,758
Greenhouse: 149 square feet

L **D**

● What a grand plan! This
well-zoned beauty has nearly
everything going for it. Start
with the 340-square-foot country kitchen, which sports a fireplace, snack bar and greenhouse
next door. Move to the media
room, where there's a wall of
built-ins, and then on to the
combination living room/
dining area (note the sloped
ceiling, raised-hearth fireplace
and doors leading to the terrace
in back). The king-sized master
suite sports His and Hers walk-
ins and a whirlpool made for
two.

Design 3357

Square Footage: 2,913

L **D**

Design by
Home Planners

QUOTE ONE™

Cost to build? See page 230
to order complete cost estimate
to build this house in your area!

Width 82'-8"
Depth 74'

● One-story living never had it so good! From
the formal living and dining rooms to private
media room, this home is designed to be enjoyed.
The greenhouse off the kitchen adds 147 square
feet to the plan. It offers access to the clutter
room where gardening or hobby activities can
take place. At the opposite end of the house are
a master bedroom with generous bath and two
family bedrooms. Notice the wealth of built-ins
throughout the house.

Design 2879

Living Area Including Atrium: 3,173 square feet
Upper Lounge/Balcony: 267 square feet
Total: 3,440 square feet

● This plush modern design seems to have it all, including an upper lounge, an atrium with a skylight, a garden court and a large covered terrace. The convenient kitchen has snack-bar service to a breakfast room and also enjoys a greenhouse window. The deluxe master suite includes its own whirlpool and a bay window. Three family bedrooms, two with window seats, share a full bath. A spacious family room shares a warming fireplace and a view of the rear covered terrace. To the front, a living room with a fireplace delights in a view of the garden court as well as the atrium.

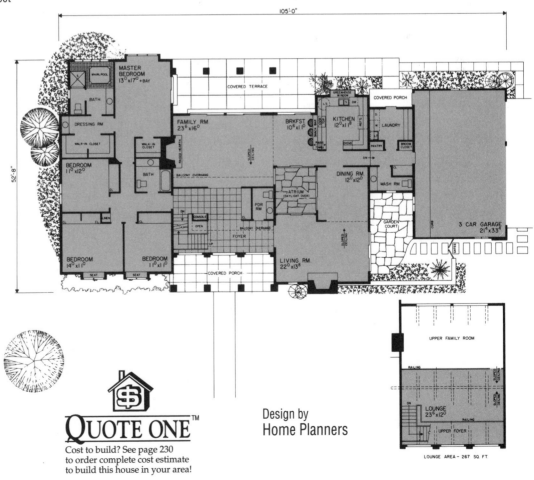

QUOTE ONE™

Cost to build? See page 230
to order complete cost estimate
to build this house in your area!

Design by
Home Planners

197

Design 2880

Square Footage: 2,758
Greenhouse: 149 square feet

L **D**

● This comfortable traditional home offers plenty of modern livability. A clutter room off the two-car garage is the perfect space for workbench, sewing, and hobbies. It includes a work island and bench space. Across the hall one finds a modern media room, the perfect place for stereo speakers, videos, and more. A spacious country kitchen off the greenhouse is a cozy gathering place for family and friends, as well as convenient work area. The 149-foot greenhouse itself easily could be the focal point of this home filled with modern amenities. The house also features a formal dining room, living room with fireplace, covered porch, and three bedrooms including a master bedroom suite.

Design by
Home Planners

Design 2977 First Floor: 4,104 square feet; Second Floor: 979 square feet; Total: 5,083 square feet

L

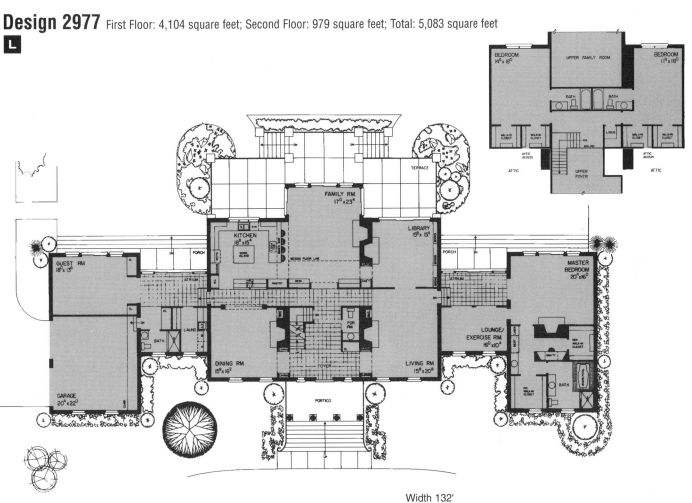

Width 132'
Depth 53'-6"

Design by
Home Planners

● Both front and rear facades of this elegant
brick manor depict classic Georgian symmetry. A
columned, Greek entry opens to an impressive
two-story foyer. Fireplaces, built-in shelves, and
cabinets highlight each of the four main gathering
areas: living room, dining room, family room,
and library.

QUOTE ONE®

Cost to build? See page 230
to order complete cost estimate
to build this house in your area!

Design 9107

First Floor: 1,584 square feet
Second Floor: 563 square feet
Total: 2,147 square feet

● A farmhouse with a wraparound veranda is hard to beat, and this one is no exception. From the central raised foyer, the plan unfolds to a living room, a dining room and an L-shaped kitchen. A full wall of glass highlights the living area and allows a private space for a garden room connected to the living room via a three-way fireplace. The breakfast room is also surrounded by glass. The master bedroom suite on the first floor has a compartmented bath and a walk-in closet. On the second floor are two additional bedrooms, a sitting area and a full bath.

Design by
Larry W.
Garnett &
Associates, Inc.

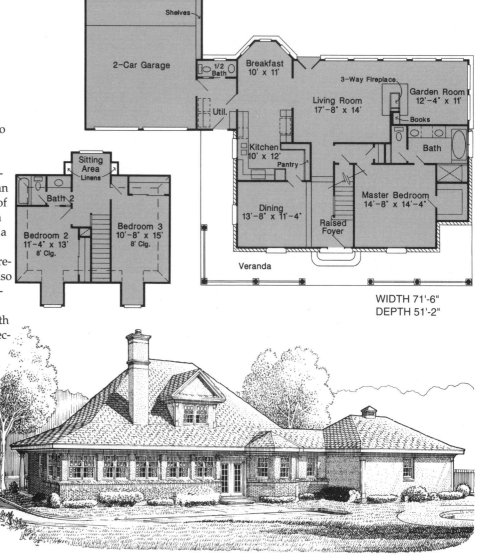

WIDTH 71'-6"
DEPTH 51'-2"

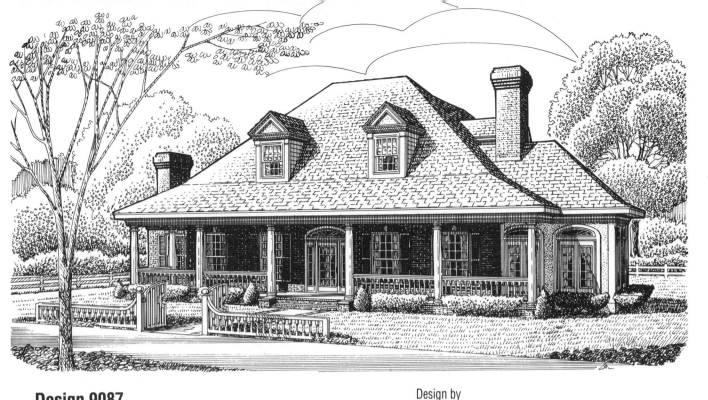

Design 9087

First Floor: 2,263 square feet
Second Floor: 787 square feet
Total: 3,050 square feet

Design by
Larry W.
Garnett &
Associates, Inc.

● Excellent outdoor living is yours with this 1½-story home. The wrapping covered front porch gives way to a center hall entry with flanking living and dining rooms. The living room features a media center, two-way fireplace and columned entry. The attached garden room has French doors to the front porch and French doors to a smaller covered porch that is also accessed through the master bedroom suite. The family room is complemented by a fireplace, built-in bookshelves and another covered porch. An angled island counter separates it from the kitchen. Upstairs are three bedrooms and two full baths. Bedroom 4 has a beautiful bumped out window while Bedrooms 2 and 3 have dormer windows.

Living Room

Width 68'-10"
Depth 52'-4"

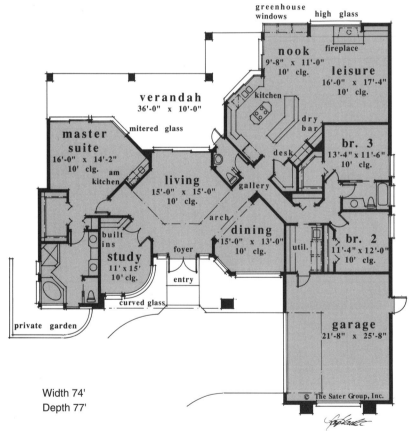

verandah
36'-0" x 10'-0"

mitered glass

master suite
16'-0" x 14'-2"
10' clg.

am kitchen

greenhouse windows

high glass

fireplace

nook
9'-8" x 11'-0"
10' clg.

leisure
16'-0" x 17'-4"
10' clg.

kitchen

dry bar

desk

br. 3
13'-4" x 11'-6"
10' clg.

living
15'-0" x 15'-0"
10' clg.

gallery

study
11' x 15'
10' clg.

built ins

arch

dining
15'-0" x 13'-0"
10' clg.

foyer

entry

util.

br. 2
11'-4" x 12'-0"
10' clg.

private garden

curved glass

garage
21'-8" x 25'-8"

© The Sater Group, Inc.

Width 74'
Depth 77'

Design 6605

Square Footage: 2,762

L

● A different and exciting floor plan and specialized windows define this three-bedroom home. Clear and simple rooflines and a large welcoming entryway make it unique. A large archway frames the dining room entry to the gallery hall. The hall leads past the kitchen toward the infomal leisure and nook area. High glass above the built-in fireplace allows for natural light and rear views. Greenhouse-style garden windows light the nook. The large master suite has a morning kitchen and a sitting area. The bath features a make-up space, a walk-in shower and a private garden tub. An adjacent study has French doors, built-in bookshelves and curved-glass windows.

Design by
The Sater
Design Collection

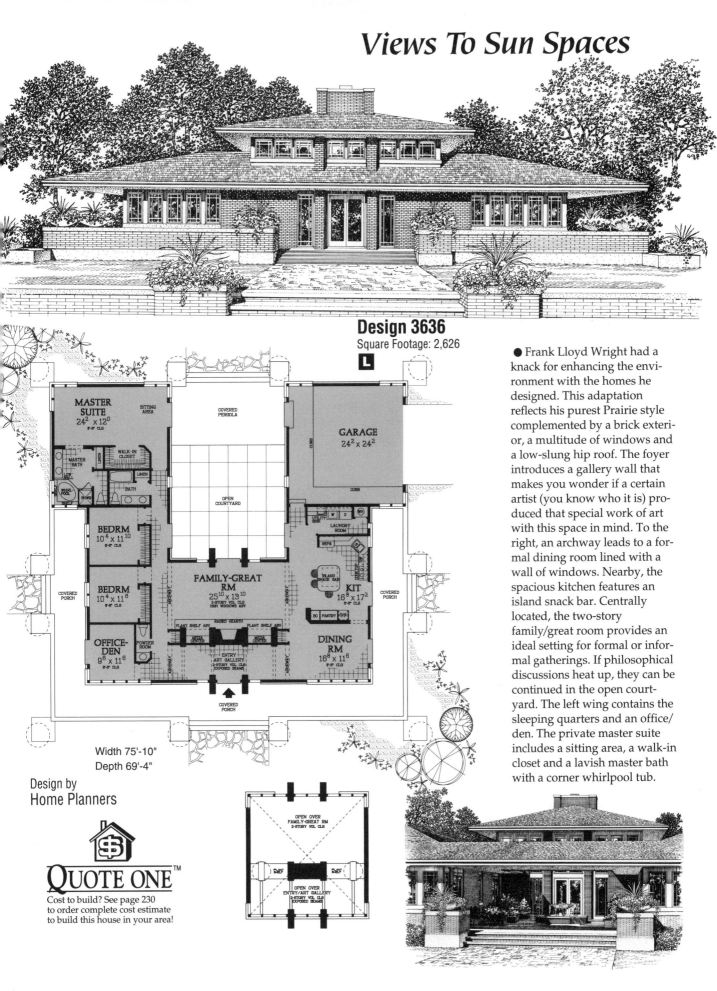

Views To Sun Spaces

Design 3636
Square Footage: 2,626

L

MASTER SUITE
24² x 12⁰
8'-8" CLG

SITTING AREA

MASTER BATH

WALK-IN CLOSET

LINEN

BATH

LINEN

WHIRL-POOL

LOW WALL

SHWR

COVERED PERGOLA

OPEN COURTYARD

GARAGE
24² x 24²

CURB

CURB

BEDRM
10⁴ x 11¹⁰
8'-6" CLG

UTILITY SINK

W   D

LAUNDRY ROOM

REFG

COVERED PORCH

BEDRM
10⁴ x 11⁶
8'-6" CLG

FAMILY-GREAT RM
25¹⁰ x 13¹⁰
2-STORY VOL CLG
HIGH WINDOWS ABV

ISLAND SNACK BAR

KIT
18⁸ x 17²

COVERED PORCH

RAISED HEARTH

PANTRY   OVN

BC

PLANT SHELF ABV

PLANT SHELF ABV

OFFICE-DEN
9⁸ x 11⁶
8'-6" CLG

POWDER ROOM

ENTRTMT CENTER

ENTRTMT CENTER

ARCHWAY

GALLERY

DINING RM
18⁸ x 11⁶
8'-8" CLG

ENTRY/ART GALLERY
2-STORY VOL CLG
EXPOSED BEAMS

ARCHWAY

COVERED PORCH

Width 75'-10"
Depth 69'-4"

Design by
Home Planners

OPEN OVER
FAMILY-GREAT RM
2-STORY VOL CLG

OPEN OVER
ENTRY/ART GALLERY
2-STORY VOL CLG
EXPOSED BEAMS

QUOTE ONE™
Cost to build? See page 230
to order complete cost estimate
to build this house in your area!

● Frank Lloyd Wright had a knack for enhancing the environment with the homes he designed. This adaptation reflects his purest Prairie style complemented by a brick exterior, a multitude of windows and a low-slung hip roof. The foyer introduces a gallery wall that makes you wonder if a certain artist (you know who it is) produced that special work of art with this space in mind. To the right, an archway leads to a formal dining room lined with a wall of windows. Nearby, the spacious kitchen features an island snack bar. Centrally located, the two-story family/great room provides an ideal setting for formal or informal gatherings. If philosophical discussions heat up, they can be continued in the open courtyard. The left wing contains the sleeping quarters and an office/den. The private master suite includes a sitting area, a walk-in closet and a lavish master bath with a corner whirlpool tub.

Design 3634

Square Footage: 3,264

● Grand style is reflected within the pediment gables, columns and keystones of this distinguished home. Inside, a formal living room, angled for interest, warmly greets friends and provides a perfect complement to the formal dining room located nearby. The island kitchen overlooks the covered entertainment terrace and easily serves both formal and informal areas. Family gatherings will be enjoyed in the light and airy family room that shares space with a bay-windowed nook. A secluded master suite features a spacious master bedroom that provides room to stretch and a walk-in closet sized for frequent shoppers. The master bath enjoys a corner whirlpool tub that overlooks the privacy patio and garden area. Two additional bedrooms, a den/study, a full bath and a powder room complete the plan.

Width 84'-4"
Depth 75'-4"

Design by
Home Planners

QUOTE ONE™

Cost to build? See page 230
to order complete cost estimate
to build this house in your area!

Design 3637

Square Footage: 3,278

L

● The landscape harmonized so well with his designs that they often seemed as one. Yes, we're talking about the Wright stuff! This Prairie-style home—with its U-shaped design—maximizes indoor-outdoor livability. Note the access provided to the central, open courtyard from the family/great room, country kitchen, bedroom, master suite and guest suite. Inside, the master suite is split for privacy, enhanced with a sitting area, a walk-in closet and a luxurious master bath. Open planning combines the country kitchen with an eating area, a snack bar and a formal dining room nearby. The family-great room separates the sleeping quarters and formal living room. Guests will feel right at home with their own private suite and pampering guest bath. Plans for a detached garage with an optional guest suite are included with the blueprints.

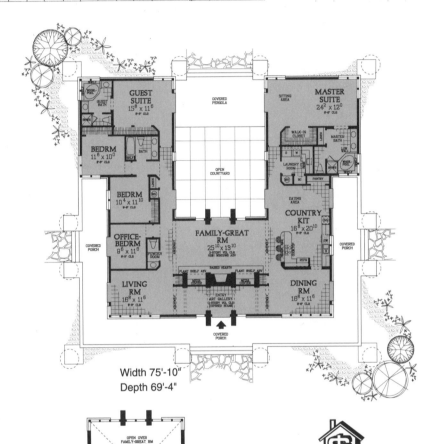

Width 75'-10"
Depth 69'-4"

Design by
Home Planners

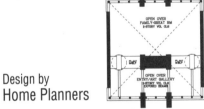

Cost to build? See page 230 to order complete cost estimate to build this house in your area!

Garage Plan G201

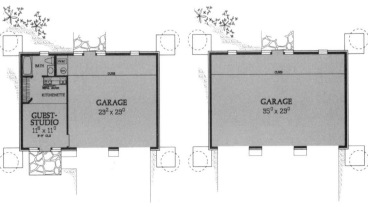

MASTER
SUITE
24² x 12⁰

SITTING
AREA

SLOPED CEILING

WALK-IN
CLOSET

LINEN

LINEN

LOW
WALL

BATH

SHWR

COVERED
ARBOR

OPEN
COURTYARD

GARAGE
24² x 24²

UTILITY
SINK

W D

LAUNDRY
ROOM

REFG

COUNTRY
KIT
16⁸ x 17⁴
SLOPED CEILING

ISLAND
SNACK BAR

COOK TOP

BEDRM
10⁴ x 11¹⁰
VOL. CLG.

PLANT SHELF ABV

BEDRM
10⁴ x 11⁶
VOL. CLG.

PLANT SHELF ABV

FAMILY-GREAT
RM
24¹⁰ x 14⁰
SLOPED CLG.

COVERED
PORCH

COVERED
PORCH

BC PANTRY OVN

DINING
RM
16⁸ x 11⁶
SLOPED CEILING

OFFICE-
DEN
9⁶ x 11⁶
VOL. CLG.

POWDER
ROOM

ARCHWAY

RAISED HEARTH

MEDIA

MEDIA

PLANT SHELF ABV

ARCHWAY

ARCHWAY

ENTRY
ART GALLERY
SLOPED CLG

ARCHWAY

COVERED
PORCH

Width 75'-2"
Depth 68'-8"

Quote One™

Cost to build? See page 230
to order complete cost estimate
to build this house in your area!

Design by
Home Planners

Design 3632

Square Footage: 2,539

L

● An open courtyard takes center-stage in this graceful Mediterranean-style home. Art collectors will appreciate the gallery that enhances the entry and showcases their favorite works. To the right is a dining room which will make every meal a special occasion and an adjacent country kitchen designed with an island snack bar and a large pantry. The centrally located family-great room supplies the nucleus for formal and informal entertaining. A raised-hearth fireplace flanked by built-in media centers adds a special touch. The sleeping wing features a master suite located to the rear for privacy. Here, you may relax in the sitting room or retire to the master bath for a pampering soak in the corner whirlpool. Two family bedrooms share a hall bath. An office/den and a powder room complete the plan.

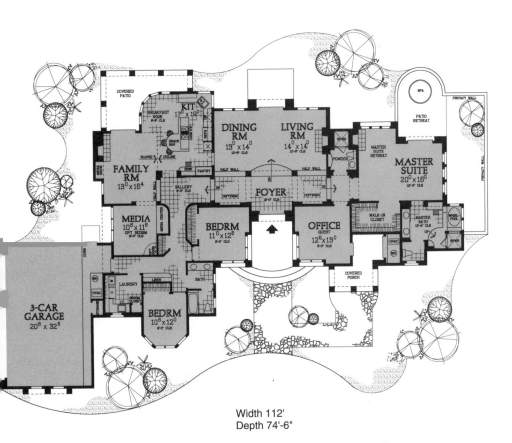

Width 112'
Depth 74'-6"

Design 3630
Square Footage: 3,034

L

● A grand entry enhances the exterior of this elegant stucco home. The office located at the front of the plan makes this design ideal for a home-based business. Formal areas combine to provide lots of space for entertaining. The kitchen, complete with a snack bar and a breakfast nook, opens to the family room which connects to the media room. The private master suite includes two retreats—one is a multi-windowed sitting area, the other contains a spa for outdoor enjoyment. Be sure to notice the walk-in closet and the luxurious bath. Two family bedrooms share a full bath.

QUOTE ONE™
Cost to build? See page 230
to order complete cost estimate
to build this house in your area!

Design by
Home Planners

Design 9082

Square Footage: 2,360

● Reminiscent of the homes built long ago in the Southwest, this Spanish adaptation has many components to draw attention to it. Note the long entry porch leading to an angled foyer flanked by a huge living room with cathedral ceiling and dining room with sloped ceiling. Across the gallery is a long porch with skylights that over-looks the tiled courtyard. The kitchen features plenty of counter space and a large pantry. To the rear, in privacy is the master bedroom suite. It has a tub area with raised gazebo ceiling and transom windows. There are also two family bed-rooms sharing a full bath with double vanities.

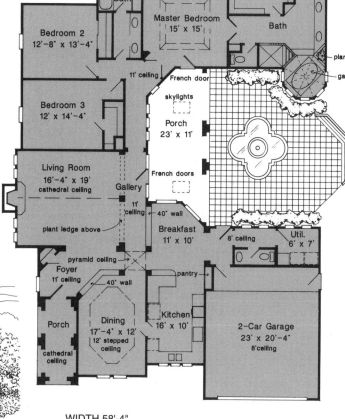

Bath

11' stepped ceiling

Master Bedroom
15' x 15'

Bath

planter

planter

gazebo

Bedroom 2
12'-8" x 13'-4"

11' ceiling

French door

skylights

Porch
23' x 11'

Bedroom 3
12' x 14'-4"

Living Room
16'-4" x 19'
cathedral ceiling

Gallery

11'
ceiling

French doors

40" wall

plant ledge above

Breakfast
11' x 10'

8' ceiling

Util.
6' x 7'

pyramid ceiling

Foyer
11' ceiling

40" wall

pantry

Porch

Dining
17'-4" x 12'
12' stepped ceiling

cathedral ceiling

Kitchen
16' x 10'

2-Car Garage
23' x 20'-4"
8' ceiling

WIDTH 58'-4"
DEPTH 73'-4"

Design by
Larry W.
Garnett &
Associates, Inc.

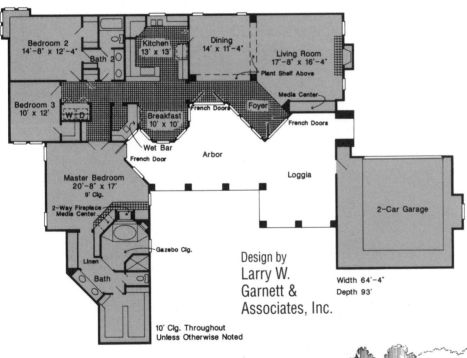

Bedroom 2
14'-8" x 12'-4"

Bath 2

Kitchen
13' x 13'

Dining
14' x 11'-4"

Living Room
17'-8" x 16'-4"

Plant Shelf Above

Bedroom 3
10' x 12'

W D

Breakfast
10' x 10'

French Doors

Media Center

Foyer

French Doors

Wet Bar

French Door

Arbor

Master Bedroom
20'-8" x 17'
9' Clg.

Loggia

2-Car Garage

2-Way Fireplace
Media Center

Gazebo Clg.

Linen

Bath

Design by
Larry W.
Garnett &
Associates, Inc.

Width 64'-4"
Depth 93'

10' Clg. Throughout
Unless Otherwise Noted

Design 9083
Square Footage: 2,176

● This grand Southwestern design caters to outdoor lifestyle with areas that invite visitation. The front entry opens to a beautiful and characteristic Spanish courtyard with loggia, arbor and spa area. The foyer runs the length of the home and leads from open living and dining areas to convenient kitchen and breakfast nook, then back to the sleeping quarters. The master suite is especially notable with its luxurious bath and ample closet space. Note the many extras in the plan: fireplace and media center in the living room and in the master bedroom, wet bar at the breakfast nook, oversized pantry in the kitchen.

QUOTE ONE®

Cost to build? See page 230
to order complete cost estimate
to build this house in your area!

Design 3486
Square Footage: 2,000

● This classic stucco design provides a cool retreat in any climate. From the covered porch, enter the skylit foyer to find an arched ceiling leading to the central gathering room with its raised-hearth fireplace and terrace access. A connecting corner dining room is conveniently located near the amenity-filled kitchen that features an abundant pantry, a snack bar and a separate breakfast area. The large master bedroom includes terrace access and a master bath with a whirlpool tub, a separate shower and plenty of closet space. A second bedroom and a study that can be converted to a bedroom complete this wonderful plan.

Design by
Home Planners

QUOTE ONE™

Cost to build? See page 230 to order complete cost estimate to build this house in your area!

Width 75'
Depth 55'

Design 3642

Square Footage: 2,945

● This Santa Fe delivers great livability. From three bedrooms for the family and a beautiful master suite for Mom and Dad to formal and informal living areas, the floor plan is designed for today's lifestyles. The living room opens directly from the foyer and is defined by a curve of glass overlooking the front entry. Across the hall and through double columns is the dining room which overlooks the rear patio. The family room is mega-sized and contains a wet bar, curved fireplace and other built-ins. It leads, through a utility area, to the three-car garage. The kitchen overlooks the rear patio and connects to a glass-walled breakfast nook. Don't miss the double walk-in closets in the master suite.

Design by
Home Planners

Width 73'
Depth 68'-10"

Design 6611

Square Footage: 3,104

L

● Brick accents warm the exterior of this captivating Floridian home. A feeling of elegance makes a fine first impression upon entering the grand foyer. It opens to the formal living and dining room through columns and archways. Step out onto the verandah and enjoy the cooling breezes. It is accessible from the formal living area, the private master suite or the cheerful breakfast nook. The spacious kitchen is a cook's delight with its large pantry, an island cooktop and garden greenhouse window. The leisure room hosts a fireplace with built-in shelves and convenient access to an outdoor patio and grill, making it a favorite for informal gatherings. The sumptuous master wing features a bayed study and a master suite with a stepped ceiling, a huge walk-in closet and plenty of space for a sitting area. The master bath enjoys a relaxing tub with a private garden view, a separate shower and a compartmented toilet. This home will please even the most discriminating homeowner.

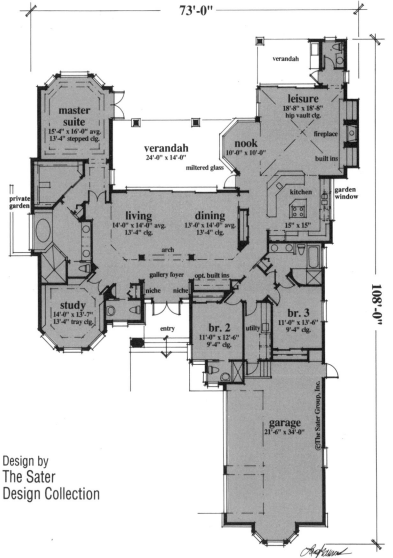

Design by
The Sater
Design Collection

66'-8"

Design 8620
Square Footage: 2,454

● This one-story sports many well-chosen, distinctive exterior details including a cameo window and hipped rooflines. The dining and living rooms flank the foyer. A tray ceiling in the living room adds further enhancement. The bayed breakfast area admits light softened by the patio. Secluded from the main house, the master bedroom comes with a tray ceiling and fireplace through to the master bath. A raised tub, double vanity and immense walk-in closet highlight the bath.

Design by
Home Design
Services, Inc.

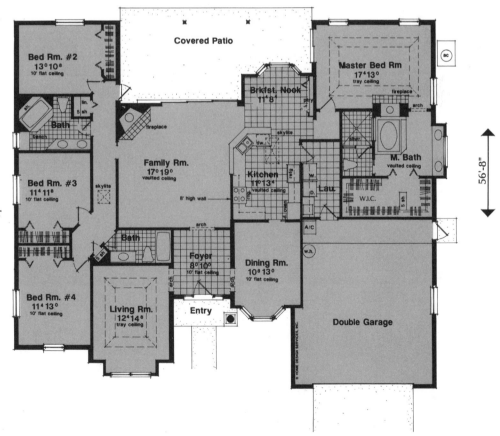

56'-8"

Covered Patio

Bed Rm. #2
13⁰10⁶
10' flat ceiling

Master Bed Rm
17⁴13⁰
tray ceiling

Brkfst. Nook
11⁴8²

fireplace

Family Rm.
17⁰19⁰
vaulted ceiling

Kitchen
11⁰13⁴
vaulted ceiling

M. Bath
vaulted ceiling

Bed Rm. #3
11⁴11⁸
10' flat ceiling

skylite

W.I.C.

8' high wall

Bath

arch

Foyer
8⁰10⁰
10' flat ceiling

Dining Rm.
10⁸13⁰
10' flat ceiling

Bed Rm. #4
11⁴13⁰
10' flat ceiling

Living Rm.
12⁴14⁸
tray ceiling

Entry

Double Garage

213

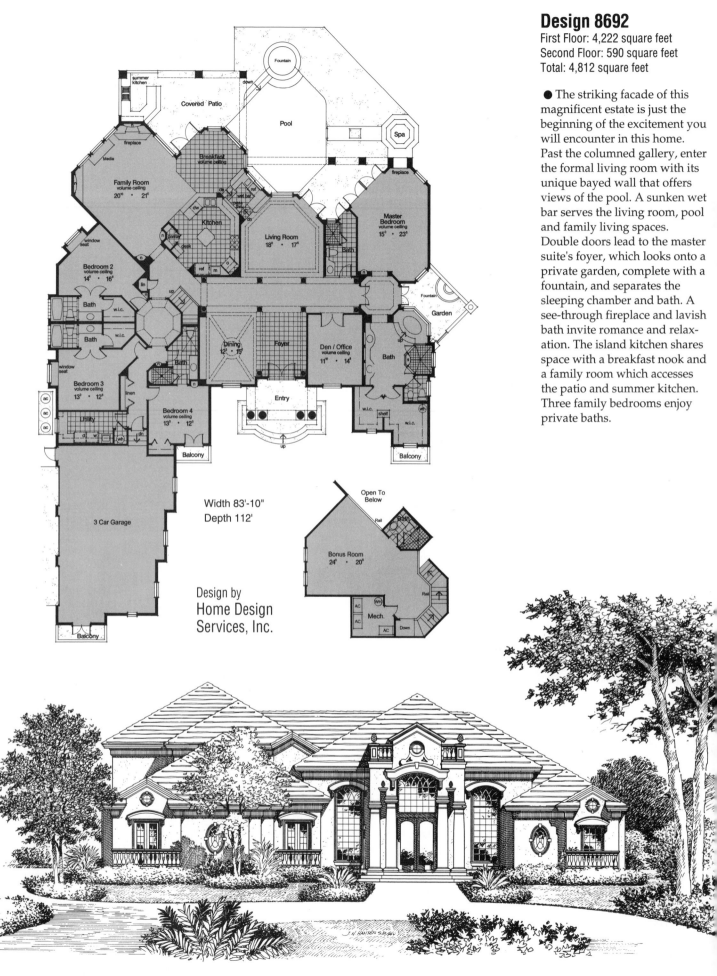

Design 8692

First Floor: 4,222 square feet
Second Floor: 590 square feet
Total: 4,812 square feet

● The striking facade of this magnificent estate is just the beginning of the excitement you will encounter in this home. Past the columned gallery, enter the formal living room with its unique bayed wall that offers views of the pool. A sunken wet bar serves the living room, pool and family living spaces. Double doors lead to the master suite's foyer, which looks onto a private garden, complete with a fountain, and separates the sleeping chamber and bath. A see-through fireplace and lavish bath invite romance and relaxation. The island kitchen shares space with a breakfast nook and a family room which accesses the patio and summer kitchen. Three family bedrooms enjoy private baths.

Width 83'-10"
Depth 112'

Design by
Home Design
Services, Inc.

Design 8084

First Floor: 3,328 square feet
Second Floor: 868 square feet
Total: 4,196 square feet

● The combination of stucco, stacked stone and brick adds texture and character to this Country French home. Columns with connecting arches define the entrances to the dining room and living room. Double French doors open to the study with built-in bookcases and a window seat. A see-through fireplace serves both the living room and the study. The master suite is enhanced by a raised, corner fireplace and a bath with an exercise room.

Design by
Larry E. Belk
Designs

Width 108'-2"
Depth 61'-6"

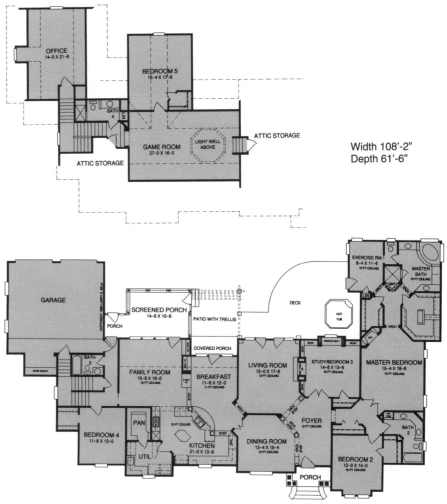

215

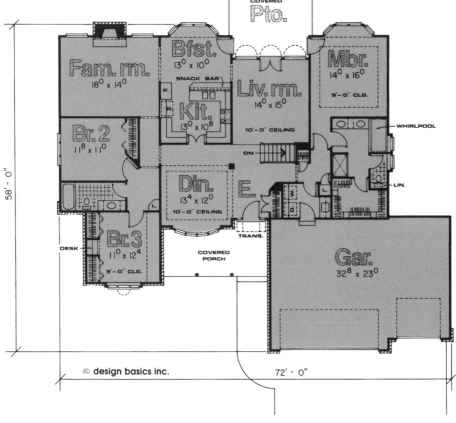

Design 7275

Square Footage: 2,132

● Amenities fill this ranch-style home, from the covered porch to the covered patio. Upon entering, the oak entry opens onto a formal dining room enhanced by a wall of bowed windows. To the rear is a living room filled with light, compliments of a glass wall. Casual times will be enjoyed in the family room with its warming fireplace. The adjacent kitchen is planned for maximum counter space and serves the bay-windowed breakfast room as well as the formal and informal living areas. Split for privacy, the master suite enjoys a bay window that fills the room with the hues of early morning light or cool blue shades of evening. A pampering master bath completes the suite. Two bedrooms share a hall bath.

Design by
Design
Basics,
Inc.

Design 9113
Square Footage: 1,496

● This great one-story design fits well on a narrow lot. From the covered front porch, the foyer opens to living areas on the left. These areas include a living room with a fireplace and a pass-through bar to the kitchen, as well as a glass-surrounded dining area with a French door. A utility area leads to the two-car garage out back. Three bedrooms complete the living space and include a master bedroom that fancies its own bath: a garden tub, dual vanities and a separate shower set the stage in this bath. Note, too, the French door that leads to the tiled courtyard. Two family bedrooms share a full hall bath. Bedroom 2 even has a walk-in closet. Bedroom 3 features a built-in desk.

WIDTH 43'-8"
DEPTH 74'-8"

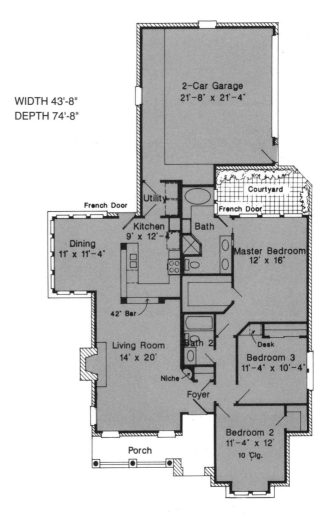

Design by
Larry W.
Garnett &
Associates, Inc.

Design 9821 First Floor: 2,070 square feet; Second Floor: 790 square feet; Total: 2,860 square feet

● The striking combination of wood frame, shingles and glass create the exterior of this classic cottage. The foyer opens to the main-level layout. To the left of the foyer is a study with a warming hearth and vaulted ceiling. To the right is the formal dining room. A great room with an attached breakfast area is to the rear near the kitchen. A guest room is nestled in the rear of the plan for privacy. The master suite provides an expansive tray ceiling, a glass sitting area and easy passage to the outside deck. Upstairs, two bedrooms are accompanied by a loft for a quiet getaway. This home is designed with a basement foundation.

Width 58'-4"
Depth 54'-10"

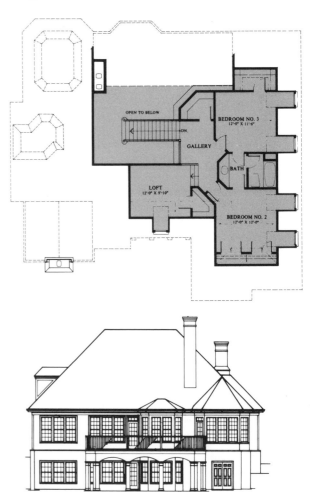

Design by
Design Traditions

QUOTE ONE®
Cost to build? See page 230
to order complete cost estimate
to build this house in your area!

Design 3600/3601

Square Footage: 2,258/2,424

● This unique one-story plan seems tailor-made for a small family or for empty-nesters. Formal areas are situated well for entertaining—living room to the right and formal dining room to the left. A large family room is found to the rear. It has access to a rear wood deck and is warmed in the cold months by a welcome hearth. The U-shaped kitchen features an attached morning room for casual meals. Bedrooms are split. The master suite sits to the right of the plan and has a walk-in closet and a fine bath. A nearby office has a private porch. One family bedroom is on the other side of the home and also has a private bath.

Design by
Home Planners

Design 3601

Quote One™

Cost to build? See page 230 to order complete cost estimate to build this house in your area!

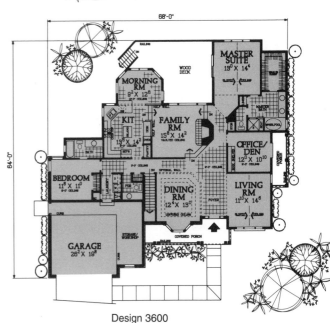

Design 3600

Design 3600 Rear Elevation

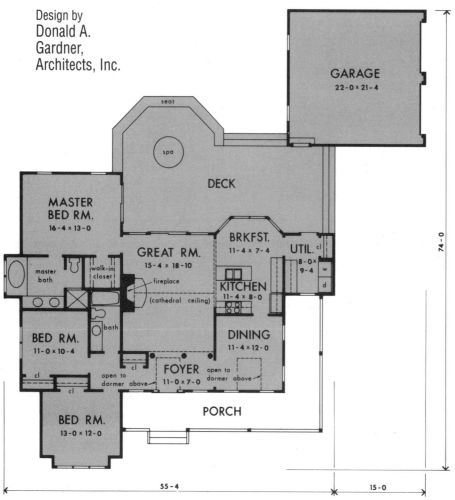

Design by
Donald A.
Gardner,
Architects, Inc.

GARAGE
22-0 x 21-4

seat

spa

DECK

**MASTER
BED RM.**
16-4 x 13-0

GREAT RM.
15-4 x 18-10

BRKFST.
11-4 x 7-4

UTIL. cl
8-0 x
9-4

master
bath

walk-in
closet

fireplace

(cathedral   ceiling)

KITCHEN
11-4 x 8-0

w
d

bath

BED RM.
11-0 x 10-4

DINING
11-4 x 12-0

cl

cl

cl

open to
dormer above

FOYER
11-0 x 7-0

open to
dormer above

cl

BED RM.
13-0 x 12-0

PORCH

55-4

15-0

74-0

Design 9713
Square Footage: 1,590

● The open floor plan of
this country farmhouse packs
in all of today's amenities in
only 1,590 square feet.
Columns separate the foyer
from the great room with its
cathedral ceiling and fireplace. Serving meals has
never been easier—the
kitchen makes use of direct
access to the dining room as
well as a breakfast nook
overlooking the deck and
spa. A handy utility room
even has room for a counter
and cabinets. Three bed-
rooms make this an especially desirable design. The master bedroom, off of the great
room, provides private
access to the deck. This
design is flexible enough to
be accommodated by a nar-
row lot if the garage is relo-
cated. This plan includes a
crawl-space foundation.

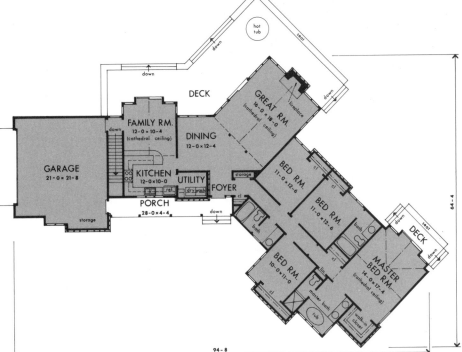

Design 9601
Square Footage: 1,988

● This country-style ranch is the essence of excitement with its combination of exterior building materials and interesting shapes. Because it is angled, it allows for flexibility in design—the great room and/or the family room can be lengthened to meet family space requirements. The master bedroom has a cathedral ceiling, a walk-in closet, a private deck and a spacious master bath with a whirlpool tub. There are three family bedrooms, two of which share a full bath and one having a private bath. An expansive deck area with space for a hot tub wraps around the interior family gathering areas. Both the family room and the great room have cathedral ceilings; the great room has a fireplace. Please specify crawlspace or basement foundation when ordering.

Design by
Donald A.
Gardner,
Architects, Inc.

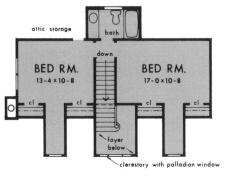

attic storage

bath

down

BED RM.
13-4 × 10-8

BED RM.
17-0 × 10-8

cl cl cl cl

foyer
below

clerestory with palladian window

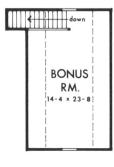

BONUS
RM.
14-4 × 23-8

down

Design by
Donald A.
Gardner,
Architects, Inc.

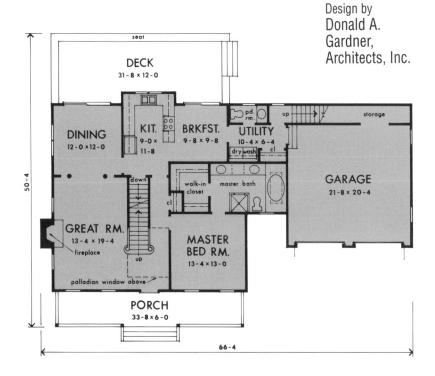

seat

DECK
31-8 × 12-0

DINING
12-0 × 12-0

KIT.
9-0 ×
11-8

BRKFST.
9-8 × 9-8

pd.
rm.

UTILITY
10-4 × 6-4

up

storage

dry wash cl

walk-in
closet

master bath

GARAGE
21-8 × 20-4

down

cl

GREAT RM.
13-4 × 19-4

fireplace

MASTER
BED RM.
13-4 × 13-0

up

palladian window above

PORCH
33-8 × 6-0

50-4

66-4

Design 9606

First Floor: 1,289 square feet
Second Floor: 542 square feet
Total: 1,831 square feet
Bonus Room: 393 square feet

● This cozy country cottage is
perfect for the growing family—
offering both an unfinished basement option and a bonus room.
Enter through the two-story foyer
with a Palladian window in a
clerestory dormer above. The master suite is on the first floor for privacy and accessibility. Its accompa-
nying bath boasts a whirlpool tub
with a skylight above and a double-bowl vanity. The second floor
contains two bedrooms, a full bath
and plenty of storage. Note that all
first-floor rooms except the kitchen
and utility room boast nine foot
ceilings. This plan is available with
either a basement or crawlspace
foundation. Please specify when
ordering.

Quote One®

Cost to build? See page 230
to order complete cost estimate
to build this house in your area!

Design 3606

First Floor: 1,969 square feet
Second Floor: 660 square feet
Total: 2,629 square feet
Bonus Room: 360 square feet

L **D**

● Entertaining and comfortable living are the by-words for this gracious home. From the two-story foyer, enter the living room with its bay window, or the spacious family/great room with its central fireplace. Here, access is provided to the enclosed sun room. The U-shaped kitchen features a center island, a large pantry, a writing desk and a snack bar. Access to the garage is provided via a decorative arbor. The first-floor master suite includes a pampering master bath with a whirlpool and a walk-in closet. Both the bedroom and the bathroom access the private master suite veranda. The home office easily converts to a fourth bedroom. Two additional bedrooms and a full bath are found on the second floor. A bonus room provides additional space over the garage.

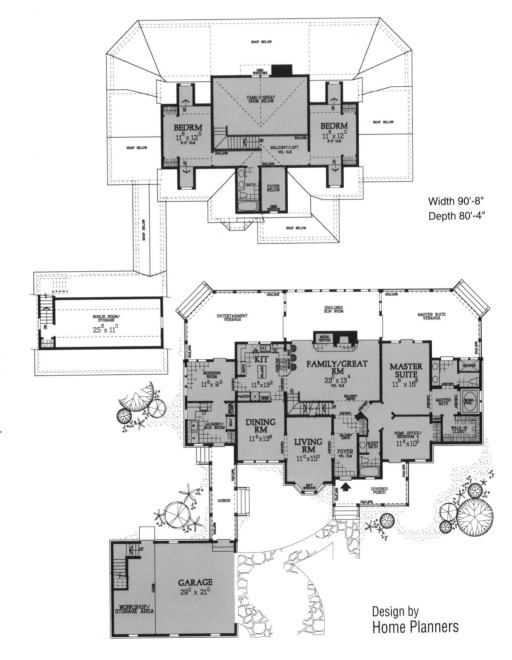

Width 90'-8"
Depth 80'-4"

Design by
Home Planners

Quote One™

Cost to build? See page 230 to order complete cost estimate to build this house in your area!

Design 3565

First Floor: 1,248 square feet
Second Floor: 1,012 square feet
Total: 2,260 square feet

L **D**

● Every detail of this plan speaks of modern design. The exterior is simple yet elegant, while interior floor planning is thorough yet efficient. The formal living and dining rooms are to the left of the home, separated by columns. The living room features a wall of windows and a fireplace. The kitchen with island cooktop is adjacent to the large family room with terrace access. A study with additional terrace access completes the first floor. The master bedroom features a balcony and a spectacular bath with whirlpool tub, shower with seat, separate vanities and a walk-in closet. Two family bedrooms share access to a full bath. Also notice the three-car garage.

QUOTE ONE™

Cost to build? See page 230 to order complete cost estimate to build this house in your area!

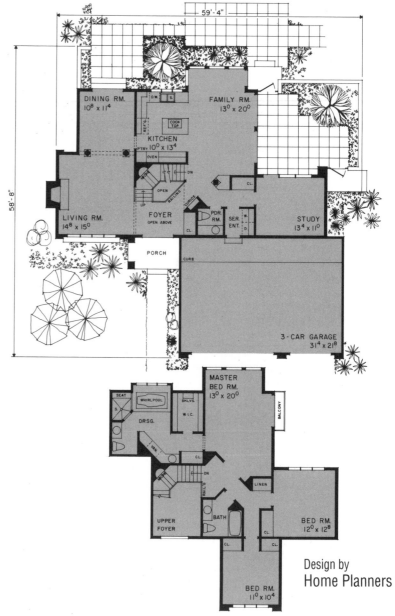

Design by
Home Planners

Design 2902
Square Footage: 1,632

L

● A sun space highlights this passive solar design. It has access from the kitchen, dining room and garage. It will be a great place to enjoy meals because of its location. Three skylights highlight the interior - one in the kitchen, laundrey and master bath. An air-locked vestibule helps this design's energy efficiency. Interior livability is excellent. The living/dining room has a sloping ceiling, fireplace and two sets of sliding glass doors to the terrace. This area will cater to numerous family activities. Additional activities can take place in the basement. Note its open staircase. Three bedrooms are in the sleeping wing. The square footage of the sun space is 216 and is not included in the above figure.

Width 59'
Depth 56'-8"

Design by
Home Planners

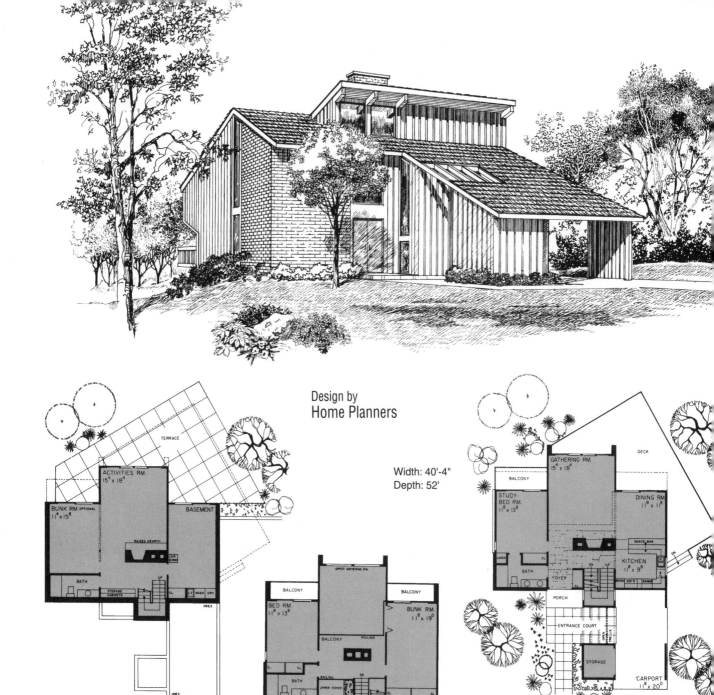

Design by
Home Planners

Width: 40'-4"
Depth: 52'

TERRACE

ACTIVITIES RM.
15⁴ x 18⁴

BASEMENT

BUNK RM. OPTIONAL
11⁴ x 15⁸

RAISED HEARTH

AIR CONC.

BATH

STORAGE CABINETS

UP

CL.

LT. WASH DRY.

UNEX.

UNEX.

GATHERING RM.
15⁵ x 18⁴

DECK

BALCONY

STUDY-BED RM.
11⁸ x 13⁸

DINING RM.
11⁸ x 11⁸

SNACK BAR

LINEN

CL.

KITCHEN
11⁸ x 9⁸

BATH

FOYER

DN UP

ENTRY REF'G RANGE

CL.

PORCH

ENTRANCE COURT

OPEN TRELLIS

STORAGE

CARPORT
11⁸ x 20⁰

UPPER GATHERING RM.

BALCONY

BALCONY

BED RM.
11⁸ x 13⁸

BUNK RM.
11⁸ x 19⁰

CL.

CL.

BALCONY

RAILING

BATH

RAILING

UPPER FOYER

DN

CL.

CL.

Design 2511

Main Level: 1,043 square feet; Upper Level: 703 square feet
Lower Level: 794 square feet; Total: 2,540 square feet

L **D**

● Though not a large house in square footage, this
shed-roof style offers three levels of livability. Living
areas are on the main level
with sleeping areas above
and a casual activities
room below. Large bal-
conies and a covered
lower terrace enhance
outdoor living. The
gathering room is a
full two stories high.

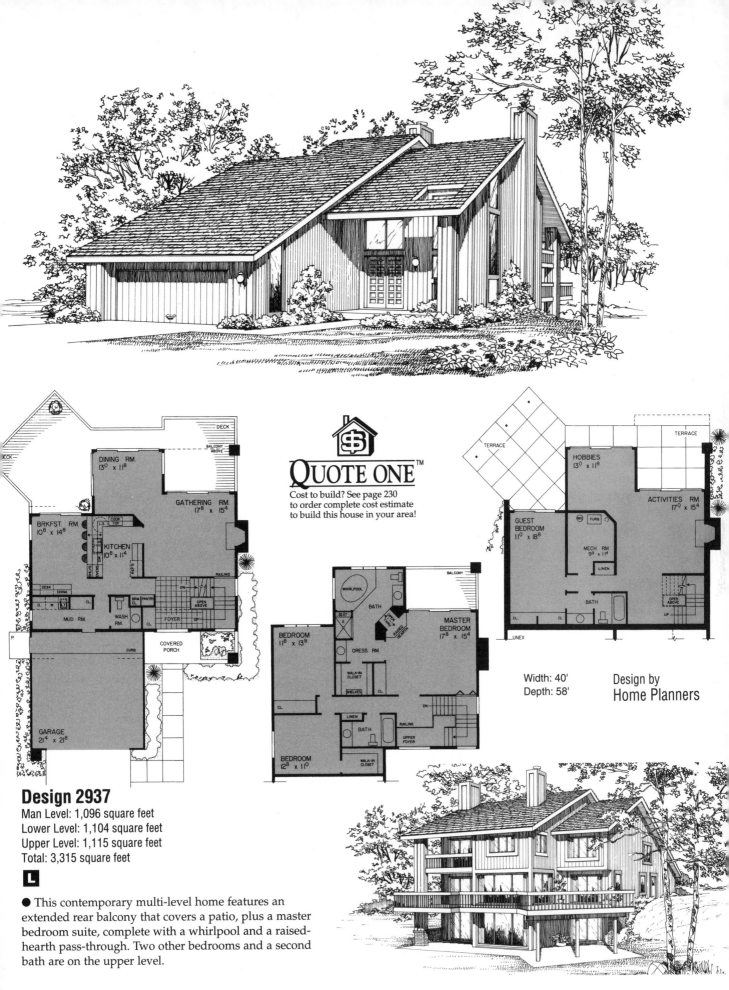

QUOTE ONE™

Cost to build? See page 230
to order complete cost estimate
to build this house in your area!

DECK

BALCONY ABOVE

DECK

DINING RM.
13⁰ x 11⁸

GATHERING RM.
17⁸ x 15⁴

BRKFST. RM.
10⁸ x 14⁸

KITCHEN
10⁸ x 11⁴

DESK CHINA
CL.

D. W

MUD RM.

WASH RM.
CL.

BRM PANTRY
CL.

FOYER

OPEN ABOVE

RAILING

ON. UP

COVERED PORCH

CURB

P

GARAGE
21⁴ x 21⁸

WHIRLPOOL

BATH

SEAT

RAISED HEARTH

BEDROOM
11⁸ x 13⁸

DRESS. RM.

WALK-IN CLOSET

SHELVES

CL.

LINEN

BATH

BEDROOM
12⁸ x 11⁰

WALK-IN CLOSET

BALCONY

MASTER BEDROOM
17⁸ x 15⁴

DN.

RAILING

UPPER FOYER

TERRACE

TERRACE

HOBBIES
13⁰ x 11⁸

ACTIVITIES RM.
17⁰ x 15⁴

GUEST BEDROOM
11⁰ x 18⁸

FURN

MECH. RM.
9⁰ x 11⁴

LINEN

BATH

CL. CL.

OPEN ABOVE

UP

CL.

UNEX.

Width: 40'
Depth: 58'

Design by
Home Planners

Design 2937

Man Level: 1,096 square feet
Lower Level: 1,104 square feet
Upper Level: 1,115 square feet
Total: 3,315 square feet

L

● This contemporary multi-level home features an
extended rear balcony that covers a patio, plus a master
bedroom suite, complete with a whirlpool and a raised-
hearth pass-through. Two other bedrooms and a second
bath are on the upper level.

LET US SHOW YOU OUR HOME BLUEPRINT PACKAGE.

Building a home? Planning a home? Our Blueprint Package has nearly everything you need to get the job done right, whether you're working on your own or with help from an architect, designer, builder or subcontractors. Each Blueprint Package is the result of many hours of work by licensed architects or professional designers.

QUALITY

Hundreds of hours of painstaking effort have gone into the development of your blueprint set. Each home has been quality-checked by professionals to insure accuracy and buildability.

VALUE

Because we sell in volume, you can buy professional quality blueprints at a fraction of their development cost. With our plans, your dream home design costs only a few hundred dollars, not the thousands of dollars that architects charge.

SERVICE

Once you've chosen your favorite home plan, you'll receive fast, efficient service whether you choose to mail or fax your order to us or call us toll free at 1-800-521-6797. For customer service, call toll free 1-888-690-1116.

SATISFACTION

Over 50 years of service to satisfied home plan buyers provide us unparalleled experience and knowledge in producing quality blueprints.

ORDER TOLL FREE
1-800-521-6797

After you've looked over our Blueprint Package and Important Extras on the following pages, simply mail the order form on page 237 or call toll free on our Blueprint Hotline: 1-800-521-6797. We're ready and eager to serve you. For customer service, call toll free 1-888-690-1116.

Each set of blueprints is an interrelated collection of detail sheets which includes components such as floor plans, interior and exterior elevations, dimensions, cross-sections, diagrams and notations. These sheets show exactly how your house is to be built.

AMONG THE SHEETS INCLUDED MAY BE:

FRONTAL SHEET

This artist's sketch of the exterior of the house gives you an idea of how the house will look when built and landscaped. Large floor plans show all levels of the house and provide an overview of your new home's livability, as well as a handy reference for deciding on furniture placement.

FOUNDATION PLANS

This sheet shows the foundation layout including support walls, excavated and unexcavated areas, if any, and foundation notes. If slab construction rather than basement, the plan shows footings and details for a monolithic slab. This page, or another in the set, may include a sample plot plan for locating your house on a building site.

DETAILED FLOOR PLANS

These plans show the layout of each floor of the house. Rooms and interior spaces are carefully dimensioned and keys are given for cross-section details provided later in the plans. The positions of electrical outlets and switches are shown.

HOUSE CROSS-SECTIONS

Large-scale views show sections or cut-aways of the foundation, interior walls, exterior walls, floors, stairways and roof details. Additional cross-sections may show important changes in floor, ceiling or roof heights or the relationship of one level to another. Extremely valuable for construction, these sections show exactly how the various parts of the house fit together.

INTERIOR ELEVATIONS

Many of our drawings show the design and placement of kitchen and bathroom cabinets, laundry areas, fireplaces, bookcases and other built-ins. Little "extras," such as mantelpiece and wainscoting drawings, plus molding sections, provide details that give your home that custom touch.

EXTERIOR ELEVATIONS

These drawings show the front, rear and sides of your house and give necessary notes on exterior materials and finishes. Particular attention is given to cornice detail, brick and stone accents or other finish items that make your home unique.

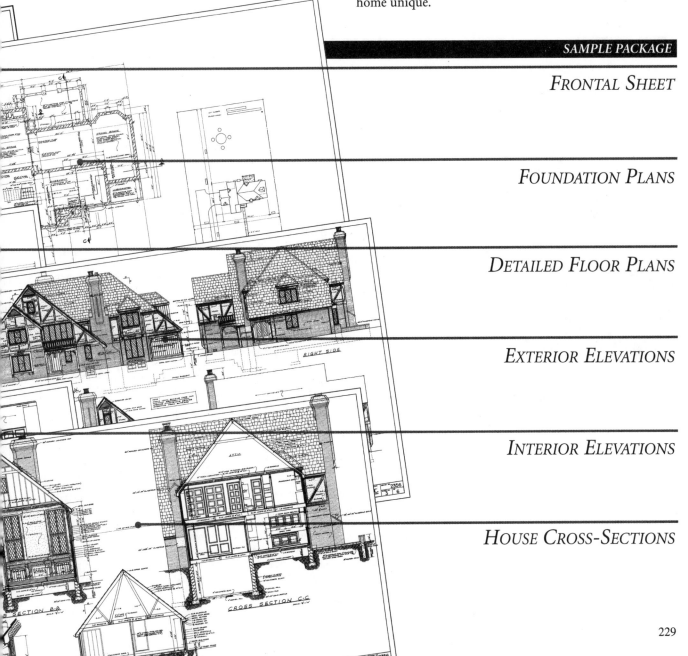

SAMPLE PACKAGE

FRONTAL SHEET

FOUNDATION PLANS

DETAILED FLOOR PLANS

EXTERIOR ELEVATIONS

INTERIOR ELEVATIONS

HOUSE CROSS-SECTIONS

INTRODUCING EIGHT IMPORTANT PLANNING AND CONSTRUCTION AIDS DEVELOPED BY OUR PROFESSIONALS TO HELP YOU SUCCEED IN YOUR HOME-BUILDING PROJECT

MATERIALS LIST

(Note: Because of the diversity of local building codes, our Materials List does not include mechanical materials.)

For many of the designs in our portfolio, we offer a customized materials take-off that is invaluable in planning and estimating the cost of your new home. This Materials List outlines the quantity, type and size of materials needed to build your house (with the exception of mechanical system items). Included are framing lumber, windows and doors, kitchen and bath cabinetry, rough and finish hardware, and much more. This handy list helps you or your builder cost out materials and serves as a reference sheet when you're compiling bids. A Materials List cannot be ordered before blueprints are ordered.

SPECIFICATION OUTLINE

This valuable 16-page document is critical to building your house correctly. Designed to be filled in by you or your builder, this book lists 166 stages or items crucial to the building process. It provides a comprehensive review of the construction process and helps in choosing materials. When combined with the blueprints, a signed contract, and a schedule, it becomes a legal document and record for the building of your home.

QUOTE ONE®

SUMMARY COST REPORT / MATERIALS COST REPORT

A new service for estimating the cost of building select designs, the Quote One® system is available in two separate stages: The Summary Cost Report and the Materials Cost Report.

The **Summary Cost Report** is the first stage in the package and shows the total cost per square foot for your chosen home in your zip-code area and then breaks that cost down into various categories showing the costs for building materials, labor and installation. The report includes three grades: Budget, Standard and Custom. These reports allow you to evaluate your building budget and compare the costs of building a variety of homes in your area.

Make even more informed decisions about your home-building project with the second phase of our package, our **Materials Cost Report.** This tool is invaluable in planning and estimating the cost of your new home. The material and installation (labor and equipment) cost is shown for each of over 1,000 line items provided in the Materials List (Standard grade), which is included when you purchase this estimating tool. It allows you to determine building costs for your specific zip-code area and for your chosen home design. Space is allowed for additional estimates from contractors and subcontractors, such as for mechanical materials, which are not included in our packages. This invaluable tool includes a Materials List. For most plans, a Materials Cost Report cannot be ordered before blueprints are ordered. Call for details. In addition, ask about our Home Planners Estimating Package.

The Quote One® program is continually updated with new plans. If you are interested in a plan that is not indicated as Quote One; please call and ask our sales reps. They will be happy to verify the status for you. To order these invaluable reports, use the order form on page 237 or call 1-800-521-6797.

CONSTRUCTION INFORMATION

If you want to know more about techniques—and deal more confidently with subcontractors—we offer these useful sheets. Each set is an excellent tool that will add to your understanding of these technical subjects. These helpful details provide general construction information and are not specific to any single plan.

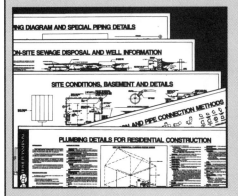

PLUMBING

The Blueprint Package includes locations for all the plumbing fixtures, including sinks, lavatories, tubs, showers, toilets, laundry trays and water heaters. However, if you want to know more about the complete plumbing system, these Plumbing Details will prove very useful. Prepared to meet requirements of the National Plumbing Code, these fact-filled sheets give general information on pipe schedules, fittings, sump-pump details, water-softener hookups, septic system details and much more. Sheets also include a glossary of terms.

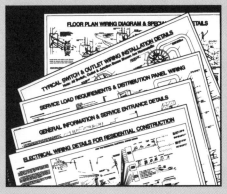

ELECTRICAL

The locations for every electrical switch, plug and outlet are shown in your Blueprint Package. However, these Electrical Details go further to take the mystery out of household electrical systems. Prepared to meet requirements of the National Electrical Code, these comprehensive drawings come packed with helpful information, including wire sizing, switch-installation schematics, cable-routing details, appliance wattage, doorbell hook-ups, typical service panel circuitry and much more. A glossary of terms is also included.

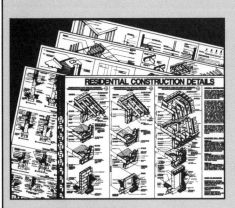

CONSTRUCTION

The Blueprint Package contains everything an experienced builder needs to construct a particular house. However, it doesn't show all the ways that houses can be built, nor does it explain alternate construction methods. To help you understand how your house will be built—and offer additional techniques—this set of Construction Details depicts the materials and methods used to build foundations, fireplaces, walls, floors and roofs. Where appropriate, the drawings show acceptable alternatives.

MECHANICAL

These Mechanical Details contain fundamental principles and useful data that will help you make informed decisions and communicate with subcontractors about heating and cooling systems. Drawings contain instructions and samples that allow you to make simple load calculations, and preliminary sizing and costing analysis. Covered are today's most commonly used systems from heat pumps to solar fuel systems. The package is filled with illustrations and diagrams to help you visualize components and how they relate to one another.

PLAN-A-HOME®

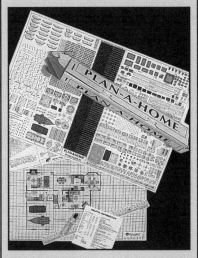

PLAN-A-HOME® is an easy-to-use tool that helps you design a new home, arrange furniture in a new or existing home, or plan a remodeling project. Each package contains:

✓ **MORE THAN 700 REUSABLE PEEL-OFF PLANNING SYMBOLS** on a self-stick vinyl sheet, including walls, windows, doors, all types of furniture, kitchen components, bath fixtures and many more.

✓ **A REUSABLE, TRANSPARENT, ¼" SCALE PLANNING GRID** that matches the scale of actual working drawings (¼" equals one foot). This grid provides the basis for house layouts of up to 140'x92'.

✓ **TRACING PAPER** and a protective sheet for copying or transferring your completed plan.

✓ **A FELT-TIP PEN**, with water-soluble ink that wipes away quickly.

Plan-A-Home® lets you lay out areas as large as a 7,500 square foot, six-bedroom, seven-bath house.

To Order, Call Toll Free 1-800-521-6797

To add these important extras to your Blueprint Package, simply indicate your choices on the order form on page 237. Or call us toll free 1-800-521-6797 and we'll tell you more about these exciting products. For customer service, call toll free 1-888-690-1116.

THE DECK BLUEPRINT PACKAGE

Many of the homes in this book can be enhanced with a professionally designed Home Planners Deck Plan. Those home plans highlighted with a **D** have a matching Deck Plan, sold separately, which includes a Deck Plan Frontal Sheet, Deck Framing and Floor Plans, Deck Elevations and a Deck Materials List. A Standard Deck Details Package, also available, provides all the how-to information necessary for building *any* deck. Our Complete Deck Building Package contains one set of Custom Deck Plans of your choice, plus one set of Standard Deck Building Details, all for one low price. Our plans and details are carefully prepared in an easy-to-understand format that will guide you through every stage of your deck-building project. This page contains a sampling of six different Deck layouts (and a front-yard landscape) to match your favorite house. See page 234 for prices and ordering information.

EUROPEAN-FLAIR HOME
Landscape OLA088

WEEKEND-ENTERTAINER DECK
Deck ODA013

CENTER-VIEW DECK
Deck ODA015

KITCHEN-EXTENDER DECK
Deck ODA016

SPLIT-LEVEL ACTIVITY DECK
Deck ODA018

TRI-LEVEL DECK WITH GRILL
Deck ODA020

CONTEMPORARY LEISURE DECK
Deck ODA021

THE LANDSCAPE BLUEPRINT PACKAGE

For the homes marked with an **L** in this book, Home Planners has created a front-yard Landscape Plan that matches or is complementary in design to the house plan. These comprehensive blueprint packages include a Frontal Sheet, Plan View, Regionalized Plant & Materials List, a sheet on Planting and Maintaining Your Landscape, Zone Maps and Plant Size and Description Guide. These plans will help you achieve professional results, adding value and enjoyment to your property for years to come. Each set of blueprints is a full 18" x 24" in size with clear, complete instructions and easy-to-read type. Six of the forty front-yard Landscape Plans to match your favorite house are shown below.

Regional Order Map

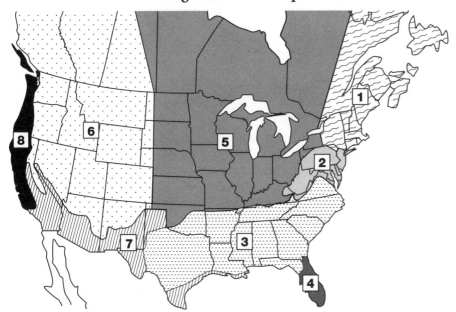

Most of the Landscape Plans shown on these pages are available with a Plant & Materials List adapted by horticultural experts to 8 different regions of the country. Please specify the Geographic Region when ordering your plan. See page 237 for prices, ordering information and regional availability.

Region	1	Northeast
Region	2	Mid-Atlantic
Region	3	Deep South
Region	4	Florida & Gulf Coast
Region	5	Midwest
Region	6	Rocky Mountains
Region	7	Southern California & Desert Southwest
Region	8	Northern California & Pacific Northwest

CAPE COD COTTAGE
Landscape OLA003

GAMBREL-ROOF COLONIAL
Landscape OLA004

CENTER-HALL COLONIAL
Landscape OLA005

CLASSIC NEW ENGLAND COLONIAL
Landscape OLA006

COUNTRY-STYLE FARMHOUSE
Landscape OLA008

TRADITIONAL SPLIT-LEVEL
Landscape OLA029

HOUSE BLUEPRINT PRICE SCHEDULE

Prices guaranteed through December 31, 2000

TIERS	1-SET STUDY PACKAGE	4-SET BUILDING PACKAGE	8-SET BUILDING PACKAGE	1-SET REPRODUCIBLE	HOME CUSTOMIZER® PACKAGE
P1	$20	$50	$90	$140	N/A
P2	$40	$70	$110	$160	N/A
P3	$60	$90	$130	$180	N/A
P4	$80	$110	$150	$200	N/A
P5	$100	$130	$170	$230	N/A
P6	$120	$150	$190	$250	N/A
A1	$400	$440	$500	$600	$650
A2	$440	$480	$540	$660	$710
A3	$480	$520	$580	$720	$770
A4	$520	$560	$620	$780	$830
C1	$560	$600	$660	$840	$890
C2	$600	$640	$700	$900	$950
C3	$650	$690	$750	$950	$1000
C4	$700	$740	$800	$1000	$1050
L1	$750	$790	$850	$1050	$1100
L2	$800	$840	$900	$1100	$1150
L3	$900	$940	$1000	$1200	$1250
L4	$1000	$1040	$1100	$1300	$1350

OPTIONS FOR PLANS IN TIERS A1–L4

Additional Identical Blueprints in same order for "A1–L4" price plans ....$50 per set

Reverse Blueprints (mirror image) with 4- or 8-set order for "A1–L4" price plans ....$50 fee per order

Specification Outlines ....$10 each

Materials Lists for "A1–C3" price plans ....$60 each

Materials Lists for "C4–L4" price plans ....$70 each

OPTIONS FOR PLANS IN TIERS P1–P6

Additional Identical Blueprints in same order for "P1–P6" price plans ....$10 per set

Reverse Blueprints (mirror image) for "P1–P6" price plans ....$10 per set

1 Set of Deck Construction Details ....$14.95 each

Deck Construction Package ....add $10 to Building Package price
 (includes 1 set of "P1–P6" price plans, plus
 1 set Standard Deck Construction Details)

1 Set of Gazebo Construction Details ....$14.95 each

Gazebo Construction Package ....add $10 to Building Package price
 (includes 1 set of "P1–P6" price plans, plus
 1 set Standard Gazebo Construction Details)

IMPORTANT NOTES

The 1-set study package is marked "not for construction."
Prices for 4- or 8-set Building Packages honored only at time of original order. All Donald A. Gardner basement foundations will incur a $225 surcharge. Right-reading reverse blueprints, if available, will incur a $165 surcharge.

INDEX

To use the Index below, refer to the design number listed in numerical order (a helpful page reference is also given). Note the price index letter and refer to the House Blueprint Price Schedule above for the cost of one, four or eight sets of blueprints or the cost of a reproducible drawing. Additional prices are shown for identical and reverse blueprint sets, as well as a very useful Materials List for some of the plans. Also note in the Index below those plans that have matching or complementary Deck Plans or Landscape Plans. Refer to the schedules above for prices of these plans. All plans in this publication are customizable. However, only Home Planners plans can be customized with the Home Planners Home Customizer® Package. These plans are indicated below with the letter "Y." See page 237 for more information. The letter "Y" also identifies plans that are part of our Quote One® estimating service and those that offer Materials Lists. See page 230 for more information.

To Order: Fill in and send the order form on page 237—or call toll free 1-800-521-6797 or 520-297-8200. FAX: 1-800-224-6699 or 520-544-3086

DESIGN	PRICE	PAGE	MATERIALS LIST	CUSTOMIZABLE	QUOTE ONE	DECK	DECK PRICE	LANDSCAPE	LANDSCAPE PRICE	REGIONS
3458	C1	148	Y	Y	Y	ODA006	P2	OLA023	P3	123568
3459	C3	166	Y	Y	Y			OLA021	P3	123568
3461	C1	136	Y	Y	Y			OLA005	P3	123568
3467	C1	14	Y	Y	Y			OLA004	P3	123568
3471	L1	59	Y	Y	Y			OLA037	P4	347
3479	C1	36	Y	Y	Y	ODA012	P3	OLA001	P3	123568
3486	A3	210	Y	Y	Y					
3488	C1	169	Y	Y	Y	ODA013	P2	OLA021	P3	123568
3495	C3	143	Y	Y	Y	ODA012	P3	OLA001	P3	123568
3498	C2	151	Y	Y	Y					
3557	L1	45	Y	Y	Y	ODA006	P2	OLA029	P3	12345678
3558	C2	65	Y	Y	Y	ODA006	P2	OLA004	P3	123568
3560	C1	147	Y	Y	Y			OLA035	P3	12345678
3565	A4	224	Y	Y	Y	ODA011	P3	OLA034	P3	347
3573	C4	6	Y	Y	Y	ODA012	P3	OLA034	P3	347
3600	A4	219	Y	Y	Y			OLA001	P3	123568
3601	A4	219	Y	Y	Y			OLA001	P3	123568
3606	C2	223	Y	Y	Y	ODA011	P2	OLA025	P3	123568
3608	C3	137	Y	Y	Y			OLA024	P4	123568
3615	A3	15	Y	Y	Y			OLA001	P3	123568
3630	C3	207	Y	Y	Y			OLA010	P3	1234568
3632	C2	206	Y	Y	Y			OLA038	P3	7
3634	C4	204	Y	Y	Y			OLA025	P3	123568
3636	C2	203	Y	Y	Y			OLA039	P3	3478
3637	C3	205	Y	Y	Y			OLA036	P4	123568
3638	C3	157	Y	Y	Y			OLA016	P4	1234568
3639	C2	23	Y	Y	Y			OLA018	P3	12345678
3642	C3	211	Y	Y	Y					
6602	C2	159						OLA004	P3	123568
6605	C1	202						OLA012	P3	12345678
6606	C1	117						OLA008	P4	1234568
6607	A4	146			Y			OLA012	P3	12345678
6608	C1	158	Y					OLA008	P4	1234568
6611	C2	212						OLA012	P3	12345678
6613	A4	25						OLA001	P3	123568
6615	C2	118	Y		Y			OLA024	P4	123568
6618	C2	119						OLA024	P4	123568
6619	C4	53	Y		Y			OLA024	P4	123568
6620	C4	12						OLA004	P3	123568
6621	C2	52	Y		Y			OLA024	P4	123568
6622	C1	13	Y		Y					
6628	C2	116						OLA001	P3	123568
6633	C2	28						OLA014	P4	12345678
6642	C3	31						OLA014	P4	12345678
6646	C3	47						OLA008	P4	1234568
6647	C3	55								
6649	C3	41						OLA012	P3	12345678
6650	C3	46								
7214	A3	90	Y							
7217	C1	88	Y							
7245	C3	96	Y							
7273	C2	67	Y							
7274	A4	94	Y							
7275	C1	216	Y							
7276	C2	93	Y							
8028	C2	104						OLA014	P4	12345678
8032	C3	29						OLA008	P4	1234568
8084	L1	215								
8086	C3	22						OLA001	P3	123568
8092	C1	100						OLA008	P4	1234568
8099	C2	105						OLA008	P4	1234568
8102	C2	168								
8109	L1	171								
8118	C1	18								
8139	C2	182								
8143	C3	64								
8144	A4	82								
8152	C3	101								
8161	C3	19								
8600	C1	156								
8603	C2	63								
8620	C1	213								
8628	L1	30								
8652	C2	21								
8663	C2	61								
8672	C1	58								
8684	A4	154								
8685	A3	155								
8686	A4	62								
8687	A4	26								
8688	C1	27								
8689	C1	40								
8690	C4	60								
8692	L1	214								
8693	A3	24								
8908	L2	8								
8932	C4	177								

DESIGN	PRICE	PAGE	MATERIALS LIST	CUSTOMIZABLE	QUOTE ONE	DECK	DECK PRICE	LANDSCAPE	LANDSCAPE PRICE	REGIONS
8960	C3	68								
9018	C1	191								
9019	A3	125								
9067	C1	134	Y							
9082	A4	208								
9083	A4	209	Y		Y					
9087	C2	201	Y		Y					
9107	A4	200								
9113	A2	217								
9124	C1	95								
9156	C1	132								
9180	A3	69								
9203	C1	124	Y							
9228	C3	87	Y							
9229	C3	9	Y							
9249	A4	84	Y							
9256	A4	91	Y							
9272	C2	85	Y							
9288	A3	16	Y							
9305	A4	89	Y							
9321	A3	186	Y							
9370	C1	86	Y							
9377	C2	92	Y							
9403	A3	153	Y					OLA001	P3	123568
9403	A3	153	Y					OLA001	P3	123568
9415	A3	49	Y					OLA001	P3	123568
9417	C3	33	Y					OLA001	P3	123568
9478	C1	48	Y					OLA001	P3	123568
9483	A4	152	Y					OLA001	P3	123568
9485	C2	32	Y					OLA004	P3	123568
9499	C1	54	Y					OLA008	P4	1234568
9504	C1	35	Y					OLA004	P3	123568
9509	A3	38	Y					OLA004	P3	123568
9536	C1	141	Y					OLA004	P3	123568
9538	C1	39	Y					OLA001	P3	123568
9554	C3	57	Y		Y					
9557	A4	140	Y		Y					
9601	A3	221	Y							
9606	A3	222	Y		Y					
9611	A3	111	Y							
9613	A3	192	Y							
9616	C1	77	Y							
9619	A4	172	Y							
9621	A3	75	Y		Y					
9623	A4	173	Y		Y					
9632	A4	71	Y		Y					
9661	A3	17	Y		Y					
9666	A3	144	Y		Y					
9673	A4	72	Y		Y					
9690	A3	135	Y		Y					
9712	A4	73	Y		Y					
9713	A3	220	Y							
9733	C1	74	Y							
9734	A3	78	Y		Y					
9738	A4	76	Y		Y					
9748	A3	80	Y							
9750	A3	81	Y							
9753	A2	109	Y		Y					
9756	A4	108	Y		Y					
9764	A3	79	Y		Y					
9767	A4	34	Y		Y					
9771	A3	107	Y							
9780	A3	110	Y		Y					
9801	C3	189								
9804	C4	180	Y		Y					
9816	C3	127	Y		Y					
9821	C3	218	Y							
9823	C3	128	Y		Y					
9826	C4	188								
9838	C4	126			Y					
9843	C2	187								
9850	C3	103	Y		Y					
9854	C1	98								
9862	C2	174	Y		Y					
9864	C3	99	Y		Y					
9869	C3	102	Y		Y					
9898	C3	97								
9908	C3	142								
9910	L1	176	Y							
9966	C3	175								
9970	C4	185								
9978	C4	181								
9979	C4	183								
9980	C3	184								
9987	C1	50								
9989	C3	51								
9990	L3	190	Y							

BEFORE FILLING OUT THE COUPON AT RIGHT OR CALLING US ON OUR TOLL-FREE BLUEPRINT HOTLINE, YOU MAY WANT TO LEARN MORE ABOUT OUR SERVICES AND PRODUCTS. HERE'S SOME INFORMATION YOU WILL FIND HELPFUL.

OUR EXCHANGE POLICY
Since blueprints are printed in response to your order, we cannot honor requests for refunds. However, we will exchange your entire first order for an equal or greater number of blueprints within our plan collection within 90 days of the original order. The entire content of your original order must be returned to our offices before an exchange will be processed. If the returned blueprints look used, redlined or copied, we will not honor your exchange. Fees for exchanging your blueprints are as follows: 20% of the amount of the original order...*plus* the difference in cost if exchanging for a design in a higher price bracket or *less* the difference in cost if exchanging for a design in lower price bracket. (**Reproducible blueprints are not exchangeable.**) Please add $25 for postage and handling via Regular Service; $35 via Priority Service; $45 via Express Service. Shipping and handling charges are not refundable.

ABOUT REVERSE BLUEPRINTS
If you want to build in reverse of the plan as shown, we will include any number of reverse blueprints (mirror image) from a 4- or 8-set package for an additional fee of $50. Although lettering and dimensions will appear backward, reverses will be a useful aid if you decide to flop the plan.

REVISING, MODIFYING AND CUSTOMIZING PLANS
The wide variety of designs available in this publication allows you to select ideas and concepts for a home to fit your building site and match your family's needs, wants and budget. Like many homeowners who buy these plans, you and your builder, architect or engineer may want to make changes to them. Some changes may be made by your builder, but we recommend that most changes be made by a licensed architect or engineer. If you need to make alterations to a design that is customizable, you need only order our Home Customizer® Package to get you started. As set forth below, we cannot assume any responsibility for blueprints which have been changed, whether by you, your builder or by professionals selected by you or referred to you by us, because such individuals are outside our supervision and control.

ARCHITECTURAL AND ENGINEERING SEALS
Some cities and states are now requiring that a licensed architect or engineer review and "seal" a blueprint, or officially approve it, prior to construction due to concerns over energy costs, safety and other factors. Prior to application for a building permit or the start of actual construction, we strongly advise that you consult your local building official who can tell you if such a review is required.

ABOUT THE DESIGNS
The architects and designers whose work appears in this publication are among America's leading residential designers. Each plan was designed to meet the requirements of a nationally recognized model building code in effect at the time and place the plan was drawn. Because national building codes change from time to time, plans may not comply with any such code at the time they are sold to a customer. In addition, building officials may not accept these plans as final construction documents of record as the plans may need to be modified and additional drawings and details added to suit local conditions and requirements. We strongly advise that purchasers consult a licensed architect or engineer, and their local building official, before starting any construction related to these plans.

LOCAL BUILDING CODES AND ZONING REQUIREMENTS
At the time of creation, our plans are drawn to specifications published by the Building Officials and Code Administrators (BOCA) International, Inc.; the Southern Building Code Congress (SBCCI) International, Inc.; the International Conference of Building Officials (ICBO); or the Council of American Building Officials (CABO). Our plans are designed to meet or exceed national building standards. Because of the great differences in geography and climate throughout the United States and Canada, each state, county and municipality has its own building codes, zone requirements, ordinances and building regulations. Your plan may need to be modified to comply with local requirements regarding snow loads, energy codes, soil and seismic conditions and a wide range of other matters. In addition, you may need to obtain permits or inspections from local governments before and in the course of construction. Prior to using blueprints ordered from us, we strongly advise that you consult a licensed architect or engineer—and speak with your local building official—before applying for any permit or beginning construction. We authorize the use of our blueprints on the express condition that you strictly comply with all local building codes, zoning requirements and other applicable laws, regulations, ordinances and requirements. **Notice: Plans for homes to be built in Nevada must be re-drawn by a Nevada-registered professional. Consult your building official for more information on this subject.**

FOUNDATION AND EXTERIOR WALL CHANGES
Depending on your specific climate or regional building practices, you may wish to change a full basement to a slab or crawlspace foundation. Most professional contractors and builders can easily adapt your plans to alternate foundation types. Likewise, most can easily change 2x4 wall construction to 2x6, or vice versa.

DISCLAIMER
We and the designers we work with have put substantial care and effort into the creation of our blueprints. However, because we cannot provide on-site consultation, supervision and control over actual construction, and because of the great variance in local building requirements, building practices and soil, seismic, weather and other conditions, WE CANNOT MAKE ANY WARRANTY, EXPRESS OR IMPLIED, WITH RESPECT TO THE CONTENT OR USE OF OUR BLUEPRINTS, INCLUDING BUT NOT LIMITED TO ANY WARRANTY OF MERCHANTABILITY OR OF FITNESS FOR A PARTICULAR PURPOSE.

TERMS AND CONDITIONS
These designs are protected under the terms of United States Copyright Law and may not be copied or reproduced in any way, by any means, unless you have purchased Sepias or Reproducibles which clearly indicate your right to copy or reproduce. We authorize the use of your chosen design as an aid in the construction of one single family home only. You may not use this design to build a second or multiple dwellings without purchasing another blueprint or blueprints or paying additional design fees.

HOW MANY BLUEPRINTS DO YOU NEED?
A single set of blueprints is sufficient to study a home in greater detail. However, if you are planning to obtain cost estimates from a contractor or subcontractors—or if you are planning to build immediately—you will need more sets. Because additional sets are cheaper when ordered in quantity with the original order, make sure you order enough blueprints to satisfy all requirements. The following checklist will help you determine how many you need:

___ Owner

___ Builder (generally requires at least three sets; one as a legal document, one to use during inspections, and at least one to give to subcontractors)

___ Local Building Department (often requires two sets)

___ Mortgage Lender (usually one set for a conventional loan; three sets for FHA or VA loans)

___ TOTAL NUMBER OF SETS

Have You Seen Our Newest Designs?

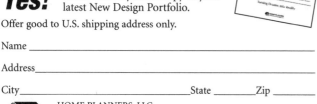

At least 50 of our latest creations are featured in each edition of our New Design Portfolio. You may have received a copy with your latest purchase by mail. If not, or if you purchased this book from a local retailer, just return the coupon below for your FREE copy. Make sure you consider the very latest of what Home Planners has to offer.

Yes! Please send my FREE copy of your latest New Design Portfolio.

Offer good to U.S. shipping address only.

Name _____

Address_____

City_____ State _____ Zip _____

HOME PLANNERS, LLC
Wholly owned by Hanley-Wood, LLC
3275 WEST INA ROAD, SUITE 110
TUCSON, ARIZONA 85741

Order Form Key

HPT14

☎ TOLL FREE 1-800-521-6797

REGULAR OFFICE HOURS:
8:00 a.m.-12:00 a.m. EST, Monday-Friday, 10:00 a.m.-7:00 p.m. EST Sat & Sun.

If we receive your order by 3:00 p.m. EST, Monday-Friday, we'll process it and ship within **two business days**. When ordering by phone, please have your credit card ready. We'll also ask you for the Order Form Key Number at the bottom of the coupon.

By FAX: Copy the Order Form on the next page and send it on our FAX line:
1-800-224-6699 or 520-544-3086.

Canadian Customers — Order Toll Free 1-877-223-6389

For faster service, Canadian customers may now call in orders directly to our Canadian supplier of plans and charge the purchase to a credit card. Or, you may complete the order form at right, adding the current exchange rate to all prices and mail in Canadian funds to:

Home Planners Canada, c/o Select Home Designs
301-611 Alexander Street • Vancouver, BC, Canada • V6A 1E1

OR: Copy the Order Form and send it via our FAX line: 1-800-224-6699.

The Home Customizer®

"This house is perfect...if only the family room were two feet wider." Sound familiar? In response to the numerous requests for this type of modification, Home Planners has developed **The Home Customizer® Package**. This exclusive package offers our top-of-the-line materials to make it easy for anyone, anywhere to customize any Home Planners design to fit their needs. Check the index on page 234-235 for those plans which are customizable.

Some of the changes you can make to any of our plans include:

- exterior elevation changes
- kitchen and bath modifications
- roof, wall and foundation changes
- room additions and more!

The Home Customizer® Package includes everything you'll need to make the necessary changes to your favorite Home Planners design. The package includes:

- instruction book with examples
- architectural scale and clear work film
- erasable red marker and removable correction tape
- ¼"-scale furniture cutouts
- 1 set reproducible drawings
- 1 set study blueprints for communicating changes to your design professional
- a copyright release letter so you can make copies as you need them
- referral letter with the name, address and telephone number of the professional in your region who is trained in modifying Home Planners designs efficiently and inexpensively.

The Home Customizer® Package will not only save you 25% to 75% of the cost of drawing the plans from scratch with an architect or engineer, it will also give you the flexibility to have your changes and modifications made by our referral network or by the professional of your choice. Now it's even easier and more affordable to have the custom home you've always wanted.

 **ORDER TOLL FREE!**
FOR INFORMATION ABOUT ANY OF OUR SERVICES OR TO ORDER CALL

1-800-521-6797 OR 520-297-8200
Browse our website:
www.homeplanners.com

BLUEPRINTS ARE NOT REFUNDABLE EXCHANGES ONLY

FOR CUSTOMER SERVICE,
CALL TOLL FREE 1-888-690-1116.

HOME PLANNERS, LLC wholly owned by Hanley-Wood, LLC
3275 WEST INA ROAD, SUITE 110 • TUCSON, ARIZONA • 85741

THE BASIC BLUEPRINT PACKAGE
Rush me the following (please refer to the Plans Index and Price Schedule in this section):
___Set(s) of blueprints for plan number(s) _____. $_____
___Set(s) of reproducibles for plan number(s) _____. $_____
___Home Customizer® Package for plan(s)_____. $_____
___Additional identical blueprints (standard or reverse) in same order @ $50 per set. $_____
___Reverse blueprints @ $50 fee per order. Right-reading reverse @ $165 surcharge $_____

IMPORTANT EXTRAS
Rush me the following:
___Materials List: $60 (Must be purchased with Blueprint set.) Add $10 for Schedule C4–L4 plans. $_____
___**Quote One®** Summary Cost Report @ $29.95 for one, $14.95 for each additional,
  for plans _____ $_____
  Building location: City _____ Zip Code _____
___**Quote One®** Materials Cost Report @ $120 Schedules P1–C3; $130 Schedules C4–L4,
  for plan_____(Must be purchased with Blueprints set.) $_____
  Building location: City _____ Zip Code _____
___Specification Outlines @ $10 each. $_____
___Detail Sets @ $14.95 each; any two $22.95; any three $29.95; all four for $39.95 (save $19.85). $_____
  ❏ Plumbing ❏ Electrical ❏ Construction ❏ Mechanical
___Plan-A-Home® @ $29.95 each. $_____

DECK BLUEPRINTS
(Please refer to the Plans Index and Price Schedule in this section)
___Set(s) of Deck Plan _____. $_____
___Additional identical blueprints in same order @ $10 per set. $_____
___Reverse blueprints @ $10 per set. $_____
___Set of Standard Deck Details @ $14.95 per set. $_____
___Set of Complete Deck Construction Package (Best Buy!) Add $10 to Building Package
  Includes Custom Deck Plan _____ Plus Standard Deck Details

LANDSCAPE BLUEPRINTS
(Please refer to the Plans Index and Price Schedule in this section)
___Set(s) of Landscape Plan _____. $_____
___Additional identical blueprints in same order @ $10 per set. $_____
___Reverse blueprints @ $10 per set. $_____
Please indicate the appropriate region of the country for Plant & Material List.
(See map on page 233): Region _____

POSTAGE AND HANDLING	1–3 sets	4+ sets
Signature is required for all deliveries. **DELIVERY** No CODs (Requires street address—No P.O. Boxes)		
•Regular Service (Allow 7–10 business days delivery)	❏ $20.00	❏ $25.00
•Priority (Allow 4–5 business days delivery)	❏ $25.00	❏ $35.00
•Express (Allow 3 business days delivery)	❏ $35.00	❏ $45.00
OVERSEAS DELIVERY	fax, phone or mail for quote	

Note: All delivery times are from date Blueprint Package is shipped.

POSTAGE (From box above) $_____
SUBTOTAL $_____
SALES TAX (AZ & MI residents, please add appropriate state and local sales tax.) $_____
TOTAL (Subtotal and tax) $_____

YOUR ADDRESS (please print)
Name _____
Street_____
City _____ State_____ Zip _____
Daytime telephone number (_____) _____

FOR CREDIT CARD ORDERS ONLY
Credit card number _____ Exp. Date: (M/Y) _____
Check one ❏ Visa ❏ MasterCard ❏ Discover Card ❏ American Express

Signature_____
Please check appropriate box: ❏ Licensed Builder-Contractor ❏ Homeowner

ORDER TOLL FREE!
1-800-521-6797 or 520-297-8200

Order Form Key

HPT14

HOME PLANNERS WANTS YOUR BUILDING EXPERIENCE TO BE AS PLEASANT AND TROUBLE-FREE AS POSSIBLE.

That's why we've expanded our library of Do-It-Yourself titles to help you along. In addition to our beautiful plans books, we've added books to guide you through specific projects as well as the construction process. In fact, these are titles that will be as useful after your dream home is built as they are right now.

BIGGEST & BEST  1001 of our best-selling plans in one volume. 1,074 to 7,275 square feet. 704 pgs $12.95 1K1	**ONE-STORY**  450 designs for all lifestyles. 800 to 4,900 square feet. 384 pgs $9.95 OS	**MORE ONE-STORY**  475 superb one-level plans from 800 to 5,000 square feet. 448 pgs $9.95 MOS	**TWO-STORY**  443 designs for one-and-a-half and two stories. 1,500 to 6,000 square feet. 448 pgs $9.95 TS
VACATION  465 designs for recreation, retirement and leisure. 448 pgs $9.95 VSH	**HILLSIDE**  208 designs for split-levels, bi-levels, multi-levels and walkouts. 224 pgs $9.95 HH	**FARMHOUSE**  200 country designs from classic to contemporary by 7 winning designers. 224 pgs $8.95 FH	**COUNTRY HOUSES**  208 unique home plans that combine traditional style and modern livability. 224 pgs $9.95 CN

BUDGET-SMART  200 efficient plans from 7 top designers, that you can really afford to build! 224 pgs $8.95 BS	**BARRIER FREE**  Over 1,700 products and 51 plans for accessible living. 128 pgs $15.95 UH	**ENCYCLOPEDIA**  500 exceptional plans for all styles and budgets—the best book of its kind! 528 pgs $9.95 ENC	**ENCYCLOPEDIA II**  500 completely new plans. Spacious and stylish designs for every budget and taste. 352 pgs $9.95 E2
AFFORDABLE  Completely revised and updated, featuring 300 designs for modest budgets. 256 pgs $9.95 AF	**VICTORIAN**  160 striking Victorian & Farmhouse designs from three leading designers. 192 pgs $12.95 VDH	**ESTATE**  Dream big! Twenty-one designers showcase their biggest and best plans. 208 pgs $15.95 EDH	**LUXURY**  154 fine luxury plans—loaded with luscious amenities! 192 pgs $14.95 LD2

EUROPEAN STYLES  200 homes with a unique flair of the Old World. 224 pgs $15.95 EURO	**COUNTRY CLASSICS**  Donald Gardner's 101 best Country and Traditional home plans. 192 pgs $17.95 DAG	**WILLIAM POOLE**  70 romantic house plans that capture the classic tradition of home design. 160 pgs $17.95 WEP	**TRADITIONAL**  85 timeless designs from the Design Traditions Library. 160 pgs $17.95 TRA
COTTAGES  25 fresh new designs that are as warm as a tropical breeze. A blend of the best aspects of many coastal styles. 64 pgs $19.95 CTG	**CLASSIC**  Timeless, elegant designs that always feel like home. Gorgeous plans that are as flexible and up-to-date as their occupants. 240 pgs $9.95 CS	**CONTEMPORARY**  The most complete and imaginative collection of contemporary designs available anywhere. 240 pgs. $9.95 CM	**EASY-LIVING**  200 efficient and sophisticated plans that are small in size, but big on livability. 224 pgs $8.95 EL

SOUTHERN  207 homes rich in Southern styling and comfort. 240 pgs $8.95 SH	**SOUTHWESTERN**  138 designs that capture the spirit of the Southwest. 144 pgs $10.95 SW	**WESTERN**  215 designs that capture the spirit and diversity of the Western lifestyle. 208 pgs $9.95 WH	**NEIGHBORHOOD**  170 designs with the feel of main street America. 192 pgs $12.95 TND
CRAFTSMAN  170 Home plans in the Craftsman and Bungalow style. 192 pgs $12.95 CC	**COLONIAL HOUSES**  181 Classic early American designs. 208 pgs $9.95 COL	**DUPLEX & TOWNHOMES**  Over 50 designs for multi-family living. 64 pgs $9.95 DTP	**WATERFRONT**  200 designs perfect for your waterside wonderland. 208 pgs $10.95 WF

Design 9621

OVER 3 MILLION BLUEPRINTS SOLD

"We instructed our builder to follow the plans, including all of the many details which make this house so elegant. . . . Our home is a fine example of the results one can achieve by purchasing and following the plans which you offer. . . . Everyone who has seen it has assured us that it belongs in 'a picture book.' I truly mean it when I say that my home 'is a DREAM HOUSE.' "

> S.P.
> Anderson, SC

"We have had a steady stream of visitors, many of whom tell us this is the most beautiful home they've seen. Everyone is amazed at the layout and remarks on how unique it is. Our real estate attorney, who is a Chicago dweller and who deals with highly valued properties, told me this is the only suburban home he has seen that he would want to live in."

> W. & P.S.
> Flossmoor, IL

"Your blueprints saved us a great deal of money. I acted as the general contractor and we did a lot of the work ourselves. We probably built it for half the cost! We are thinking about more plans for another home. I purchased a competitor's book but my husband wants only your plans!"

> K.M.
> Grovetown, GA

"We are very happy with the product of our efforts. The neighbors and passersby appreciate what we have created. We have had many people stop by to discuss our house and kindly praise it as being the nicest house in our area of new construction. We have even had one person stop and make us an unsolicited offer to buy the house for much more than we have invested in it."

> K. & L.S.
> Bolingbrook, IL

"The traffic going past our house is unbelievable. On several occasions, we have heard that it is the 'prettiest house in Batavia.' Also, when meeting someone new and mentioning what street we live on, quite often we're told, 'Oh, you're the one in the yellow house with the wrap-around porch! I love it!' "

> A.W.
> Batavia, NY

"I have been involved in the building trades my entire life. . . . Since building our home, we have built two other homes for other families. Their plans from local professional architects were not nearly as good as yours. For that reason we are ordering additional plan books from you."

> T.F.
> Kingston, WA

"The blueprints we received from you were of excellent quality and provided us with exactly what we needed to get our successful home-building project underway. We appreciate your invaluable role in our home-building effort."

> T.A.
> Concord, TN